LONDON
SUBURBAN

LONDON SUBURBAN

An illustrated history of the capital's commuter lines since 1948

Frank Hornby

Silver Link Publishing Ltd

First published in August 1995

British Library Cataloguing in Publication Data

A catalogue record for this book is available from the British Library.

ISBN 1 85794 039 3

Silver Link Publishing Ltd
Unit 5
Home Farm Close
Church Street
Wadenhoe
Peterborough PE8 5TE
Tel/fax (01832) 720440

Printed and bound in Great Britain

ACKNOWLEDGEMENTS

My grateful thanks are due to Mr N. L. Browne for his many helpful comments and suggestions; also to those who have kindly contributed photographs from their collections, as credited.

BIBLIOGRAPHY

In compiling this work, in addition to numerous maps and timetables, the following sources of information have proved invaluable:

BR Diary 1979-1985, J. Glover
British Electric Trains, H. Linecar
British Rail Motive Power (Ian Allan)
LCGB Bulletin 1979-1994
London and its Railways, R. Davies and M. D. Grant
London's Railway History, H. P. White
London's Termini, Alan A. Jackson
'London Suburban Railway' Series, V. Mitchell and K. Smith (Middleton Press)
Motive Power Recognition - DMUs and EMUs, C. J. Marsden

Modern Railways 1962-1964
Railway Magazine 1931-1994
Railway Observer 1948-1994
RCTS Locomotive Histories, LBSC, LSWR, SECR
Railways of South East England
Railway World 1961-1985
Regional History of Railways - Southern England, H. P. White
Register of Closed Stations, C. R. Clinker
Southern Electric 1909-79, G. T. Moody
The Great Eastern Railway, C. J. Allen
The North London Railway, M. Robbins
The South Eastern & Chatham Railway, O. S. Nock
The South Western Railway, C. H. Ellis
Trains Illustrated 1954-1964

CONTENTS

INTRODUCTION

When the first passenger railways opened for business in London in the 1830s, the population of the capital was around 1¾ millions, concentrated in an area of some 20 square miles. Most people still lived within walking distance of their work, while those wealthy enough to reside in the villas of outlying districts enjoyed the convenience of their own carriages.

Not surprisingly therefore, the first trunk lines, expanding towards Birmingham and Bristol, Norwich and Southampton, gave little thought to potential revenue from short-distance passengers; indeed, the termini in Euston Square and Paddington were then quite close to the fringes of the built-up area. At first, on the London & Birmingham, there was only Harrow station south of Watford, with just five trains stopping in each direction daily, while on the Great Western there was initially only West Drayton - joined shortly afterwards by Ealing, Hanwell and Southall - between Paddington and Slough.

But there were other lines of a very different character; the London & Greenwich, London & Blackwall and London & Croydon spring instantly to mind as examples of those catering for the first 'commuters' - long before that word was dreamed of! The London & Greenwich, built on viaducts throughout its 3¾ miles and opened in 1836, was exclusively for passengers, offering a 15-minute-interval service from the beginning, as did the 5-foot-gauge London & Blackwall, opened in July 1840. The latter, also on viaducts and embankments, 3½ miles in length, was initially worked by cable haulage, while the London & Croydon, rather longer at 8¾ miles with four intermediate stations, was converted to atmospheric traction in 1844-45. Fortunately for the future, both these experiments were abandoned in favour of conventional steam haulage when the lines were extended and linked with others.

The relentless population growth and outward movement of London's boundaries during the mid-Victorian era, with speculative building sometimes following and sometimes followed by new lines of railway, resulted in the greater part of today's suburban network being in place by the end of the 1870s. The construction of joint lines, such as the West London, North & South Western Junction, Tottenham & Hampstead Junction and Metropolitan Widened Lines, resulted in a proliferation of cross-London services. Some were short-lived, such as Broad Street to Windsor, while others succumbed to tram, bus and Underground competition during the Edwardian era, or to cut-backs during the First World War. The North London Railway, opened in stages from 1847 onwards, was particularly renowned for the penetration of its trains far beyond the limits of its own rails.

The growth of suburban traffic during Victoria's reign was such that, by 1858, out of 340 trains using London Bridge station daily, only 58 were of the 'main-line' variety. Across the river at Liverpool Street, which replaced Bishopsgate as the GER terminus in 1875, workmen's cheap fares boosted traffic from Bishopsgate's two million passengers in 1855 to 65 million by 1902 - of whom 90 per cent travelled 12 miles or less.

While, in reaction to road competition, particularly from tramways, the LBSCR and LSWR opted for electrification just prior to and during the Great War, the GER chose a different solution. With careful planning the so-called 'Jazz' service, introduced in 1920, enabled steam trains seating 850 (with standing room for many more) to enter or leave the terminus at 2-minute intervals. Some years earlier, in 1902, in a gallant attempt to prove that steam could rival the acceleration of electric trains, the 'Decapod' 0-10-0T emerged from Stratford Works only to be converted within four years into a 0-8-0 tender locomotive, and, in the event, the 'Jazz' trains were successfully handled by much smaller designs.

North of the river, the LNWR alone electrified its suburban lines, between Euston, Broad Street, Watford and Richmond, commencing in 1914 and completed under LMS auspices in 1927. The GWR, wedded to steam, was content to share, with the Metropolitan Railway, ownership of the Hammersmith & City line, electrified in 1906.

When the Southern Railway was formed in 1923

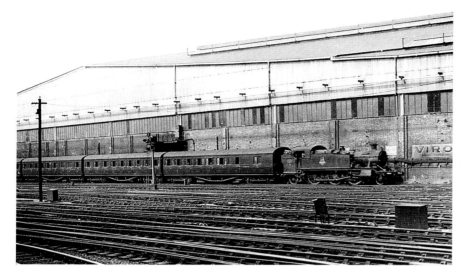

The way it was: purpose-built in the early 1930s for the GWR's London Division suburban services, Collett's '61XX' 2-6-2Ts performed admirably for 30 years on duties such as this, a 'local' seen arriving at Paddington *circa* 1955 with a typical rake of compartment stock. Note the pre-war 'searchlight' signals and the impressive backdrop of Paddington Goods Station. *A. J. Pike*

Under the stewardship of British Railways from 1948 until the recent onset of 'privatisation', the London suburban system has seen great changes, first in the elimination of steam traction, then the extension of electrification, and the replacement of older stock by a fleet of modern multiple units. It is indeed a far cry from the 'quad-arts' of yesteryear to the 'Networkers' of today!

Mercifully, line closures have been relatively few, and of several listed in the Beeching proposals (Romford-Upminster, Watford-St Albans, Clapham Junction-Olympia and Broad Street-Richmond) only the short section from Broad Street to Dalston Junction has succumbed. The first outward sign of nationalisation came with new liveries for rolling-stock in 1948 - maroon, lined gold and black for suburban hauled stock and green for multiple units - retaining the 'status quo' for Southern electrics until 'Rail Blue' appeared in late 1966. Then, after a period of blue and grey, the colourful red, white and blue as adopted by Network SouthEast has enlivened the scene since June 1986.

Equally drastic changes to the infrastructure have produced results that, as regards the stations, have been very mixed indeed. It is symptomatic of the times that, as throughout BR, some station buildings have either been replaced by functional shelters, or are locked, barred, unmanned and fair game for vandals. On the other hand, full credit must be given for the impressive transformations of major stations such as Euston and Liverpool Street, as well as of many smaller ones, made more 'customer friendly' by NSE (passengers became 'customers' in 1983!). Apart from liberal applications of red paint, improved lighting and the installation of public address systems are two of the more positive benefits.

Modernisation of signalling systems has resulted in the wholesale removal of the old-style manually worked boxes and their replacement by 'Signalling Centres' controlling wide areas, so that the few remaining semaphores are indeed an endangered species.

the new management pressed ahead with suburban electrification, speedily extended into the South Eastern section, adopting the LSWR 600V DC third-rail system in preference to the LBSCR overhead catenary fed at 6,600V AC. The increase in traffic fully justified the expense, and by 1930 the third rail had been laid throughout the suburban network.

Concurrently with the 19th-century expansion of surface lines there was similar activity below ground, commencing with the opening of the first section of the Metropolitan Railway between Paddington and Farringdon Street in 1863. The Inner Circle, serving several main-line termini and jointly owned by the Metropolitan and District railways, was opened throughout by 1884. While these two companies were extending their trackage - then still steam-operated - into what was in some areas almost virgin countryside to the north-west and west, deep 'tube' lines were also under construction. The City & South London opened in 1890 the first section of what would eventually become the Northern Line, initially worked by four-wheeled electric locomotives, later replaced by multiple units. Built to a smaller loading gauge, the Underground lines multiplied during Edwardian years, eventually 'coming up for air' in the suburbs, with Bakerloo trains emerging at Queens Park to share LNWR tracks to Watford from 1917. Later, early in the Second World War, extensions of the Northern Line replaced LNER steam services to High Barnet and Mill Hill East, with the Central Line following suit to Hainault and Epping in 1948/49, as well as to West Ruislip in the west.

The formation of the London Passenger Transport Board in 1933 had brought the Metropolitan, District and 'Underground' lines under one umbrella with buses, trains and trolleybuses, to create a public service that became the envy of the world.

Representing the future for suburban rail travel is the Docklands Light Railway. This is Tower Gateway station on 22 May 1991, and twin articulated units Nos 08 and 14 are of the first and second batches in service respectively. *F. Hornby*

Generally services have been improved in both speed and frequency, sometimes to be adversely affected later due to enforced economies. During the period under review, London's population has dwindled from over eight million to less than seven million, the greatest reduction being in the inner suburbs. Many thousands now commute daily over distances of 80 miles or more, though swingeing increases in Season Ticket prices and the recent recession have hit hard. In spite of the growth of private motoring, the decade to 1962 saw daily peak-time rail commuting boosted from 750,000 to 900,000, with BR's share up by 24 per cent, as many more firms elected to have their offices in the City or West End - a trend that has since been reversed. However, inflation throughout the 1970s fuelled fare increases ranging from 9 to 20 per cent, and reaching 24 per cent for short journeys in the South East in November 1980.

The widespread introduction of the five-day week virtually eliminated the need for peak-hour 'extras' on Saturdays, while more recently flexi-time has helped to spread the weekday load - a critical factor when demands on rolling-stock are more than doubled for just a few hours daily. Perhaps reflecting social changes, 'Workmen's' tickets were re-styled 'Early Morning' in October 1950 - and withdrawn from 1 January 1962. Meanwhile, 3rd Class had become 2nd in June 1956, known more diplomatically today as 'Standard'!

Looking back over the years, one is reminded of the incessant strikes, lightning stoppages and 'work to rule' campaigns, most prevalent in the 1970s and early 1980s, often compounded by disruptions arising from severe weather or equipment failures. The introduction of new rolling-stock or signalling systems almost invariably resulted in 'teething troubles' and one can only offer unstinted praise to those who laboured mightily to keep the wheels turning in spite of all these obstacles.

On the brighter side it is pleasing to record the revival during the 1980s of north-south cross-London services, doubtless expedited by the formation of Network SouthEast in 1986, cutting across the old regional boundaries. 'Thameslink' reinvents and indeed improves on some of the services that disappeared years ago, and we now look forward to 'Crossrail' to provide similar east-west facilities some time in the future.

Having set the scene, let us now look in greater detail in the ensuing chapters at how London suburban services have fared during the years since nationalisation.

LONDON SUBURBAN STEAM LOCOMOTIVE TYPES

Region	Class	Type	Designer	Introduced (year)	Cylinders (No) (in x in)	Boiler pressure (lb/sq in)	Driving wheels (ft-in)	Weight (tons-cwt)	Tractive effort (lb)
WR	61XX	2-6-2T	Collett	1931	(2) 18 x 30	225	5-8	78-9	27340
	54XX	0-6-0PT	Collett	1931	(2) 16½ x 24	165	5-2	46-12	14780
	14XX	0-4-2T	Collett	1932	(2) 16 x 24	165	5-2	41-6	13895
LMR	4P	2-6-4T	Fowler	1928	(2) 19 x 26	200	5-9	86-5	23125
	4P	2-6-4T	Stanier	1934	(3) 16 x 26	200	5-9	92-5	24600
	4P	2-6-4T	Stanier	1935	(2) 19⅜ x 26	200	5-9	87-17	24670
	4P	2-6-4T	Fairburn	1945	(2) 19⅜ x 26	200	5-9	85-5	24670
	3P	2-6-2T	Fowler	1930	(2) 17½ x 26	200	5-3	71-16	21486
	3P	2-6-2T	Stanier	1935	(2) 17½ x 26	200	5-3	71-5	21486
	2P	2-6-2T	Ivatt	1946	(2) 16 x 24	200	5-0	63-5	17400
	2P	0-4-4T	Stanier	1932	(2) 18 x 26	160	5-7	58-1	17099
	3P	4-4-2T	Whitelegg	1923	(2) 19 x 26	170	6-6	71-10	17390
ER	A5	4-6-2T	Robinson	1911	(2) 20 x 26	180	5-7	85-18	23743
	L1	2-6-4T	Thompson	1945	(2) 20 x 26	225	5-2	89-9	32080
	C14	4-4-2T	Robinson	1907	(2) 18 x 26	160	5-7	71-0	17100
	N1	0-6-2T	Ivatt	1907	(2) 18 x 26	170	5-8	65-17	17900
	N2	0-6-2T	Gresley	1920	(2) 19 x 26	170	5-8	71-9	19945
	N5	0-6-2T	Parker	1889	(2) 18 x 26	160	5-1	62-12	18781
	N7	0-6-2T	Hill	1915	(2) 18 x 24	180	4-10	64-17	20512
	F5	2-4-2T	Holden	1903	(2) 17½ x 24	180	5-4	56-8	17571
BR	4P	2-6-4T	Riddles	1952	(2) 18 x 28	225	5-8	86-13	25100

1

LINES FROM PADDINGTON

PADDINGTON-READING
WEST EALING-GREENFORD
WEST DRAYTON-STAINES WEST AND UXBRIDGE (VINE STREET)
SLOUGH-WINDSOR AND SLOUGH TRADING ESTATE
MAIDENHEAD-MARLOW AND HIGH WYCOMBE
TWYFORD-HENLEY-ON-THAMES
OLD OAK COMMON-HIGH WYCOMBE VIA GREENFORD

If there were league tables for the suburban traffic handled by the London termini, Paddington would barely scrape into the second division, let alone be in contention with the 'front runners' like Liverpool Street and Waterloo. In the early years of the Great Western Railway, with sights set firmly on Bristol and points west, scant regard was shown for the modest communities between London and Reading - even Royal Windsor was bypassed and had to be content with a branch line from Slough - and the 1839 timetable listed just four 'short trains' daily, between Paddington and West Drayton. In more recent times the popular GWR image was one of splendid trains hauled by locomotives with regal (or saintly) names, and to the lineside spotter the 'locals' behind their less glamorous tank engines were scarcely worth a glance!

By the 1930s ribbon development along the arterial roads west of London had attracted concentrations of industry to locations such as Southall, Hayes and Slough, so that while this brought short-distance custom to the railway, much of it was between these and other intermediate stations. Moreover, interchange with the District and Central Lines at Ealing Broadway siphoned many passengers away from Paddington. Nevertheless, as the towns along the line grew steadily, so did the traffic, requiring progressively heavier and more frequent trains.

By 1951 suburban traffic was up by 25 per cent as compared with pre-war years, and although adversely affected by the motoring boom in the 1960s, revived again, notably with a further 25 per cent increase in the five years from 1986. By then the population of Slough had topped the 100,000 mark, with Reading approaching double that figure and Maidenhead reaching 60,000 - a far cry from the small towns and villages along Brunel's 'Great Way to the West'!

ROUTES AND INFRASTRUCTURE

The 36 miles of main line between Paddington and Reading have been four-tracked since 1893, soon after the abolition of the broad gauge, providing a separate pair for stopping passenger and goods trains. With easy gradients - no steeper than 1 in 1200 - and with only 15 intermediate stations, a reasonably smartly timed service is possible.

At Paddington the suburban station has none of the grandeur of its main-line counterpart, to which it is linked only by a footbridge. It formed a separate entity known as Bishop's Road until it was rebuilt and enlarged in 1933, since when it has consisted of two 600-foot island platforms with faces numbered 13-16, originally serving four through tracks, the inner pair for the GWR and the outer for the Metropolitan's Hammersmith & City line trains, allowing cross-platform interchange. After extensive alterations, completed in November 1967, the tracks at platforms 13 and 14 became terminal roads for Western Region use, while those at Nos 15 and 16 remained through lines for the Hammersmith & City service. Some outer suburban trains operate from platforms in the main station, usually Nos 11 or 12.

The 1967 reorganisation provided separate tracks for the Metropolitan, passing through Royal Oak station a mere quarter of a mile away before burrowing beneath the BR running lines at Subway Junction to emerge at Westbourne Park. A long footbridge linked the Metropolitan and BR stations here until the latter, 1¼ miles from Paddington, closed in March 1992.

At Old Oak Common Junction the erstwhile direct line to Birmingham diverges from the Reading main line, which continues due west through Acton and Ealing Broadway, a busy interchange station

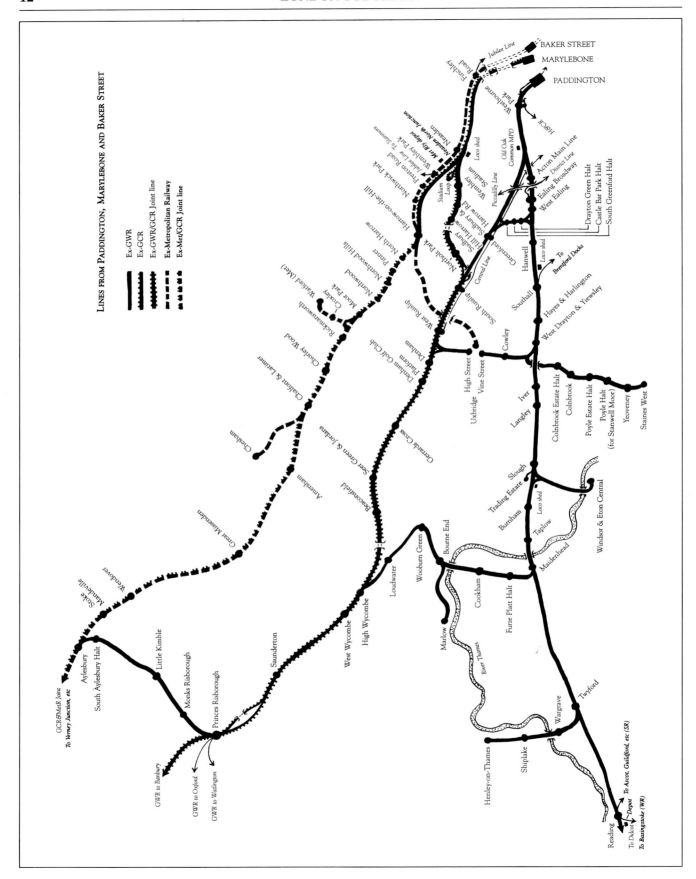

LINES FROM PADDINGTON, MARYLEBONE AND BAKER STREET

Ex-GWR
Ex-GCR
Ex-GWR/GCR Joint line
Ex-Metropolitan Railway
Ex-Met/GCR Joint line

SUBURBAN LINES FROM PADDINGTON, MAIN LINE AND BRANCHES

Miles	Name	Opened	Closed	Notes
From Paddington				
0	Paddington	6/1838		Present station opened 1854
1¼	Westbourne Park	10/1871	3/1992	
4¼	Acton main line	2/1868		
5¾	Ealing Broadway	12/1838		
6½	West Ealing	3/1871		'Castle Hill Ealing' to 1899
7¼	Hanwell & Elthorne	12/1838		
9	Southall	5/1839		
10¾	Hayes & Harlington	5/1864		
13¼	West Drayton	6/1838		'West Drayton & Yiewsley' to 5/1974
14¾	Iver	12/1924		
16¼	Langley	1845		
18½	Slough	6/1838		
21	Burnham	1899		'Burnham Beeches' to 9/1930; 'Burnham (Bucks)' to 5/1975
22½	Taplow	6/1838		Originally 'Maidenhead'
24¼	Maidenhead	7/1839		Original station closed 1871
31	Twyford	7/1839		
36	Reading	3/1844		'Reading General' to 5/1973
Paddington to High Wycombe				
9¼	Greenford	1904		
10¼	Northolt	5/1907	11/1948	
11¾	South Ruislip	1908		
12¼	Ruislip Gardens	7/1934	7/1958	
13½	West Ruislip for Ickenham	1906		
16¼	Denham for Harefield	4/1906		GW&GC Joint
17¼	Denham Golf Club Platform	1912		
19	Gerrards Cross	1906		
21¼	Seer Green	1915		
23¼	Beaconsfield for Penn	1906		
28	High Wycombe	1854		
Greenford loop				
	West Ealing			
½	Drayton Green	3/1905		
1	Castle Bar Park	5/1904		
1¾	South Greenford	9/1926		
2¾	Greenford	10/1904		
Uxbridge branch				
	West Drayton			
1½	Cowley	10/1904	9/1962	
2½	Uxbridge (Vine St)	9/1856	9/1962	'Uxbridge' to 5/1907
Staines West branch				
	West Drayton			
2½	Colnbrook Estate Halt	5/1961	3/1965	
3	Colnbrook	8/1884	3/1965	
3¼	Poyle Estate Halt	1/1954	3/1965	
3¾	Poyle Halt for Stanwell Moor	6/1927	3/1965	
5¼	Yeoveney	3/1892	3/1965	
6¼	Staines West	11/1885	3/1965	

Table continued overleaf

Miles	Name	Opened	Closed	Notes
Windsor branch				
	Slough			
2¾	Windsor & Eton Central	10/1849		'Windsor & Eton' to 1/1950
Henley-on-Thames branch				
	Twyford			
1¾	Wargrave	1900		
2¾	Shiplake	6/1857		
4½	Henley-on-Thames	6/1857		
Bourne End, Marlow and High Wycombe branches				
	Maidenhead			
1¼	Furze Platt Halt	7/1937		
3	Cookham	8/1854		
4½	Bourne End	8/1854		'Marlow Road' to 1874
2¼	Marlow	6/1873		
5¾	Wooburn Green	8/1854	5/1970	
7¼	Loudwater	8/1854	5/1970	
(9	High Wycombe)			
From Slough				
¼	Slough Trading Estate	1919	1/1956	

where the District and Central Lines have terminal platforms. Ealing Broadway was extensively modernised in 1965 with shops and kiosks sharing the entrance hall with the booking office. More recently this and other stations have had their platforms resurfaced and lengthened in preparation for the 'Network Turbos'.

The next station is West Ealing, beyond which the Greenford loop branches off in a northerly direction to join up the two main lines, serving three intermediate halts in 2 miles before terminating in a bay platform at Greenford (Central Line) station. The loop, double track throughout, opened in 1903 and is mostly on embankments, with a 320-foot viaduct over the River Brent and a girder bridge across Western Avenue. At South Greenford the southbound platform was temporarily demolished in 1993 so that intending passengers for the Ealing direction had first to go northwards to Greenford and return from there! Triangular junctions at both ends make the loop a useful diversionary route when required.

Back on the main line, Hanwell station still retains much of its 'GWR' atmosphere, with original buildings and modern lighting in the shape of old gas lamps! After crossing Wharncliffe Viaduct we reach Southall, 9 miles from Paddington, where the one-time locomotive depot of post-war construction still stands, on the south side of the line in the 'vee' of the junction with the Brentford branch. The latter lost its passen-

Left Drayton Green is one of the three 'halts' on the Greenford Loop, and is near the triangle junction with the main line at West Ealing. In this view, *circa* 1953, Collett 0-4-2T No 1446, in pristine condition, is in charge of an auto-saloon on a Greenford service. Note the junction in the background, the corrugated iron shelter, and the gas lighting. *Lens of Sutton*

ger service in 1942, and proposals for its reopening in 1954 did not come to fruition.

Two stations further on, West Drayton was until the 1960s the junction for two branches, one south to Staines West - still partly open for freight traffic - and the other north to Uxbridge (Vine Street). Trains for both branches were accommodated at the outer face of the up island platform, and they shared a common exit from the west end before the Staines branch swung away to dive under the main line and continue south for 6¼ miles.

Opened throughout in 1885 with single standard-gauge track, the passenger service to Staines lasted for 80 years. There was one intermediate station with a passing loop at Colnbrook, then three 'halts' of which the request stop at Yeoveney, with a platform just 20 feet long, was surely the smallest to feature in our 'London Suburban' survey. A wartime spur, removed in 1959, connected with the Southern Region's Staines-Windsor branch, which passes close to the Staines West terminus. The station building here began its existence as a mill manager's house, conveniently situated for conversion when the railway arrived!

By contrast, the Uxbridge (Vine Street) branch, opened in 1856 and converted from the broad gauge in 1871, was doubled in 1880, being much the busier of the two. The only intermediate station in its 2½-mile length was at Cowley, and the terminus consisted of an island platform with adjacent goods yard. Passenger services ceased on 8 September 1962, though freight traffic continued until July 1964.

Another 9½ miles and five stations to the west is Slough, with four through platforms, an east-facing bay on the up side for terminating trains, and another on the down side at the west end for the Windsor branch. The station is a well-preserved example of classical red-bricked GWR architecture. Until closure in June 1964 a five-road loco-motive shed occupied a site adjacent to a triangular junction giving access to the branch from both directions. Later, diesel multiple units were stabled on sidings inside the triangle; the western arm, once used by excursions from far and near, has since been removed.

Prominently displaying reporting number '2A82', railcar W55023 of Pressed Steel construction awaits departure from Staines West on 26 April 1963. The station building pre-dated the railway and was adapted from commercial use. Note the London Transport double-decker parked outside - a welcome example of road-rail co-operation. J. M. Tolson

The 2¾-mile Windsor branch opened in 1849 with no stations en route (a short-lived one opened at Chalvey in 1929) and was double track until singled in 1963. Windsor & Eton Central terminus was an altogether superior affair, approached on brick arches with a 200-foot bowstring girder bridge across the Thames. The station was rebuilt in 1897, very much with Royal travellers in mind, boasting five platform faces, a Royal waiting room, and an arched roof, a la Paddington in miniature, over the entrance. Although now reduced to one platform, at least it is still open, with a more frequent service than it enjoyed in its prime, though such events as 'Jubilee'-hauled excursions arriving via Slough West curve are but distant memories. In recent years part of the station was incorporated into a museum, complete with 'Royal Train' and waxwork passengers and staff!

Mention should also be made of another short and less well known branch from Slough to the Trading Estate 1½ miles to the west. Before closure in January 1956 it had an island platform at the terminus for its unadvertised passenger service.

Continuing down the main line through Burnham (Bucks) and Taplow, the Thames is crossed by Brunel's famous arched bridge, widened when the relief lines were laid. At Maidenhead station, some way beyond the river, there is cross-platform connection on the 'up' side with trains for the branch north to Bourne End - now a two-track terminus where reversal is necessary for those continuing along the further short branch to Marlow.

The line was opened from Maidenhead through to High Wycombe as the independent Wycombe Railway in August 1854, worked from the outset by the Great Western Railway, which absorbed it in February 1867. It was converted to standard gauge in 1870. There is a

halt at Furze Platt and a station at Cookham, followed by a bridge across the Thames at Bourne End where, in its through station days, there was an impressive track layout and an array of lower quadrant signals.

The Marlow branch parts company with the Maidenhead line at the platform ends and closely follows the river for 2¾ miles before terminating at a single platform, short of the site of the original station. This had been the epitome of the branch-line terminus so beloved by modellers, with a small locomotive shed, closed in 1961. The branch train, affectionately known locally as the 'Marlow Donkey', is recorded for posterity (with artist's licence!) on the inn sign of a nearby hostelry.

Before closure in May 1970 the 5½-mile continuation northward from Bourne End passed through two stations, with single platforms and sidings, at Wooburn Green and Loudwater, before climbing out of the valley of the River Wye at the approach to High Wycombe. The local service to and from Maidenhead was supplemented by through trains between Paddington and High Wycombe or Aylesbury.

Next along the main line is Twyford, 31 miles from Paddington and yet another junction, this time for a branch that curves away sharply to head north for 4½ miles to Henley-on-Thames of regatta fame. The line is in close proximity to the river, which it crosses between the two intermediate stations. Opened in June 1857, it had a chequered history, being doubled after conversion from broad to standard gauge in 1876, only to be singled again many years later in June 1961. Special trains, not shown in the public timetable, have run during the regatta week and in 1948 many services were designated as having 'limited accommodation', indicating the use of AEC railcars on the branch at that time. The terminus, originally with three platform faces, boasted a Brunelian roof until the old station was demolished in 1975.

Westwards from Twyford the main line passes through the steep-sided Sonning Cutting for 2 miles before emerging into open country at the approach to Reading, the outer limit for many stopping services. Some local trains terminate in a bay platform at the London end of this extremely busy station, while others are dealt with at through platforms. The depot for diesel units is on the site of the old steam shed, west of the station in the junction of the Bristol and 'Berks & Hants' main lines.

Retracing our steps to Old Oak Common Junction, the former Birmingham main line is now closely paralleled by London

Above left Windsor station in its heyday had the look of a lesser Paddington, with a splendid glass-roofed edifice and well-protected platforms. The Swindon 'Cross Country' DMU is on an enthusiasts' rail tour, while a Pressed Steel three-car unit on the Slough shuttle service can be seen in the left background. *F. Hornby*

Left Only the Great Western and its Western Region successor could offer such an evocative scene within the 'London Suburban' area! Class '14XX' 0-4-2T No 1448 has arrived at Marlow from Bourne End on 17 November 1951 in charge of an auto-saloon, the ensemble being known locally as the 'Marlow Donkey'. *A. J. Pike*

Underground's Central Line, opened throughout to West Ruislip in November 1948. In consequence the GWR local services were withdrawn and the stations and halts as far as Greenford closed six months prior to nationalisation. The junction with the loop line at Greenford has already been mentioned, while a fly-over junction at Northolt, 2½ miles further on, marks the beginning of the line opened jointly by the GWR and GCR in 1906. This was used by express trains from both Paddington and Marylebone, so was laid out for fast running with easy gradients and loop lines at the stations for stopping trains. The through tracks have since been lifted, leaving only the platform lines in situ. The station buildings owe far more to the GWR than to the GCR, and though now served exclusively by trains from Marylebone, the neat brick buildings with wide canopies are unmistakeable in their origin.

A 2-mile branch from a junction between West Ruislip and Denham terminated in a small station at Uxbridge (High Street), opened in 1907. The meagre passenger service from Denham ceased on the outbreak of war in September 1939, though coal traffic was still handled until July 1964. A scheme to link the High Street and Vine Street stations was abandoned after some preliminary work had been started.

The line beyond Denham on to High Wycombe traverses patches of still attractive countryside and will receive further attention in the next chapter, dealing with the services out of Marylebone.

Think of typical GWR signalling and in one's mind's eye one sees lower quadrant semaphores on white posts topped with tall finials, controlled from boxes of red brick and cream-painted woodwork. But electric power signals were installed between Paddington and Southall as long ago as 1932, and new power boxes were provided at Paddington the following year. By early BR days the station approach tracks were signalled by multiple-aspect colour-lights, and the writing was on the wall for traditional methods of train control, although the transformation was gradual. Both suburban and long-distance traffic benefited from the changes, commencing in 1959 when multiple-aspect signals were installed eastwards from Acton, and authority was given to commence work on the 27 miles from Southall to Reading. A new power installation, commissioned at Slough on 13 October 1963, replaced 20 boxes controlling the main line from Hayes to Twyford and the Windsor branch, while track improvements enabled the speed limit over much of the relief lines to be raised to 75 mph. Meanwhile, on the Henley branch a computerised, electronically interlocked control system installed in 1962 was claimed to be the first of its kind in the world.

From September 1967 a new panel box at Old Oak Common took over control of the line in stages between Paddington and Hayes, linking with Slough box and, from March 1972, with Reading. A further remodelling of tracks and signalling from Paddington to West Drayton was commenced in the spring of 1992, the cost of £40 million being shared between Network SouthEast and InterCity. Preliminary work has also started on the Heathrow link, which, subject to funding, is forecast for completion in 1995/6. This involves installation of a flyover junction west of Hayes & Harlington, and eventual construction of 100 mph three-car electric units that will require only 17 minutes 'under the catenary' for the journey.

SERVICES

The Western Region timetable for Summer 1948, in the first year of British Railways, listed 75 weekday suburban arrivals at Paddington from the Reading direction. Thirteen of these, in the early morning, were 'Workmen's', none of the 40 arrivals on Sunday being so designated. Reading was the starting point for 19, the slowest being the all-stations 09.05, allowed 103 minutes for the 36 miles, a modest 21 mph. There were of course others from beyond Reading, calling at Slough and Ealing Broadway en route and taking only half that time. Three more came from Henley-on-Thames, providing 1st Class accommodation - then denied to the strictly 'suburban' traveller - while one was through from Marlow and five from High Wycombe. One of these gave the fastest service from Maidenhead, covering the 24¼ miles in 36 minutes, with one stop (40.4 mph).

Windsor had four through trains, one being non-stop from Slough in 26 minutes for 18 miles (41.5 mph). Of the 18 tabled as starting from Slough, two in the afternoon peak actually came from the Trading Estate branch, though not advertised as such. Eleven started from Uxbridge (Vine Street) - some pausing for a few minutes at West Drayton before continuing - and another 11 from Hayes & Harlington. There was just one up from Southall, and additionally there were a few short workings along the main line terminating at Slough, Ealing Broadway, etc, and making connections with Paddington trains. A solitary Reading to Twyford train continued thence along the branch to Henley-on-Thames after reversal.

All in all, this judicious mix of semi-fast and stopping trains ensured that most stations from Reading up to West Drayton had one or more reasonably fast services to Town during the morning peak hours.

Weekday suburban arrivals at Paddington from High Wycombe or beyond via Denham numbered 21, only five of which - four from Princes Risborough and one from High Wycombe - took the direct route through Park Royal. Journey time from High Wycombe ranged from 55 to 62 minutes for 28 miles. The remainder, inclusive of two from Princes Risborough, five from West Ruislip and nine from Northolt, were routed via the Greenford loop. Several of these made calls at the halts along the loop, thus supplementing the 16 daily trains from West Ruislip or Northolt to Ealing Broadway. After the Central Line extension opened on 21 November 1948 these latter started from Greenford, and from 4 July of the following year all stopping trains between High Wycombe and Paddington via Denham were withdrawn and the service concentrated on Marylebone.

The down services on all lines closely replicated those in the up direction, save that on Saturdays there were more trains around lunchtime and fewer in the late afternoon. The Sunday frequency was about half that on weekdays. The branches all enjoyed quite generous services, ranging from 16 daily between Bourne End and Maidenhead to 37 between Uxbridge and West Drayton - the latter, curiously, being the first to be closed in due course. All were still open on Sundays at that time.

Ten years later the 1958/59 timetable makes an interesting comparison, being the last in which steam traction was still pre-eminent. The 'Workmen's' designation for the early morning stopping trains had disappeared, but arrivals and departures at Paddington suburban and main-line stations were shown separately - all early morning and late evening trains being dealt with at the latter. Moreover, the through services to and from the branches were clearly identified.

As yet there were no significant changes in journey times or frequencies, save that from 1956 some off-peak branch and main-line stopping services had been reorganised on a 'regular interval' basis. Of the 76 weekday down semi-fast and stopping trains, eight went through to Uxbridge and two conveyed through coaches to Henley-on-Thames, as did five to Windsor, most of these being in the afternoon peak. High Wycombe was reached from Paddington via Maidenhead by six trains allowed between 79 and 102 minutes, as compared with around 55-60 minutes by those from Marylebone. The only services still routed by the direct line from Paddington via High Wycombe were two expresses to Birmingham and beyond, and a semi-fast to Banbury.

On the branches, Uxbridge (Vine Street) had suffered a fairly drastic reduction to 25 trains daily due to falling patronage, whereas Windsor had benefited by an increase to 41. An additional halt had opened at Poyle Estate on the Staines West branch, the overall journey time being increased by 2 or 3 minutes in consequence.

By the close of 1959 new diesel multiple units were appearing on some semi-fast turns, and within the next two years had taken over practically all suburban duties between London and Reading. A morning train between Maidenhead and High Wycombe was so worked from 21 November 1960, as were others on that line soon afterwards, including a round trip from Paddington, out via Maidenhead and back via Greenford. Even the 'Marlow Donkey' ceased to be steam-worked after 8 July 1962, in favour of a single railcar working through to and from Maidenhead.

Regrettably the transformation from steam to diesel traction was far from trouble-free, as the new suburban units were prone to breakdowns, requiring frequent substitutions by the dwindling fleet of '61XX' 2-6-2Ts with compartment stock. Later, in 1964, faced with mounting deficits, an attempt was made to win back lost custom with a more intensive service - publicised as the 'Western Commuteroutes' - providing a quarter-hourly peak-time frequency at most stations. The DMUs took over some longer runs from locomotive-hauled trains, a move resented by Season Ticket-holders accustomed to a higher standard of comfort. Matters eventually improved when, in 1968, some of the more 'customer friendly' Class 123 InterCity units were transferred to the London Division. The brunt of the work, however, continued to be borne by the Class 117 'High Density' units, which gave yeoman service for three decades - longer than their steam predecessors - until in turn displaced by a new generation of 'Network Turbos'.

In the interim there have been various timetable adjustments prompted by the constant pursuit of greater efficiency, or by problems arising from staff shortages. As previously mentioned, Uxbridge lost its passenger service in September 1962, followed by the Staines West branch in March 1965 and the Bourne End to High Wycombe line in May 1970. Cuts were proposed for the Windsor and Greenford services in 1963 and on the main line in the summer of 1968. A recasting of the timetable in May 1973 provided for a half-hourly stopping service between Paddington and Slough, connecting there with outer-suburban trains to and from Didcot. Windsor had its first off-season Sunday trains restored, but they were withdrawn from the Henley branch as of 1 January 1976. In that year ten weekday stopping trains were withdrawn on the main line, and through trains on the Henley, Marlow and Windsor branches also suffered cuts.

As from 4 March 1967, following the withdrawal of the Birkenhead expresses, a service of Birmingham 'semi-fast' trains via the direct line was introduced, giving High Wycombe the benefit of six 'non-stops' to and from Paddington. This was later reduced to four, and still further reduced in 1973 when all but one each way were diverted via Reading.

The 'Network Turbo' diesel units went into service early in 1992, initially on outer-suburban turns and eventually all but eliminating their predecessors (now, by a masterly piece of public relations, dubbed 'Heritage' units) by the end of the year. Initially, any advantage derived from their superior performance was partially offset by delays due to major track and signalling alterations at and near to Paddington.

If we conclude our survey by examining the timetable current at the time of writing in 1994 we find ample evidence of the changes over the years - not only in the trains themselves but also in travelling patterns. Of the 158 weekday arrivals listed in the Reading-Paddington table, no fewer than 54 have come from further down the line, including those from Westbury and the 'Turbo Expresses' from Oxford, all of which call at Slough. The remainder comprise 32 from Reading, two each from Maidenhead and Marlow, 35 from Slough, 32 from Greenford and one - the 'Regatta Express' - from Henley-on-Thames. Journey time from Reading with eight stops is 54 minutes - down by half an hour from the 1948 schedules. Naturally there is less scope for improvement on the remaining branches, on which the level of services does not differ radically from those of 45 years previously. Windsor has more trains daily (42 as against 36) and Henley rather fewer (23 as against 26), some of the latter being to and from Reading, reversing at Twyford. There are, however, significantly fewer through services between these branches and Paddington (Windsor has one down train but no corresponding one up).

Off peak the 'regular-interval' principle is firmly established, with four trains per hour from Reading in the weekday suburban timetable, one of which is a 'Turbo Express' from Oxford. Two connect at Slough with half-hour stopping trains, omitting Acton Main Line. The latter is served by the half-hourly Greenford-Paddington trains, connecting with main-line trains at Ealing Broadway.

On the old Birmingham direct line just one service survives, in the shape of the 09.15 Paddington-Aylesbury, reaching High Wycombe in 32 minutes with one intermediate stop and returning from Aylesbury at 10.33.

TRACTION AND TRAINS

Among the locomotive fleet inherited by BR from the Great Western Railway in 1948 was a class of 70 '61XX' 2-6-2Ts, designed in 1931 specifically for the London suburban services. At nationalisation they were allocated to Old Oak (19), Southall (14), Slough (28), and Reading (9), with the remainder at Oxford. With 5 ft 8 in driving wheels and a boiler pressure of 225 lb per sq in they could cope with 300-ton trains at speeds in excess of 60 mph when required, and were responsible for most of the stopping and semi-fast services on both the Reading and High Wycombe lines. By 1950 two were sub-shedded at Aylesbury, and several were moved away from the London Division in 1956.

Additionally, Southall had 13 of the auto-fitted '54XX' 0-6-0PTs, employed mostly on the Ealing Broadway-West Ruislip 'shuttles' of one or two saloons, while eight of the handy little '14XX' 0-4-2Ts, also auto-fitted, were distributed between Southall, Slough and Reading sheds. They shared duties on the branches with the AEC diesel railcars, but it is worth mentioning that they were similar in size to the little 'Metro' 2-4-0Ts that worked main-line stopping trains prior to the introduction of the '61XXs'!

Various other classes lent a hand, ranging from 'Hall' 4-6-0s on semi-fasts, including those to and from Henley, to the post-war Hawksworth '94XX' 0-6-0PTs, noted on the Henley branch in 1950. In January

---

WESTERN REGION: PADDINGTON-SLOUGH (18.5 MILES)
WEEKDAY DOWN TRAINS

Year Traction	1948 Steam	1966 DMUs (first generation)	1994 DMUs ('Network Turbos')
Total (all trains)	53	74	126
No of intermediate stops	10	10	8
Fastest time (mins)	48	45	37
Average speed (mph)	21.8	23.3	28.3
Slowest time (mins)	64	53	41*
Average speed (mph)	17.3	19.8	22.2

* 9 intermediate stops

of that year a '54XX' 0-6-0PT appeared on the Windsor branch with one auto-trailer, substituting for the usual '61XX' and two coaches.

Personal notes of journeys made in the earlier years mention a 'Hall' leaving platform 2 at Paddington with a 'stopper' to Slough in December 1948, while in March 1949 a '61XX' was found working West Ruislip trains via the Greenford loop. At about the same time pannier tank No 3704 gave a lively performance on a down local - a tribute to the versatility of the small engine, though doubtless hardly popular with the crew! In March 1950 a '54XX' with one auto-trailer was working West Drayton-Uxbridge shuttles, and a year later a visit was made to Henley-on-Thames behind 0-6-0PT No 5763 with two corridor coaches, the return to Twyford being in the pioneer AEC railcar No W1, built at Southall in 1933.

Another class not generally associated with the London area was the '45XX' small 2-6-2T, but a few of these gravitated to Southall in later years and one of the '55XX' series worked the last train on the Uxbridge (Vine Street) branch in September 1962.

Coaching stock consisted of several groups of non-corridor bogie compartment vehicles, mostly of pre-war build, the oldest of which were the 'Toplight' sets

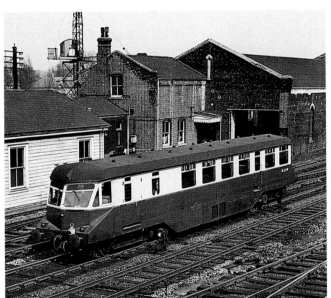

Middle left Mainly confined to the branch lines, the AEC diesel-mechanical railcars played a minor role in the WR London suburban scene. No W21W has ventured on to the Up Relief and is seen passing the goods shed at Southall on 4 April 1959. The vehicle was one of a Swindon-built batch with AEC engines, and the angular style of bodywork applied to those built from 1940 onwards. *F. Hornby*

Left For a short while after nationalisation a push-pull service operated between Paddington and West Ruislip along the old Birmingham direct line, ceasing with the extension of the Central Line in November 1948. A '54XX' 0-6-0PT of 1931 design propels an auto-saloon through the semi-derelict station at Park Royal, closed since 1937. *Lens of Sutton*

of six 48-foot close-coupled coaches built in 1921 and withdrawn around 1956. Three six-coach articulated sets, also of 48-footers dating from 1925, lasted until 1960. Of the same vintage were rakes of four 57-foot coaches comprising two Brake 3rds and two Composites seating 300 all told, while later sets built in 1931 were made up of flush-sided 60-footers. Further variations were of 1937 design and lasted until 1962, except for some eight-compartment '1sts' that were broken up around 1957; 1st class, incidentally, which had been withdrawn from suburban trains at the outbreak of war, was restored in September 1950, a measure doubtless welcomed by the more affluent commuters.

Post-war vehicles of Hawksworth design included ten-compartment 100-seater 3rds and Brake 3rds, some 100 coaches in all. They were a timely addition to the fleet in view of increasing traffic, though destined for a short life of no more than 11 years. Inevitably a wholesale withdrawal of suburban stock followed dieselisation in 1959-61, including the auto-trailers, among them the batch built as recently as 1951-52. These roomy vehicles attracted some attention in their carmine and cream livery, especially as two were named after birds - 'Thrush' and 'Wren'.

Generally the suburban trains, not infrequently strengthened by a corridor coach, compared favourably for comfort with their contemporaries on some other lines - and indeed, with their diesel successors, in the opinion of many travellers!

The first of the latter into service were Gloucester RCW single cars of the 55000 series (later classified 122), sometimes used with driving trailers, which replaced AEC railcars on the Henley branch in October 1958. They were followed a year later by the 'High Density' sets (Class 117), built by Pressed Steel Co, with two 300 hp Leyland engines giving a maximum speed of 70 mph. The three cars comprised a Driving Motor Brake Second (DMBS), Trailer Composite (TS) and Driving Brake Second (DBS), with doors to each bay and a total seating capacity of 202 2nd and 22 1st Class. The fleet, consisting of 122 vehicles in all, bore the brunt of the London

Division suburban duties into the early 1990s, supplemented by the rather more spacious 'Low Density' Metro-Cammell units (Class 101) of identical power and speed capability.

Several variations of driving and trailer cars were produced, forming two-car or three-car sets, capable of working singly or in multiple. A typical three-car formation would seat 158 2nd and 24 1st Class passengers, making them rather more suited to the semi-fast duties, shared with six of the Gloucester RCW 'Cross Country' three-car units, transferred to Reading depot in 1959.

The Pressed Steel single railcars of the 55020 series (Class 121) of 1960 became the logical successors to the auto-trains on the services between Greenford and Ealing Broadway or Paddington as well as on the branches. The DMBSs and the Driving Trailer Seconds (DTS) seat 65 and 91 respectively, and, as their maximum speed of 70 mph matches that of the multiple units, they have also been used in mixed formations with Classes 101 or 117. When first introduced they suffered from braking deficiencies and were temporarily replaced by three-car sets until the problem was solved.

As had happened in steam days, failures resulted in other forms of traction coming to the rescue, as in 1962 when some outer-suburban turns were covered for a week by 'Hymek' diesel-hydraulic locomotives with hauled stock. The final curtain came down on the old order when Southall and Reading closed to steam traction in 1965 and became diesel depots - Reading shed was demolished and replaced by a new building, although the post-war one at Southall survived. In October of that year Southall's allocation consisted of 19 Class 117 units and six Class 121 single cars, with 23 and three respectively at Reading. Four of the Class 117 units were fitted with gangway

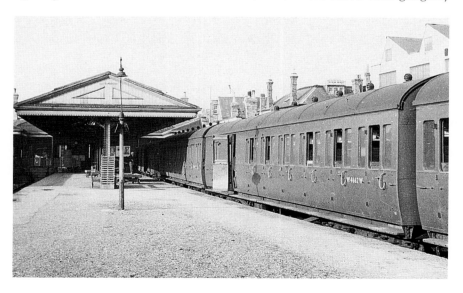

Uxbridge (Vine Street) station on 27 February 1954, consisting of an island platform alongside which is the stock for a through train to Paddington. Coach W4662W is a 1925-built 60-seater Brake 3rd. Vine Street, the terminus of a 2½-mile branch from West Drayton, saw its last passenger train in September 1962. *F. Hornby*

Seen from Paddington's Metropolitan Line platform 15, Class 165/1 'Network Turbo' DMU No 165132 awaits departure on a stopping service to Slough on 15 April 1993. The first appearance of these units on 'Thames Line' duties was precisely one year previously. *F. Hornby*

connections to facilitate ticket issuing and inspection, these being concentrated at Reading. Southall lost its allocation in May 1968, whereafter the whole fleet was based at Reading, joined in October 1982 by new Derby-built experimental three-car diesel-electric unit No 210 001. After extended trials this took over an outer-suburban roster, but the design was not adopted as standard, and No 210 001 was later converted into an electric multiple unit. By March 1986 Reading's allocation totalled 159 vehicles inclusive of 30 Class 117 units, now numbered L400-29.

As further variety, in December 1990 a Class 104 BRCW two-car unit was noted working a special service between Paddington and Hayes & Harlington via the Greenford loop, using the 'rare' curves of both triangle junctions, due to engineering work in the Acton area. It was also reported that an early trip on Sunday mornings from Slough to Paddington was being covered by a London Buses 'midibus', calling at all stations plus Old Oak depot - doubtless for the benefit of staff! By this time the diesel units had been repainted in Network SouthEast livery and sported the 'Thames Line' logo.

It was not until 1992 that the next major change came with the gradual introduction of the Class 165 'Network Turbo' units in April, closely followed by the 165/1 series in two and three-car formations. Two of the latter in multiple unit provide 500 seats in '3+2' layout as compared with 642 seats in ten hauled coaches, and their maximum speed of 90 mph - 20 mph faster than their predecessors - makes them specially

welcome in view of the 25 per cent increase in passenger journeys since 1986. Initially they were rostered for the longer runs to Didcot and Oxford, and by 3 January 1992, when the last loco-hauled 'Network Express' left Paddington, there were 25 three-car units available, including some on loan from the Chiltern Line. By the end of the year they were taking over the Reading services from the long-suffering 117s, relegating that class to the branches, but even these last bastions of the 'Heritage' units were under threat when a 'Turbo' took over the Slough-Windsor run at weekends in January 1993. The weekdays 07.32 Henley-Paddington 'Regatta Express' was also entrusted to the newcomers.

In May 1983 the first of the Class 166 variation with 400 hp motors appeared on the scene, and these, with a more roomy '2+2' seating formation and 1st Class accommodation, were allocated to the longer runs, freeing more Class 165s for the stopping services. These commenced operation on the Greenford loop in October 1993, at which time the last preserve of the 117s was on the Marlow branch. With a full complement of 65 'Turbo' units available at Reading depot, 'Driver Only' operating was introduced on 'Thames Line' services in the same month.

In conclusion, we began this survey by commenting on the relatively lowly position held by the Western Region in the 'London commuter league table', but have hopefully charted the steady but impressive transformation that has taken place since 1948. In spite of the loss of the High Wycombe traffic to Marylebone and branch line closures, there are now more trains, well patronised throughout the day, with a fleet of 1990s construction under the control of a thoroughly modernised signalling system. 'Thames Line' is thus well placed to cope with whatever demands the future may hold.

2

LINES FROM MARYLEBONE

MARYLEBONE-AYLESBURY VIA AMERSHAM
NEASDEN JUNCTION-AYLESBURY VIA HIGH WYCOMBE
WEMBLEY STADIUM LOOP

During the early 1990s Marylebone has been tastefully modernised, as befits a station catering for the growing clientele using the new and smartly timed 'Chiltern Line' 'Turbo' trains. Considering that not so long ago it was threatened with closure on more than one occasion, this represents a remarkable turn-round in its fortunes.

When the Great Central (nee Manchester, Sheffield & Lincolnshire) Railway pushed southwards towards the metropolis from Nottingham in 1899 it reached its goal by sharing the existing tracks of the Metropolitan Railway for 42 miles from Quainton Road to Canfield Place, needing only 2 miles of new line for the last lap into its brand new terminus. The fact that the entrepreneurial Sir Edward Watkin was chairman of both companies doubtless greatly facilitated this arrangement, made with the proviso that GCR trains would not call at stations in the 9¼ miles between Harrow and Marylebone, along which stretch two extra tracks were provided for the newcomer.

As the Metropolitan had reached Aylesbury in 1892 and was already offering an adequate service thereto, the prospects for the GCR in building up any worthwhile suburban traffic were clearly limited; indeed, in the earlier years the 13 daily arrivals and departures at Marylebone were all of a 'long-distance' character. But in spite of its fast and comfortable trains between Manchester and London, the competition from

three other trunk lines proved too formidable for the newcomer to make a convincing breakthrough and, even many years later, humorists referred to Marylebone station as an 'oasis of peace amidst London's noise and bustle'.

However, in the two decades between the World Wars, the Metropolitan had successfully promoted the advantages of living along its line, under the 'Metroland' banner, which inevitably brought some benefit to the GCR and its LNER successor, as partners on the Aylesbury route. Meanwhile the line through High Wycombe, opened jointly by the GWR and GCR in 1906, had also generated useful traffic. Even in pre-grouping days all 21 of Robinson's handsome 4-6-2Ts were based at Neasden shed for suburban traffic, joined by newly built engines in LNER years so that by nationalisation there were some 30 of the class available. Also, in 1937 the LNER had taken over the responsibility of handling the Metropolitan trains between Rickmansworth and Aylesbury, acquiring most of the motley fleet of steam locomotives from the 'Met' in the process. From the foregoing it can be seen that the suburban services out

Seen from the Jubilee Line platform at West Hampstead, a BR train from High Wycombe hurries towards Marylebone on the ex-GCR segregated tracks on 19 July 1986. The down Metropolitan track is between the BR and Jubilee lines, the corresponding up track being out of sight on the far right-hand side. *F. Hornby*

SUBURBAN LINES FROM MARYLEBONE TO AYLESBURY VIA AMERSHAM AND VIA HIGH WYCOMBE AND PRINCES RISBOROUGH

Miles	Name	Opened	Closed	Notes
From Marylebone via Amersham				
	Marylebone	3/1899		
9¼	Harrow-on-the-Hill			
13½	Northwood			
17	Rickmansworth			
19¼	Chorley Wood	To GCR		
21½	Chalfont & Latimer	traffic		
23½	Amersham	3/1906		
28¾	Great Missenden			
33¼	Wendover			
35½	Stoke Mandeville			
37¾	Aylesbury			
From Chalfont				
4	Chesham	1889		Met Rly
From Marylebone via High Wycombe				
6¼	Wembley Stadium	4/1923	9/1969	Station on loop; last used 8/5/1968
6½	Wembley Stadium	3/1906		'Wembley Hill' to 5/78; 'Wembley Complex' to 5/87
8	Sudbury & Harrow Road	3/1906		
8¾	Sudbury Hill Harrow	3/1906		
9¾	Northolt Park	3/1906		'For Northolt Village' to 6/55
11¾	South Ruislip	1908		
12¼	Ruislip Gardens	1934	7/1958	
13½	West Ruislip	4/1906		Originally 'For Ickenham'
16¼	Denham	4/1906		Originally 'For Harefield'
17	Denham Golf Club Platform	1912		
18¾	Gerrards Cross	4/1906		GW&GC Joint (then GW&LNER Joint)
21½	Seer Green	1915		Originally 'For Penn'
23	Beaconsfield	4/1906		Date opened to GC traffic
27¾	High Wycombe	4/1906		
30	West Wycombe	8/1862	11/1958	
33	Saunderton	8/1862		
36	Princes Risborough	10/1863		
37½	Monks Risborough	11/1929		Originally GWR broad gauge; standard
39	Little Kimble	6/1872		gauge from 10/1868; GW&GC Joint since
42½	South Aylesbury Halt	2/1933	6/1967	1907

of Marylebone have always been - both for historical and geographical reasons - very much of an 'outer' nature, Aylesbury being 37¾ miles by one route and 43¼ miles by the other from the London terminus.

During BR years the former GCR line - initially part of the Eastern Region - became something of a political football, passed from one administration to another; the first major upheaval was in July 1949 when Marylebone annexed from Paddington the services to High Wycombe and Princes Risborough via Ruislip. Then in April 1950 the honours went slightly the other way when Marylebone to Northolt Junction

and Neasden to Harrow (exclusive) were transferred to the Western Region, though remaining in the Eastern Region operating area. The London Midland Region gained control eight years later (in February 1958), and in 1963 Marylebone came under LM 'Western Lines' jurisdiction. Meanwhile, as from 11 September 1961 the LMR took over all services north of Amersham from London Transport's Metropolitan line, coincidental with the extension of electrification to that point.

These changes were reflected in the variety of steam motive power employed - fascinating for the

Although this has the appearance of an outward-bound suburban train, the insignia on the smokebox door of Fairburn Class '4' 2-6-4T No 42256 identifies it as a 'special' heading for the Wembley Stadium loop. It is passing a semaphore-signalled Neasden Junction on 2 May 1959 - Cup Final day! *B. W. Brooksbank*

enthusiast but surely a headache for the maintenance staff at Neasden shed who, at one time or another, had ER, LMR, WR and BR Standard locomotives under their charge.

In the early 1960s there was a steady and deliberate run-down of the long-distance services culminating in the withdrawal of the few remaining Nottingham semi-fasts on 5 September 1966, after which the line beyond Aylesbury was closed to passenger traffic. The Marylebone to Aylesbury direct route was thus left with only the 'outer-suburbans', dieselised since 1961, so that the situation was thus exactly the opposite of that in the early GCR years. Nevertheless uncertainty persisted, with proposals in 1969 to divert trains on the High Wycombe line back to Paddington, leaving Baker Street to deal with all Aylesbury traffic, while the Neasden to Northolt Junction link would close. Reprieve came after due consideration in 1972, on the grounds of hardship to passengers using the four threatened stations, plus the expenditure that would be incurred, but by 1984 Marylebone was once again under sentence of closure. This time it was the extra revenue generated by the introduction of Travel Cards that saved the day, and the closure notice was eventually withdrawn in April 1986.

Next came regional boundary changes from 11 October 1987, whereby Marylebone-Aynho Junction via High Wycombe, Neasden Junction-Claydon Junction via Aylesbury, and Greenford-Northolt Junction were transferred from the London Midland to the Western Region. By this time 'Network SouthEast' had been launched, and plans were laid for the replacement of the ageing fleet of diesel units and for improvements to Marylebone station. While work on tracks and signalling was in progress trains were indeed diverted into Paddington in fulfilment of the 1969 proposals, but only on Sundays and only temporarily!

ROUTES AND INFRASTRUCTURE

Historically the services out of Marylebone make use of stations of Metropolitan and Great Western

Railway origin on the Aylesbury direct route and the line via High Wycombe respectively, with only the four stations between the Neasden and Northolt Junctions, plus the terminus itself, built exclusively for GCR purposes.

Hidden behind the imposing frontage of a hotel building - latterly headquarters of the British Railways Board - Marylebone station is of modest proportions and its four platform faces are adequate, even today with more trains in and out than ever before. It has recently been extensively modernised, and a booking office on the concourse - perhaps more convenient but less imposing than the original - doubles for BR and for London Underground's Bakerloo Line below.

A new 60-lever mechanical signal box came into use in 1967 controlling the station, the approaches and access to the diesel depot. Colour-light signalling was installed in September/October 1990 and stabling sidings for the 'Turbo' trains were provided on the west side, at which time the diesel depot closed.

Half a mile or so out of the station the lines plunge into a series of shallow tunnels beneath St John's Wood and Lord's cricket ground (fulfilling a solemn pledge that the coming of the railway would not desecrate the sacred pitch!) before climbing up alongside the Metropolitan and Jubilee lines near Finchley Road. The 'Chiltern Line' tracks remain independent out to Harrow-on-the-Hill, beyond which the double track to Rickmansworth was shared by BR and Metropolitan trains until quadrupling took place between 1959 and 1962. Thereafter one pair has been allotted to BR and to Metropolitan fast trains, leaving the other tracks free for Metropolitan stopping ser-

For a map of the lines from Marylebone to Aylesbury and High Wycombe, see page 12.

vices. Passing Neasden the site of the former steam shed (closed in 1966) can be seen on the down side, closely followed by the divergence of the link line to Northolt Junction.

Harrow-on-the-Hill, 9¼ miles from Marylebone, is the first stop for 'Chiltern Line' trains. The station was reconstructed in stages by London Transport between 1938 and 1948 and has six platform faces, providing interchange with the Metropolitan Line. A busy bus station in the yard makes it an admirable centre for rail and road public transport.

Onwards from Harrow the fast lines bypass the next four stations out to Moor Park, noted for its golf courses. Beyond here the four tracks merge into two between the South and North Junctions for the Metropolitan branch to Watford.

Then comes Rickmansworth, currently the second stopping place out of Marylebone, at the foot of a 7-mile climb through Chalfont & Latimer to Amersham. Chalfont is the junction for a 4-mile Metropolitan single-track branch to Chesham, on which, prior to electrification in August 1960, shuttle services were worked by a BR steam locomotive with Metropolitan stock. Amersham, a town of 17,000 inhabitants, became the outer terminus for Metropolitan services in September 1960. From here there are only three stations in the remaining rather thinly populated 14 miles to Aylesbury. From a summit between Great Missenden and Wendover it is downhill at 1 in 117 over the final 7 miles.

Aylesbury, the county town of Buckinghamshire, has grown considerably in post-war years and now has 50,000 inhabitants. The station has been modernised without seriously interfering with its traditional architecture, and a new depot has been built nearby where the 'Turbo' diesel units are maintained. There is, however, no trace of the small two-road steam shed that once occupied a site alongside the station on the down side.

Until recent years much of the direct route to Aylesbury was still mechanically signalled, save that a new box controlling colour-lights came into use at Amersham in 1960. The semaphores have now made way for three-aspect colour-lights, and a power box has been commissioned on the platform at the London end of Aylesbury station. The maximum line speed has been upgraded to 75 mph, to the benefit of the 'Turbo' units.

To consider the other route to Aylesbury, via High Wycombe, we must retrace our steps to Neasden,

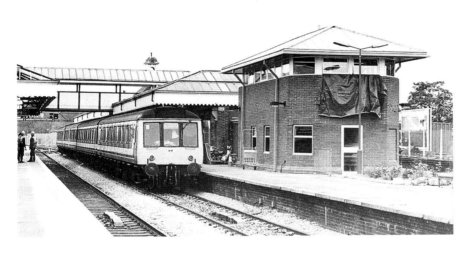

Above left Rebuilding at Aylesbury is well advanced on 30 May 1991 as a Class 115 DMU awaits departure time alongside the new signal box. The unit, in NSE livery, bears the name *Aylesbury College, Silver Jubilee 1987* on the leading power car. *F. Hornby*

Left When the Neasden-Northolt Junction line was opened the stations were quite lavish, in expectation of building development at a later date. Although now surrounded by housing they have been drastically 'rationalised' - as evidenced by this view of the rebuilt Sudbury & Harrow Road on 18 January 1994, the new island platform occupying the site of the former through roads. The 'Turbo' unit on a service from High Wycombe has not deigned to stop! *F. Hornby*

where it branches off the direct route to link, 6½ miles further on, with the ex-GWR line from Paddington by a flying junction at Northolt. There are four stations between the two junctions, only two of which - Wembley Stadium and Northolt Park - are now served outside peak hours. This stretch is not unlike its near neighbour, the WR Greenford loop, in its urban surroundings, though the stations as built were - unnecessarily as it turned out - far more lavish and have been much simplified in recent years.

At least passing notice should also be taken of the Wembley Stadium loop, which, although concerned only with special events, made heavy demands on suburban stock and motive power on those occasions. The loop, about a mile in length, diverged at Neasden North Junction from the Northolt Junction line, which it rejoined, facing Neasden, some 600 yards further on. The special trains, running at intervals of only a few minutes when required, traversed it in a clockwise direction, calling at the single-platform Stadium station before doubling back to Marylebone. It had opened in April 1923 in time for the first FA Cup Final, and closed in September 1969.

From Northolt Junction through High Wycombe to Princes Risborough we are on the erstwhile GWR&GCR Joint line of 1906, which received due notice in the previous chapter by virtue of the fact that for a short while after nationalisation it was served by stopping trains from Paddington as well as from Marylebone. Though undulating, the line is easily graded with a summit near Beaconsfield, and some of the long-distance expresses from Marylebone took this route, which had the advantage of avoiding possible delays from Metropolitan trains.

Most off-peak trains make eight stops in the 28 miles to and from High Wycombe, about half as many as in a comparable distance from Liverpool Street or Victoria, emphasising the contrast in the catchment areas served. South and West Ruislip became

interchange stations when the Central Line extension was completed in November 1948. Beyond Ruislip the line crosses the River Colne, then reaches Beaconsfield, with 13,000 inhabitants, and High Wycombe itself, a sprawling conurbation of 70,000 souls, both places contributing their valuable quotas of daily commuters.

The station layout at High Wycombe was duly 'rationalised' during May 1990, when the centre roads were removed and replacement of the many GWR-type semaphore signals began. The up and down platforms here are staggered, with a terminal bay at the London end of the down platform, long enough for a pair of two-car diesel units.

All told, inclusive of station refurbishments between West Ruislip and High Wycombe and the removal of mechanical signal boxes, some £70 million has been expended on a thorough-going modernisation programme.

From High Wycombe there are now only four stations in the remaining 15½ miles to Aylesbury, two others - West Wycombe and South Aylesbury Halt - having been closed in 1958 and 1967 respectively.

Above right After a major football match this platform at Wembley Stadium would have been thronged with jubilant (or disappointed) crowds awaiting transport back to Marylebone. No doubt due to the increasing popularity of road transport, the station and loop closed in September 1969. *Lens of Sutton*

Right West Ruislip station on the one-time GW&GCR Joint line still displays a strong GWR influence, on the up platform at least. This view towards High Wycombe shows the modern overbridge linking the 'Chiltern Line' station with the Central Line terminus on the left-hand side. *F. Hornby*

There is a rising gradient from High Wycombe to Saunderton, then a fairly steep fall, on average at 1 in 100. For some 3 miles beyond Saunderton the up and down lines diverge, the latter being the 1862 original while the up line was laid in the early 1900s. They come together again at Princes Risborough, the second of the stations still open.

Princes Risborough was in its heyday the junction for a branch to Watlington and for a secondary line to Oxford via Thame, which lost their passenger services in 1961 and 1963 respectively. The mechanical signalling equipment here, rendered redundant by the installation of MAS (multiple-aspect signalling) has been acquired by a local preservation association.

The main line onwards to Banbury and Birmingham is of course still open and used by the hourly service to and from Marylebone, but we turn due north along the remaining sparsely populated 7 miles to Aylesbury. This is single track across mainly flat country and of Great Western origin, albeit originally opened in 1863 by the independent Wycombe Railway. There is a descent at 1 in 50 beyond Little Kimble, the second of the two stations, and the direct route via Amersham is joined close to Aylesbury station.

SERVICES

For some years following nationalisation in 1948, so long as steam traction prevailed there was no great change in the services on the Aylesbury direct line, either in speed or frequency. As an example of the prevailing standards, the 1953 timetable showed only 11 weekday stopping trains each way, taking from 88 to 101 minutes for the 37¾ miles with from eight to ten stops en route. Other than a solitary through train from Chesham for the early risers, the first arrival at Marylebone was at 08.51 from Aylesbury, closely followed by a faster train taking only 80 minutes with two fewer stops. However, travellers from the county town in those days also had the benefit of five fast trains originating from Woodford or points further north, with an average journey time of 1 hour.

The Saturday frequency was similar, but with adjustments, mainly in the down direction, to allow for the half-day, while on Sundays there were just two stopping and two fast trains. On this route, of course, the Metropolitan also provided a frequent service to and from Baker Street and the City.

The line via High Wycombe fared rather better, thanks to the transfer of most services from Paddington to Marylebone in 1949. In the up direction off-peak trains, inclusive of five through from Princes Risborough, left High Wycombe at 10 minutes past each hour, all stations to West Ruislip then non-stop into Marylebone. Stopping trains from West Ruislip followed 10 minutes later, taking 35 minutes for the 13¼ miles, but these were severely curtailed from January 1951, with some trains from High Wycombe making extra stops in partial compensation. Despite the growth of housing along this section over the years, it undoubtedly suffers from the close proximity of stations on the Piccadilly Line.

In the 1953 timetable, inclusive of two trains through from Aylesbury and nine from Princes Risborough, there were 31 weekday up trains all told from High Wycombe, ranging from 53 minutes with six stops to 68 minutes with 12 stops, for the 27¾ miles. The Sunday service consisted of 17 trains, of which six were through from Princes Risborough and one from Brackley.

Five years later, the pattern in the 1958/59 Winter timetable was substantially unchanged on both lines, but dieselisation was looming on the horizon, a trial run having been made by a two-car unit between Marylebone and Beaconsfield as far back as April 1954. The phasing out of steam traction began on 23 January 1961, a process completed for stopping trains on both routes by June of the following year. During the interim stages the new four-car diesel mechanical sets ran to steam-train timings, but with the completion of track qua-

Class 'A5' 4-6-2T No 69805, a Gorton product of 1911, eases into Marylebone on 10 October 1953 with a stopping train from Aylesbury comprised of Gresley stock. Although transferred away from Neasden shortly afterwards, No 69805 remained in service until September 1959. *F. Hornby*

drupling between Harrow and Watford South Junction, improvements were possible. Hitherto a few BR trains had called at stations between Harrow-on-the Hill and Rickmansworth, but this was no longer possible as only Moor Park had extra platforms on the new fast lines, for the benefit of Metropolitan trains only.

From 18 June 1961, therefore, all BR services were non-stop over this section, with hourly off-peak trains on weekdays and Saturdays to and from Aylesbury making seven stops with a 59-minute schedule. Frequency was stepped up to quarter-hourly during peak times, the total number of trains being double that of steam days, while the running time was reduced, on average, by half an hour. On Sundays there were still only two through trains in each direction, but others shuttled between Aylesbury and Amersham, connecting there with the Metropolitan services.

Initially on the High Wycombe line the diesel units showed less superiority over their steam predecessors, due to the numerous service slacks, so the average schedule of 53 minutes between High Wycombe and Marylebone was only marginally better than the fastest trains in 1953. Nevertheless the hourly interval service with extras at business times, plus the restoration of hourly stopping trains to and from West Ruislip, represented an overall improvement. Beyond High Wycombe some additional services were extended through to and from Aylesbury in 1962.

In the introductory diesel year of 1961 just 49 trains left Marylebone on weekdays, carrying some 6,000 passengers. By 1968 the total number of arrivals and departures had risen to 126, all now operating within the confines of the two routes to Aylesbury, as long-distance services had ceased two years previously.

During the remaining years in which the Derby four-car sets kept their monopoly the level of services remained fairly constant. Taking 1966 as an example, there were 26 down trains to Aylesbury on weekdays and Saturdays, calling at Harrow and all stations to Rickmansworth, while on Sundays

16 trains each way between Amersham and Aylesbury ran in connection with Metropolitan services. On the High Wycombe line there were 35 weekday down trains, ten of which went on to Princes Risborough and six more to Aylesbury. The Saturday and Sunday timetables showed 24 and 17 departures respectively, the journey time to High Wycombe being little changed at 50 minutes. Ten years later, as part of a London Midland Region economy drive, some service cuts were made as from 5 January 1976.

Moving on to the present day, following the introduction of the 'Network Turbo' diesel units, we find that Marylebone has regained something of its main-line status by virtue of the fact that in 1993 there are seven trains through to Birmingham (Snow Hill), all but one of which make three stops before High Wycombe. The off-peak pattern is for a stopping train to High Wycombe at 10 minutes past each hour and a fast train at 40 minutes past, continuing alternately to Banbury and Birmingham. There are trains to and from Aylesbury on this route at peak times only, with off-peak shuttles between Aylesbury and Princes Risborough and - as a reminder of bygone days - a morning train through from Paddington! All told, on weekdays High Wycombe sees 48 arrivals from Marylebone, while another seven provide a morning and evening service as far as Gerrards Cross only. The 'Turbo' trains have reduced the journey time to High Wycombe to 44 minutes with eight stops.

On the Aylesbury direct route, in addition to two early morning workings between Amersham and Aylesbury, there are 34 through trains on weekdays taking 55-56 minutes, eight more than in the 1960s with a slight reduction in journey times. The Sunday service is similarly improved, with 25 trains plying between Amersham and Aylesbury.

The cars on the left may give some clue as to the period of this photograph, as does the blue-grey livery, but the Derby-built Class 115 DMU could have been seen here at Marylebone at any time during three decades. The date is actually 30 March 1984, and the absence of passengers confirms, as does the distant clock, that this is an 'off-peak' scene. *F. Hornby*

TRACTION AND TRAINS

The first suburban services out of Marylebone in 1906 were worked by the then new GCR 4-4-2Ts, a few of which survived at Neasden well into the 1950s, mainly for the Chesham branch, but they were displaced from main-line duties by the imposing 'A5' 4-6-2Ts from 1911 onwards. In 1948 these locomotives were still the mainstay on both routes, but their decline was rapid after the appearance of Thompson's 'L1' 2-6-4Ts in that year, and the last two 'A5s' were transferred away from Neasden in mid-1954.

The GCR had provided four-coach bogie sets for the London area suburban trains, superior to most of their contemporaries, but in LNER days Gresley compartment stock gradually appeared on the scene. The normal loads consisted of five or six non-corridor bogies, well within the capabilities of the powerful six-coupled locomotives. Later, some 1940-built twin-articulated sets were also in use.

The effects of nationalisation were soon felt and in May 1949 a Fairburn 2-6-4T of LMS design appeared on High Wycombe duties. In July of that year a shortage of 'A5s' and 'L1s' due to maintenance arrears led to such varied types being pressed into service as 'J11' 0-6-0s, 'N2' and 'N7' 0-6-2Ts, Fowler and Stanier 2-6-4Ts (on loan from the LM Region), 'B1' 4-6-0s, and even a 'V2' 2-6-2. Also noted at this time were a pair of WR '61XX' 2-6-2Ts, sub-shedded at Aylesbury and frequently working through to Marylebone. By 1950 Neasden's allocation of 'L1s' was no fewer than 37, with the 'A5s' correspondingly reduced to five.

The stopping trains between Marylebone and West Ruislip were worked by 'N5' 0-6-2Ts of GCR origin and - after 1949 - by five 'N7' 0-6-2Ts fitted with vacuum-controlled push-pull gear. These engines also saw service on the Chesham branch, but were transferred away to King's Cross shed after the curtailment of the West Ruislip trains in January 1951.

Gresley's 'Quad-art' (four-coach articulated sets) also saw some use on this service from 1949, and were also noted, hauled by 'A5s' and 'L1s', on specials to Wembley Stadium for the 1950 Amateur Cup Final.

On a journey made to West Ruislip on 16 September 1950 a down semi-fast consisted of six coaches hauled by 'L1' No 67782, and the return on a stopping train had 'N5' No 9302 as motive power. This particular engine, still with its LNER number, was not auto-fitted, so a smart 'run round' had to be made at West Ruislip. An 'A5' 4-6-2T was noted similarly employed, but there was no sign of the 'N7s' on this occasion. As late as 1955 the ageing 'N5s' were still hard at work on the remaining West Ruislip turns.

In 1951 the ACV diesel set of three four-wheelers appeared at Marylebone and some trial runs were made on the Chesham branch before they were moved elsewhere - no doubt to the great relief of the patrons!

Although nominally powerful engines, the 'L1s' were prone to failures, frequently due to hot axleboxes, and in 1954 a critical situation was resolved by the transfer from the Tilbury section of Fairburn 2-6-4Ts, which remained on the strength until dieselisation. By 1957 Neasden's 'L1' allocation had dwindled to 17, and to a mere two within another year. In mid-1956 a batch of new BR Standard 2-6-4Ts (Nos 80137-44) also arrived, and a visit to Neasden shed in March 1957 produced 12 'L1s', nine Fairburns and five BR Standard 2-6-4Ts, with two 'C14' 4-4-2Ts keeping up the old GCR tradition. Also present were three BR Class '4' 2-6-0s, which were not infrequently used on semi-fast passenger turns.

All this changed dramatically from 1961 onwards with the introduction of the Derby-built four-car diesel mechanical units of 1960 construction - later classified 115. With two 460 hp BUT engines per unit and a maximum speed of 70 mph, they were of 'High Density' design, similar to the contemporary Western Region Class '117s', seating 302 2nd and 30 1st Class passengers per unit. In 1962 a six-road maintenance depot was constructed for them just outside Marylebone station on the up side, and this remained in

Typical of the run-down state of many locomotives in steam's last years, a filthy BR Class '4' 2-6-0 rests at the buffers at Marylebone on 1 July 1961. The six coaches of compartment stock are representative of former GCR line stopping trains over many years. *B. W. Brooksbank*

use for 30 years until the coming of the 'Turbos'. At the other end of the line, units are also stabled in the purpose-built depot at Aylesbury.

The Marylebone depot allocation in 1965 consisted of 30 Class 115 four-car units. A 1968 survey revealed that there were variations within that class, most certainly as regards livery, which, basically at that time, was 'Rail Blue'. Some had yellow panels and others full yellow ends, with the emblems on cab doors or body sides and with two different sizes of numerals!

During the 1970s and 1980s the allocation remained more or less constant, but from May 1986 the fleet was repainted in 'Network SouthEast' livery, and in June 1987 one of the driving vehicles received the name *Aylesbury College, Silver Jubilee 1987* - a first for a DMU.

In December 1989 orders were placed with BREL for the 'Network Turbo' units, and the first of Class 165 was due into service in February 1991, with a complete complement of 89 vehicles scheduled by September; however, it was not until 4 May that No 165001 made a brief appearance at Marylebone. These two- and three-car units are powered by two Perkins 350 bhp engines, giving a maximum speed of 90 mph, and are the first to be fitted with 'SELCAB' Automatic Train Protection. On 'Chiltern Line' services they display two-character headcodes between 01 and 19.

Meantime, doubtless with the 115s becoming progressively run down, Class 47 locomotives with five Mk I coaches were drafted into service on the Aylesbury direct route during November 1990. There were in fact still a few turns on this line covered by 115s at the end of 1991 due to the new units having clearance problems at Rickmansworth, but this was resolved by 20 January 1992. Some Class 165s were based at Old Oak for a time, pending full use of the new Aylesbury depot, and a 'last run' was made by a Class 115 on the 20.45 service from Aylesbury on 29 July 1992, so bringing to an end an era lasting 31 years.

Above right The six-road diesel servicing depot at Marylebone on 16 May 1978, during the 'Rail Blue' livery era. Two of the 30 Class 115 DMUs allocated here await their next assignments. *F. Hornby*

Right On 22 April 1992 brand new Class 165 two-car 'Turbo' unit No '65019' hurries through Moor Park en route from Aylesbury to Marylebone. After 30 years of 'High Density' Class 115s, the newcomers, with their 'next station' display screens and superior seating, represent a decided improvement. *F. Hornby*

3
LINES FROM EUSTON

In the two previous chapters we have been concerned with steam-hauled suburban services that were dieselised during BR years, but in turning to the lines out of Euston we encounter a fascinating combination of steam, diesel, DC and AC electric traction.

Like the Great Western, the London & North Western Railway, as successor to the London & Birmingham, was essentially a 'main-line' company in its early years, with little expectation of worthwhile revenue from the few stations serving small communities south of Watford. Indeed, in 1841 all but two of the 13 daily departures from Euston were for Rugby and beyond, but some modest development took place along the line in the 1860s as far out as Harrow. Later, with four tracks available since 1875, some kind of local service was deemed necessary and, from June 1879, hourly trains were provided between Euston and Watford. A census in 1903 showed 36 daily suburban arrivals at Euston and, during the Edwardian decade, Webb's 2-4-2Ts and 0-6-2Ts were replaced by Whales's 4-4-2 'Precursor tanks' with neat rakes of bogie stock - evidence of the increasing importance of this traffic.

Willesden Junction was rebuilt in 1894 and two additional tracks - the 'New Lines' - were completed through it from Kensal Green to Watford in February 1913, along which new stations were opened, with additional platforms at the existing ones. The planned electric services from Euston could not commence until two new single-line tunnels were completed at Primrose Hill and, with the intervention of the First World War, this was delayed until July 1922. In the meantime it fell to the Bakerloo line to operate the first electric trains along the New Lines, from Queens Park to Willesden Junction on 10 May 1915, and on to Watford Junction on weekdays in April 1917, joined in the peak hours by a few LNWR trains from Broad Street.

Within months of the start of the Euston-Watford electric service the LNWR became the largest constituent of the newly formed LMS, but the three-car multiple units, designed originally for the 1914 Willesden-Earls Court service, were still at work 25 years later when the LMS was in turn absorbed by British Railways. During those years electrification had stimulated housing developments along the line, with the fortunate residents enjoying a frequent service not only to Euston but also to Broad Street, and by Bakerloo tube via the West End to the Elephant & Castle.

On the parallel main line the outer limit for residential services had moved steadily further from London, out to Tring and Bletchley, and from 1928 onwards the new Fowler 2-6-4Ts were able to show their paces on the smartly timed semi-fasts. By 1948 the standard of service was not far short of that on offer prior to the outbreak of war in September 1939.

DC LINES

EUSTON-WATFORD, CROXLEY GREEN & RICKMANSWORTH, INCLUDING BAKERLOO LINE FROM QUEENS PARK

ROUTES AND INFRASTRUCTURE

Until the comprehensive reconstruction of 1963-68, Euston could almost rival the old Waterloo of LSWR days in being a haphazard collection of train sheds, resulting from piecemeal additions over the years.

Prior to rebuilding, the tracks at platforms 4, 5 and 7 were electrified for the DC trains, but in the modernised station two platforms, Nos 9 and 10, are deemed adequate, the three-car units appearing rather insignificant under the vast expanse of roof.

Once clear of the platforms the up and down slow

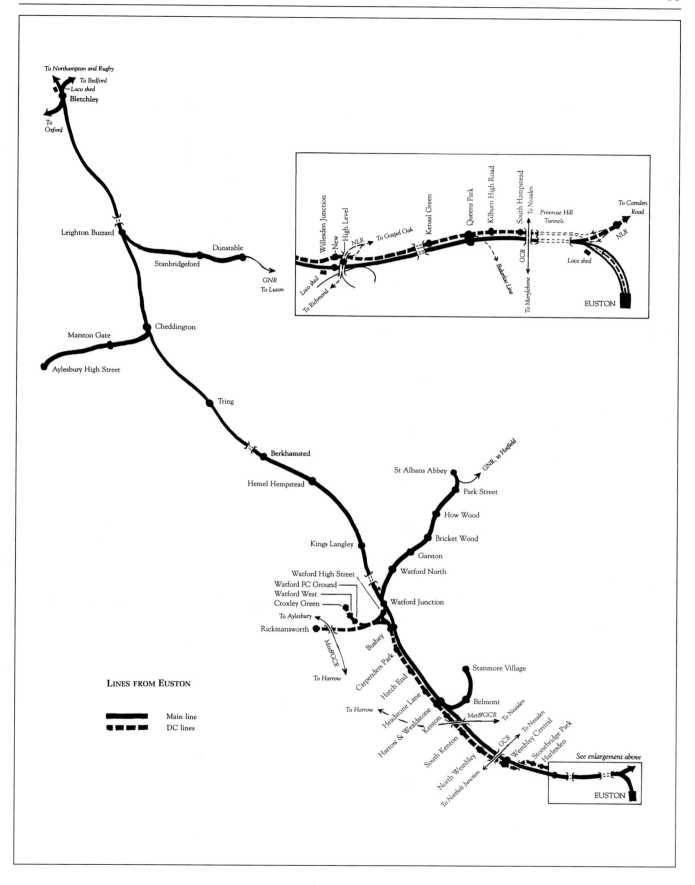

To Northampton and Rugby
To Bedford
Loco shed
Bletchley
To Oxford

Leighton Buzzard

Dunstable
Stanbridgeford

GNR
To Luton

Marston Gate
Cheddington

Aylesbury High Street

Tring

Berkhamsted

Hemel Hempstead

St Albans Abbey
Park Street

GNR to Hatfield

How Wood

Bricket Wood

Garston

Kings Langley

Watford North

Watford High Street
Watford FC Ground
Watford West
Croxley Green

To Aylesbury
Rickmansworth

Watford Junction

Bushey
Met&GCR
To Harrow

Carpenders Park
Hatch End

Stanmore Village

Headstone Lane
Harrow & Wealdstone
To Harrow
Kenton

Belmont

Met&GCR   To Neasden

South Kenton

GCR   To Neasden
Wembley Central
Stonebridge Park
Harlesden

North Wembley

To Northolt Junction

See enlargement above

EUSTON

LINES FROM EUSTON

———— Main line
- - - - DC lines

Enlargement:

Willesden Junction
New
High Level
NLR
To Gospel Oak

Kensal Green

Queens Park
Kilburn High Road
South Hampstead
To Neasden

Primrose Hill Tunnels

To Camden Road

NLR

Loco shed
To Richmond

Baker loo Line

GCR

To Marylebone

Loco shed

EUSTON

Suburban Lines from Euston:
DC lines from Euston to Watford Junction and branches

Miles	Name	Opened (New Lines)	Closed	Notes
From Euston				
0	Euston	} To DC		
2½	South Hampstead	} lines		Original main line station 1879
3¼	Kilburn High Road	} 7/1922		Original main line station 1851
3¾	Queens Park	2/1915		'Queens Park (West Kilburn)' to 12/1954
4½	Kensal Green	10/1916		
5½	Willesden Junction (New)	6/1912		
5⅞	Harlesden	6/1912		
7½	Stonebridge Park	6/1912		
8¼	Wembley Central	6/1912		'For Sudbury'
8¾	North Wembley	6/1912		
9½	South Kenton	7/1933		
10¼	Kenton	6/1912		
11½	Harrow & Wealdstone	6/1912		
12¾	Headstone Lane	2/1913		
13½	Hatch End	6/1912		'For Pinner' to 6/1956
14¾	Carpenders Park	1914		New station opened 1953
16	Bushey	2/1913		'Bushey & Oxhey'
16¾	Watford High Street	2/1913		
17¾	Watford Junction	2/1913		
Croxley Green and Rickmansworth branches				
	Watford Junction			
1½	Watford (FC station)	12/1982		
2	Watford West	6/1912		} Electrified from 10/1922
2¾	Croxley Green	6/1912		
3½	Rickmansworth Church Street	10/1862	3/1952	Electrified from 9/1927

lines are shared by AC and DC trains for a mile or so until the latter diverge on to their own tracks at Chalk Farm. Here they descend by a burrowing junction graded at 1 in 37 to re-emerge on the up (north) side of the main lines, where they are joined by a spur from the North London line, now 'freight only' but formerly used by the electric trains between Broad Street and Watford. They then pass through the twin-bore 1,220-yard Primrose Hill Tunnel and the stations at South Hampstead and Kilburn High Road, both with booking offices on overbridges at the western ends. Next is Queens Park,

Queens Park station on 14 August 1985 with a Watford-bound Class 501 three-car EMU in blue-grey livery. The 501s were Eastleigh-built in 1957-8 in line with contemporary Southern Region designs, save that screw couplings were fitted in place of buckeyes. The Bakerloo Line platforms are just visible on the left, with the main lines on the right. *F. Hornby*

SUBURBAN LINES FROM EUSTON: MAIN LINE FROM EUSTON TO BLETCHLEY AND BRANCHES

Miles	Name	Opened	Closed	Notes
From Euston				
0	Euston	7/1837		
3¾	Queens Park	1879		
5½	Willesden Junction	9/1866	12/1962	
8¼	Wembley Central	1842		'Wembley for Sudbury' to 7/1948
11½	Harrow & Wealdstone	7/1837		'Harrow' to 5/97
13½	Hatch End	8/1842		'For Pinner' to 6/1956
16	Bushey	1841		'Bushey & Oxhey'
17½	Watford Junction	7/1837		
21	Kings Langley	1909	5/1924	'& Abbots Langley' to 5/1974
23	Apsley	1938		
24½	Hemel Hempstead	7/1837		Opened as 'Boxmoor'
28	Berkhamsted	1838		
31¾	Tring	10/1837		
36	Cheddington	1839		
40¼	Leighton Buzzard	7/1837		'Leighton' 1837-59
46¾	Bletchley	1838		
Stanmore branch				
	Harrow			
1	Belmont	9/1932	10/1964	
2	Stanmore Village	12/1890	10/1964	'Stanmore' to 9/1950
St Albans branch				
	Watford Junction			
¾	Watford North	1910		
1¾	Garston (Herts)	2/1966		
3¼	Bricket Wood	1853		
4½	How Wood	10/1988		
5	Park Street	1858		'Park St & Frogmore' from 1890
6½	St Albans Abbey	1858		
Aylesbury branch				
	Cheddington			
2¾	Marston Gate	1860	2/1953	
7	Aylesbury	6/1839	2/1953	
Dunstable branch				
	Leighton Buzzard			
4¼	Stanbridgeford	1849	7/1962	Private station until 1860
7¼	Dunstable	1848	7/1962	

where the Bakerloo line surfaces between the up and down DC tracks at the London end of the station, which consists of two island platforms spanned by a wide glass canopy.

After threading the twin-bore Kensal Rise Tunnel the DC and main lines part company, with Willesden Traction & Maintenance Depot for electric and diesel locomotives between the two on a site formerly occupied by carriage sheds. The 'New Lines' Willesden New station consists of a wide island platform with two bays inset, which, in the early days were for the benefit of trains terminating there, but one track has been removed and the other sees little use. There are footbridges at both ends of the station, one leading to the booking office, the other, at the London end, linking with the high-level island platform of the North London line, which crosses at right-angles. There is a double-track electrified spur connecting

Kensal Green is typical of most of the DC line stations between Euston and Willesden Junction, with the booking office spanning the tracks. In this view on 23 August 1992 a southbound Bakerloo Line train of 1972 Mk II stock is emerging from the short twin-bore tunnel. *F. Hornby*

Kenton to cater for nearby housing estates. in 1957 annual ticket sales here reached 1.3 million, plus over 32,000 season tickets!

Next comes Bushey, where the DC lines swing sharply away from the main line to make a wide loop through Watford High Street station after crossing the River Colne on a long viaduct, then returning to terminate alongside the main line at Watford Junction.

the two lines, now little used but which once provided an alternative route for trains between Broad Street and Watford.

Beyond Willesden Junction the DC and main lines remain separated by freight yards and carriage sidings for a further 2 miles, the stations at Harlesden and Stonebridge Park being on this stretch. The DC tracks then burrow diagonally beneath the main lines, emerging on the down side and keeping parallel with them for another 8 miles. Several of the stations between Willesden New and Watford are still in the style dating from the opening of the New Lines in 1913, with two well-sheltered platforms and neat red-bricked buildings and retaining walls. One exception is Wembley Central, the first station after the lines have changed sides, where a large raft of shops and offices covers the entire platform length and spans all the running lines - the result of a property development commenced in 1963 and costing £3 million.

There are four more stations in the next 3¼ miles, the second being South Kenton, opened on 3 July 1933 with an island platform to serve a populous area close to Northwick Park. The fourth is Harrow & Wealdstone, terminus for the Bakerloo Line trains, which reverse in a siding between the running lines at the Watford end of the station. The DC and Bakerloo trains connect here with the semi-fast Milton Keynes and Northampton services on the main line.

Carpenders Park, three stations beyond Harrow, was rebuilt in 1952 to a similar style to that of South

Between the viaduct and High Street station is the junction with the 1½-mile branch to Croxley Green, opened in 1912 and electrified in October 1922. The branch has two intermediate stations, the first of which was opened as recently as December 1982 for the sole benefit of the adjacent Watford Football Club ground. Until January 1967 the same junction had also accessed a 3-mile branch westwards to Rickmansworth (Church Street). This had opened in October 1862, closely following the River Colne, with no intermediate stations, and lost its passenger service in March 1952. As laid, the junction was triangular, but when through trains between Croxley Green and Euston were discontinued, the east-west spur used by them was taken up.

Watford High Street station has an island platform with a sheltering canopy cantilevered between high retaining brick walls. It is well patronised, being much nearer the shopping centre than Watford Junction, where four terminal platforms are available for the DC trains.

As a welcome reminder that by no means all suburban stations are unstaffed and covered in graffiti, observe this splendidly maintained example at Hatch End. Built for the New Lines in 1911, its LNWR origin is proudly displayed beneath the decorative carvings. *F. Hornby*

Willesden New Station on 17 August 1988, showing the LNWR-style signal box, which has since been removed. Dual-current unit No 313002 in Network SouthEast livery is en route to Watford. The hanging baskets of greenery beneath the canopy add a pleasant touch. *F. Hornby*

On the Rickmansworth and Croxley Green branches the terminal stations were similar, with single platforms, neat buildings, run-round loops and sidings for goods traffic. Although the station at Croxley Green is still open - just - the station building was demolished in 1989. In earlier days the branches, being single track, offered the fairly rare experience of seeing the motorman 'collecting the tablet' at the junction.

Colour-light signalling on the DC lines between Camden and Watford dates back to 1933; Euston's rather archaic signalling was modernised in 1952 when an electrically operated box came into use. Thirteen years later, in conjunction with the rebuilding, it in turn was replaced, the new installation controlling the DC lines as far out as Queens Park as well as the main lines. A further advance came in January 1977 when Willesden Junction box took over from mechanical signal boxes between Queens Park and Stonebridge Park. Then in December 1988 a new power box at Willesden replaced the LNWR boxes at Willesden low level and Harrow & Wealdstone No 2, as well as two emergency ground frames - part of a £2.94 million project.

Fortunately serious accidents on the DC lines have been rare, and when mishaps have occurred the inconvenience has been minimised by the semi-fasts on the adjacent main lines making extra stops where platforms are available, at Queens Park, Wembley Central, Harrow & Wealdstone and Bushey.

SERVICES

In 1948 the DC lines timetable showed little attempt to standardise departure times, the earliest Euston-Watford service being at 05.10 with two trains in the first hour, building up to four per hour in the morning peak, then fluctuating between two and four per hour until the last departure at 00.45. South Hampstead saw its first train at 06.14 and its last at 18.57, otherwise the majority of trains called at all 17 stations. The standard timing was 45 minutes for the 17¾ miles - a respectable 23½ miles per hour with stops on average only a mile apart.

It must be remembered that in those days there were also frequent trains between Broad Street and Watford, joining the line from Euston near Chalk Farm station (renamed Primrose Hill in 1950). The weekday tally was 63 departures from Euston and 34 from Broad Street, with 60 and 44 respectively on Saturdays when, of course, there were more trains around midday and fewer in the afternoon. On Sundays there were half-hourly trains all day in and out of Euston, but the Broad Street service was confined to the afternoon and evening, and indeed was withdrawn completely by the following year.

Both the Croxley Green and Rickmansworth branches saw more trains to and from Watford Junction on Saturdays than on weekdays, doubtless with shoppers in mind; Croxley Green had 41 as against 29, while Rickmansworth had 34 as against 20. Neither branch had off-peak services on weekdays, where there was a six-hour gap from 10 am. On Sundays they both had hourly trains throughout the day.

The Rickmansworth branch was closed to passengers on 3 March 1952 and the Croxley Green service was gradually reduced - in 1953 it was down to 32 Saturday and 22 weekday trains - but there were no significant changes in the services between Watford and London at that time.

Moving on to the 1960s, the replacement of the LNWR EMUs by new Eastleigh-built units had made little difference to the journey times - just 1 minute had been shaved from the Euston-Watford schedule, but a 15-minute-interval service on this line from 7 am until midnight did represent an improvement. The 1966 timetable, as an example, listed 15 departures from Harrow & Wealdstone on the DC up line between 8 and 9 am - four each for Euston and Broad Street and three Bakerloo line trains for Elephant &

Castle. By that year the weekday Croxley Green service had been further reduced, to 14 down and 12 up trains plus one each way to and from Broad Street. The branch survived closure proposals, although the through train was withdrawn, and weekday services were maintained throughout the 1970s. However, the Saturday trains ceased to run, shoppers having presumably taken to using their cars!

Economy measures introduced in 1976 resulted in the DC lines frequency being scaled down from 15 to 20 minutes on both the Euston and Broad Street services, with a 7-hour off-peak gap in the latter. During these hours, as on Sunday mornings, the Broad Street-Richmond trains provided a connection at Willesden Junction with those between Euston and Watford. It is noteworthy that one morning train from Watford to Broad Street was routed on to the North London line via the Willesden spur, rather than via Chalk Farm. In the 1985 summer timetable, a year prior to Broad Street's closure, there remained only five up and six down trains between the City terminus and Watford, all in the Monday to Friday peak hours.

The story of Broad Street's decline belongs more appropriately to the chapter dealing with the North London line, but after its closure in June 1986 the DC line stations to Watford suffered a marked reduction in their peak-hour services. By way of partial compensation for City workers, a limited number of trains commenced running between Watford and Liverpool Street from 30 June 1986, via a new curve at Graham Road linking the North London and Great Eastern lines. This service was, however, soon reduced, and ultimately discontinued from 25 September 1992.

In the 1993/94 timetable the Monday-Saturday regular interval service of three trains per hour between Euston and Watford was still operative, reduced to half-hourly on Sundays. The future for the Croxley Green branch, however, would seem bleak, as only one train each way survived, early on weekday mornings!

The Bakerloo tube trains continued to work through to and from Watford Junction until 24 September 1982, albeit confined to four trains each way at peak hours only from October 1965. To maintain this service four trains were stabled overnight in the BR depot at Croxley Green. Prior to their withdrawal, severe weather in early 1982, combined with intermittent ASLEF strikes, had caused dislocations from time to time until mid-July.

Thereafter no Bakerloo trains ventured northwards from Queens Park on to the DC lines until 4 June 1984, when a peak-hour service was restored as far as Harrow & Wealdstone. This was extended to operate all day Mondays-Saturdays from 16 May 1988 and on Sundays from 21 May 1989.

It is interesting to recall that in 1951, during the time of the Festival of Britain, Bakerloo trains connected with special excursions on Saturday mornings at Wembley Central, and ran non-stop through to Waterloo.

TRACTION AND TRAINS

As previously mentioned, the first LNWR electric trains were introduced in May 1914 for a Willesden Junction-Earls Court service, which, incidentally, ceased to operate in October 1940, its demise hastened by air raid damage. They were three-car units of centre-gangway saloons, comprising a Motor Brake 3rd, a Trailer and a Driving Trailer, with manually operated sliding doors, some cars being divided into 1st and 3rd Class saloons. The motor coaches had a switchgear compartment and luggage space behind the driver's cabin, the electrical equipment being supplied by Oerlikon of Switzerland. Current at 630V DC was collected from an outside conductor rail, with a centre fourth rail bonded to the running lines.

Units for the Euston and Broad Street services were built to this design in batches up to 1923, plus an accident replacement in 1926, and they earned the deserved reputation of being smooth-riding and comfortable. They soldiered on throughout the 1950s, the last survivors being used on the Croxley Green 'shuttle' in 1959.

They were joined in 1927 by three-car units of compartment stock of LMS design, formed of Motor 3rds, Composite Trailers and Control Trailer 3rds, seating 240 3rd Class and 40 1st Class passengers. They rode less well than their heavier LNWR predecessors, but the late Hamilton Ellis described the 1st Class as 'sumptuous'.

Both the LMS and LNWR trains were repainted after nationalisation from LMS maroon into the BR standard green livery for multiple units. During 1957 they were joined by the first of 57 three-car slam-door sets of Eastleigh design and construction, with a marked affinity to contemporary Southern Region 'EPB' stock, with two-digit headcodes but with shorter 57-foot frames and screw couplings. They weighed 106 tons, seating 252 in what was by then designated 2nd Class accommodation, and were powered by four GEC motors rated at 740 hp, with a maximum speed of 60 mph. As delivered they were in malachite green livery, but were repainted at Wolverton in Brunswick green before 'Rail Blue' was adopted in the late 1960s, and finally blue-grey with yellow ends from the early 1980s.

Although all based at Croxley Green depot, they worked on both the Euston and Broad Street ser-

Right An Oerlikon EMU of LNWR 1914 design in BR green livery leaves Euston for Watford in September 1956. By the time they were withdrawn in 1959 these solid and comfortable units had notched up over 40 years of service, remaining substantially as built to the end. *A. J. Pike*

Middle right Wembley Central is shown here on 4 March 1961 before the start of the development that covered most of the station area within the next few years. The Euston-bound train in green livery consists of two three-car units of 1927 vintage LMS-built compartment stock. *F. Hornby*

Bottom right An almost new Eastleigh-built three-car EMU at Watford Junction on 3 May 1958 on a Croxley Green shuttle service. It is entering platform 5 (then one side of an island) from a shunt spur, removed when the station was rebuilt. *N. L. Browne*

vices and were fitted with three bars across each droplight, thanks to tight clearances in North London line tunnels. As delivered the centre trailers were compartment vehicles, but these were converted to open saloons during the 1970s. Ultimately classified 501 under the 'TOPS' scheme, they had a life of some 28 years, being phased out in 1985 when dual-current Class 313 units were transferred from the Eastern Region. Final withdrawal was delayed by a maintenance dispute, and in May 1985 all duties reverted to 501s for a short time, with the closure of Croxley Green depot deferred. The end came, however, on 30 September 1985, after which some were converted into two-car Sandite units, while others languished in Sudbury yard awaiting disposal.

During their time in service, Stonebridge Park power station, which had supplied current since LNWR days, was closed in July 1967, since when power has been taken from the National Grid. Also, from August 1970 the DC lines were converted from fourth rail to third rail operation, with the centre rail removed, save on the section shared with Bakerloo trains.

The Class 313s, originally built in 1976 by BREL York for the Great Northern inner suburban services, are 103-ton three-car units seating 232 Standard Class passengers in open saloons. They have power-operated sliding doors, end gangways between coaches and are fitted with a public address system. Eight GEC traction motors deliver 880 hp with a maximum speed capability of 75 mph, which must be very rarely attained in normal service! They currently monopolise the Euston-Watford and North London line services, 18 units being based at Bletchley for these purposes. All are in Network SouthEast livery, embellished with the 'North London Lines' logo, replacing that of the 'Harlequin Line' bestowed in June 1988.

By way of variety, during a maintenance dispute in 1987 a DMU was loaned by Bletchley depot to help out on the DC lines, together with a Class 122 single diesel car, which filled in on the Croxley branch. On Cup Final day in May 1988 a Southern Region 2EPB unit was a rare visitor, shuttling between Euston and Wembley Central. Much earlier, during 1956, while current was switched off for permanent way work, a steam-powered push-pull train plied between Wembley Central and Harrow over the DC tracks.

For many years from 1939 onwards the Bakerloo trains consisted of 1938 stock in seven-car formations, incorporating suitably modified trailers of 1927 design. In 1967 additional six-car trains were transferred on loan from the Piccadilly Line, and it was not until April 1977 that replacements in the shape of 1972 Mk II stock trains began to appear. During 1971-6 some 38 trains of 1938 stock had undergone a programme of 'extra heavy overhaul', but withdrawals commenced in 1981 and the last units were transferred to the Northern Line in 1985, where they completed 50 years of yeoman service.

In 1983 15 trains of 1959 stock were allocated to the Bakerloo Line, entering traffic on 28 February, supplemented by an additional train in 1984 when the peak-hour service to Harrow & Wealdstone was restored. They were returned to the Northern Line in 1988, when more 1972 Mk II stock became available, since when the whole service has been worked by this type. Latterly their appearance has been much improved by the application of red-painted ends and doors, and a wide blue band along the lower sides of the carriages.

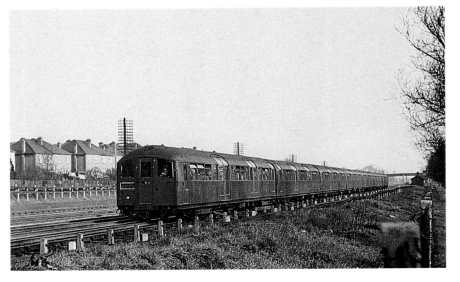

Above left Class 313 EMU No 313006, seen at South Kenton heading for Euston on 7 July 1987, was outshopped from BREL York in 1976. South Kenton station opened in 1933 to serve adjacent housing developments, with an island platform accessed by a footbridge, now replaced by a subway. *F. Hornby*

Left A Bakerloo tube train of 1938 stock on an Elephant & Castle to Watford service hurries past South Kenton on 21 March 1956. These trains performed well for some 45 years until displaced by the 1972 Mk II stock. Through running by Underground trains to Watford ceased in September 1982, marking the end of a 65-year long era. *F. Hornby*

MAIN LINES

EUSTON-BLETCHLEY AND BRANCHES
(STANMORE, ST ALBANS ABBEY, DUNSTABLE
AND AYLESBURY HIGH STREET)

ROUTES AND INFRASTRUCTURE

In the Steam Age Euston, the outer suburban trains could be found at platforms 6, 7 or 8, half-hidden between the much longer ones for the more prestigious long-distance expresses. No 7 was in fact electrified for use by the DC trains if required, but all three were of adequate length for the seven or eight coaches that constituted the normal loads. In the more systematically planned modern station the 25kV electric multiple units arrive at and depart from Nos 8 and 11, flanking the DC line platforms, and sharing with them direct access for passengers to the Underground station. Stabling sidings for the EMUs are located outside the station on the up side, and on the down side at the top of Camden bank. This 1½-mile climb is no longer the hazard it was for departing steam trains, particularly in wet and slippery conditions when help from the engine that had brought in the stock was more than welcome.

Once clear of Camden the gradients out to Bletchley are far less severe, with a steady ascent to Tring at no more than 1 in 335 and an even gentler descent thereafter. This was achieved at the expense of heavy earthworks with long tunnels at Primrose Hill and north of Watford - the latter just over a mile in length - and a deep cutting at Tring. Much work and expense was therefore incurred when the line was later quadrupled to provide relief tracks for outer suburban and freight trains.

In earlier BR years there were five stations on the main line south of Watford, reduced to four when Willesden Junction (main line station) disappeared com-

pletely after closure on 3 December 1962. Of the remainder, Harrow & Wealdstone, then as now, was the most important. On 8 October 1952 it was the scene of one of Britain's worst rail disasters, in which an up local from Tring was one of the trains involved. There are platform faces here for all six tracks, those on the fast lines being little used. On the relief lines trains on the half-hourly Milton Keynes or Northampton services call throughout the day. Wembley Central, Hatch End and Bushey each had a sparse service in steam days - the latter still sees three trains each way at peak hours - while there are platforms at Queens Park for use in emergencies.

Watford Junction station was completely rebuilt during the 1980s, incorporating a curved platform for St Albans branch trains, built on a new alignment in 1984. There are two platforms on the old alignment, of which one is a terminal bay facing the London direction, while the track has been removed from the other. A car park occupies the site of the former six-road engine shed, for so many years home to a stud of suburban tank locomotives.

The seven stations between Watford and Bletchley, six of which date back to London & Birmingham days, are all still open but show few signs of their ancestry, having been suitably modernised. Some have seen considerable growth of the towns they

This 1953 photograph vividly recalls the old sprawling Euston, as BR Class '4' 2-6-4T No 80036 storms away from platform 7 with a stopping train for Tring. A Class '5' 4-6-0 in the background, also with 'stopping train' headlamp, awaits its turn for departure. Note the DC conductor rails in the tracks for platforms 4, 5 and 7. *A. J. Pike*

Only a few months after nationalisation, this pair of Stanier '4P' 2-6-4Ts, posed outside Watford shed on 26 March 1948, still bear testimony to their LMS origins. Ironically the site of this once busy little depot is now covered by a car park! *F. Hornby*

fied at 25kV on 11 July 1988. The stations varied, from Bricket Wood, which originally had two fairly long platforms with a signal box on one of them, to the 'bus stop'-style halts. Abbey terminus had a roof spanning the island platform and one of the tracks, with run-round loops and sidings, and until 1951 was also host to two trains daily on an ER branch from Hatfield. It is now reduced to a single track and platform, while Bricket Wood has lost its loop, but at least the branch remains open, with a respectable service.

serve, notably Hemel Hempstead, which currently has a population of around 80,000. Berkhamsted with 16,000 and Leighton Buzzard with 29,000 inhabitants have similarly expanded since the 1950s, but there is still much pleasant countryside along the line, which is closely paralleled from Kings Langley to Tring by the Grand Union Canal. Cheddington and Leighton Buzzard are no longer junctions, but the former had its day of notoriety as the venue for the 'Great Train Robbery' of 1963.

Although few main-line trains now start or terminate at Bletchley, it retains its importance as the junction for Bedford and as the maintenance centre for the outer suburban EMU fleet, with a depot and extensive sidings.

All the branches south of Bletchley save that from Watford to St Albans have closed since nationalisation. The nearest to London - and the shortest - was from Harrow & Wealdstone to Stanmore, just 2 miles long. Opened in 1890, it was single track, with a passing loop at the intermediate station at Belmont, and steeply graded, Stanmore being some 260 feet above sea level. The two stations differed greatly in style, reflecting the periods in which they were built. When the line was opened great pains were taken to ensure that the small single-platform terminus at Stanmore Village should blend with its surroundings; the building was strongly reminiscent of a country church, complete with squat tower and ornamental spire. Belmont, opened in 1934, was far less ornate, with a booking office on trestles and a wooden footbridge leading to the island platform below. The passenger service was cut back to Belmont on 15 September 1952 and the branch closed completely in 1964.

The line from Watford Junction to St Albans Abbey dates from 1858 and is 6½ miles long with five intermediate stops. It is single track and was electri-

Both the branches north of Watford were rural in character. The oldest, from Cheddington to Aylesbury, 7 miles long with one intermediate station, opened in 1839 and was for many years the only railway serving the Buckinghamshire county town. The other branch, from Leighton Buzzard to Dunstable, followed in 1848 and was of similar length (7¼ miles), also with one station en route. End-on connection was made at Dunstable with a former LNER cross-country line from Hatfield via Luton. The branch was closed to all traffic in October 1967.

When describing the DC lines, mention was made of the way in which Euston's signalling system was modernised while the station was being rebuilt. Clearly such improvements benefited both suburban and inter-city traffic, and the 1965 box, on the west side of the station, had been preceded by a box at Watford, commissioned in July 1964, controlling from North Wembley to Cheddington and superseding 14 older boxes. A new form of track circuiting overcame the problem of interference arising from the proximity of DC and AC power supplies southwards from Watford. Willesden and Bletchley power boxes followed in mid-1965, controlling 13 and 33 track miles respectively and providing continuous modern colour-light signalling throughout - and well beyond - the suburban area.

On the Stanmore branch electric token block signalling had been installed in September 1938, with provision for either 'one engine in steam' or two-train working, with trains passing in the Belmont loop. This facility became superfluous when Stanmore closed and Belmont became the terminus.

Right For 12 years after the closure of Stanmore in 1952, Belmont was the terminus of the short branch from Harrow & Wealdstone. This view in February 1961 shows the former island platform and the timber structure linking it to the booking office. Note that the passing loop has been lifted. *B. W. Brooksbank*

Below right The answer to the question 'When is the next service?' could almost be 'Evensong', judging by the ecclesiastical appearance of Stanmore Village station, as seen in September 1951. Few London-bound commuters could have started their daily journeys in such attractive surroundings. *A. J. Pike*

Until removal of the Bricket Wood loop the St Albans branch was similarly worked in two sections of approximately 3 miles each. With only one train now in service at any time it is unsignalled save for automatic signals at Watford North, where a half-barrier level crossing is activated by the driver pressing a plunger.

SERVICES

When the DC electric trains commenced running between Euston and Watford in 1922, they effectively removed all inner suburban traffic from the main line. As demonstrated by the accompanying table, the growth of towns beyond Watford, notably the conurbation centred on Milton Keynes, has warranted an expansion of longer-distance residential services, facilitated by the 25kV electrification that reached Euston in November 1965.

However, this was all some way into the future at the time of nationalisation, and in the 1948 timetable Bletchley, 46¾ miles out, was considered as the limit for outer suburban traffic. Weekday down trains terminated at Watford (two), Tring (five - including two from Broad Street), Leighton Buzzard (one) and Bletchley (13). The latter were allowed as much as 108 minutes with 12 stops en route. There were, however, several additional fast trains with destinations further north, taking on average an hour to Bletchley with just one or two stops. Three trains ran 'all stations' from Watford to Bletchley, with connections at the former off the DC line. The Sunday service was sparse, with only seven departures from Euston - one

each to Watford and Tring, and the remainder to Bletchley. It should be kept in mind that on weekdays there was far more freight traffic to share the relief lines than at the present time.

The Stanmore branch was favoured with a lavish shuttle service of 51 weekday trains (52 on Saturdays, none on Sundays) plus three early morning trips to and from the intermediate station at Belmont. The through journey time ranged from 5 to 7 minutes, the latter allowing for trains to pass at Belmont.

On the Watford to St Albans branch there were 24 trains each way on weekdays and Saturdays, plus an early morning working between Watford Junction and Watford North. On Sundays there were 14 trains at hourly intervals. The journey time varied from 16 to 20 minutes according to operating needs.

North of Watford neither the Aylesbury nor the Dunstable branches contributed much in the way of commuter traffic. On the former, one train each way made London connections facilitating a through journey in just over 1½ hours, and on the latter just three down and four up trains made connections at Leighton Buzzard. The two branches lost their passenger services in 1953 and 1965 respectively.

By 1953 there was little discernible change in the main-line timetable, though there was a very slight improvement in journey times - the slowest train now reached Bletchley in 102 minutes! As to the branches, Stanmore had closed but there were still 36 daily trains shuttling over the 1 mile between Harrow and Belmont (40 on Saturdays), while the weekday service to St Albans Abbey had been enhanced to 27 trains. Patronage was increasing on this line, later rising in 1956 alone by 22 per cent.

With the introduction of the full main-line electric service on 1 March 1966 the basic off-peak timetable listed hourly trains between Euston and Bletchley taking 64 minutes with 10 stops - a respectable 43¾ mph - with another hourly train to and from Rugby via Northampton, making fewer stops and in most cases reaching Bletchley in 55 minutes at 51 mph. At peak periods the frequency was stepped up, with six departures from Euston between 17.00 and 18.00, three of which continued to Northampton or Rugby. All these were worked by the new AM10 multiple units.

LM Region: Euston-Bletchley (46.75 miles) (Weekday Down Outer Suburban Trains)		
Year	1948	1994
Traction	Steam	25kV EMUs
To Bletchley		
Total stopping trains	13	78
Fastest time (mins)	80 (4 stops)	42 (2 stops)
Average speed (mph)	35.05	66.8
Slowest time (mins)	108 (12 stops)	57 (9 stops)
Average speed (mph)	25.9	49.2
To Tring (31¾ miles)		
Total stopping trains	18	51
Fastest time (mins)	52 (3 stops)	34 (3 stops)
Average speed (mph)	36.7	56.1
Slowest time (mins)	76 (6 stops)	42 (6 stops)
Average speed (mph)	25.0	45.35
To Watford (17½ miles)		
Total stopping trains	23	83*
Fastest time (mins)	25 (non-stop)	16 (non-stop)
Average speed (mph)	42.0	66.6
Slowest time (mins)	39 (3 stops)	23 (1 stop)
Average speed (mph)	27.3	46.3
* 80 Mondays only		

Inevitably Bletchley has since been overshadowed by its near neighbour Milton Keynes, now served by half-hourly semi-fast trains to and from Euston. With a 65-minute schedule inclusive of 10 stops, the 46 mph average presents no problem to the Class 321/4 EMUs now in use. Other half-hourly trains go through alternately to Northampton and Birmingham, giving Watford and stations from Leighton Buzzard four trains per hour each way.

The Belmont branch had a frequent service right up to closure on 5 October 1964; Watford-St Albans could still boast 18 trains each way, plus a midday working as far as Bricket Wood, with 10 trains on Sundays. The line was, however, unprofitable, notwithstanding increased traffic, with a £24,000 deficit in 1965, so the branch stations became unstaffed halts to

Class AM10 unit No 070 on duty '2A04' calls at Harrow & Wealdstone on 6 August 1975 en route from Bletchley to Euston. Later classified 310, these 75 mph four-car EMUs inaugurated the 25kV outer suburban services in November 1965. *F. Hornby*

minimise losses. Nevertheless a new halt was opened at Garston on 7 February 1966 and - more recently - another at How Wood on 24 October 1988. Since electrification the service has been boosted to 26 trains each way on weekdays and Saturdays - mostly at 40-minute intervals - and 17 on Sundays, with a standard journey time of 16 minutes. The Sunday trains were withdrawn in October 1975 but, thanks to a subsidy from local councils, were reinstated two months later.

Traction and Trains

During the war one could travel between Euston and Bletchley on a 'stopper' hauled by an ex-LNWR 'Prince of Wales' 4-6-0 from Bletchley shed, but these had gone by early BR days. By this time '4P' 2-6-4Ts of Fowler, Stanier and Fairburn design were the prime movers, though Stanier Class '5' 4-6-0s were not uncommon on the longer runs. On 30 July 1949 the author was impressed to find even more prestigious power on his up stopping train in the shape of 'Jubilee' 4-6-0 No 45653 *Bahamas*.

The 2-6-4Ts were distributed between the sheds at Willesden (three), Watford (12) and Bletchley (nine), hardly prolific when compared, for instance, with the 40 suburban tanks provided for the suburban services out of Marylebone. But there was no doubting their competence, and in 1949 *The Railway Observer* was able to report a run behind one of the Fowler engines with 300 tons, covering the 5¾ miles from Willesden Junction to Harrow in 8½ minutes start to stop. With relatively so few available it was inevitable that other locomotives were pressed into service; the same source recorded a Class '4' Ivatt 2-6-0 on an evening train to Watford in 1950, and a game performance in 1953 when little '2P' 2-6-2T No 41220 hurried its train from Euston to Watford in 25 minutes - well under schedule!

During the early 1950s BR Standard types made their debut; ten Class '4' 2-6-4Ts were allocated to Watford and four to Bletchley in 1952/3, joined at the latter by 10 Class '4' 4-6-0s. The BR 2-6-4Ts almost monopolised the shorter runs thereafter; when Euston, like Marylebone, was

called upon to handle crowds of spectators for major events at Wembley Stadium with shuttle trains to and from Wembley Central, the 2-6-4Ts demonstrated their capabilities by taking loads of a dozen packed coaches in their stride.

'Super power' appeared on outer suburban trains in 1956 when the Southern Region 1-Co-Co-1 diesels Nos 10201-3 were operating on the LMR and filled in their diagrams on Bletchley locals, as did the LMS-designed Co-Cos Nos 10000-1. However, the eclipse of steam was still some years away, a start being made on 2 November 1959 when Derby-Sulzer 1,160 hp Bo-Bo diesel-electrics (later Class 24) took over some 2-6-4T turns. This was a gradual process, and unusual steam locomotives continued to enliven the scene, as for example in 1960 when Watford's '2P' 4-4-0 No 40672 made a rare appearance on an up stopping train.

Steam-hauled coaching stock consisted largely of 57-foot non-corridor compartment coaches, first introduced by the LMS in 1923 and built in batches for many years thereafter - wooden-bodied up to 1930, then with outer steel panelling, and from 1933 in a flush-sided version. Variations included nine-compartment 3rds, 1st/3rds, Brake 3rds and a few eight-compartment 1sts. As production continued until 1950 it is not surprising that they were still in evidence up to electrification. Older pre-grouping vehicles persisted well into the 1950s, low-roofed veterans of 'Midland' origin among them.

As the 25kV catenary came ever closer to London, steam shed closures came in quick succession; Watford closed on 29 March 1965 and Bletchley - to steam traction - in July of that year. The new AM10 EMUs (later Class 310), in royal blue livery, entered service from 22 November, working at first to the existing timings. These four-car units have a maxi-

Under semaphore signals, Fairburn Class '4' 2-6-4T No 42150 arrives at Watford on 4 March 1961 with a semi-fast from Euston. All seven coaches are compartment stock of LMS 56-foot standard design. *F. Hornby*

Left **During the interim between all-steam operation and the 25kV electrification, Derby-Sulzer Bo-Bo diesel-electrics replaced 2-6-4Ts and 4-6-0s on outer suburban duties. Here ML2 No D5143 (later Class 24) leaves Bletchley on an up train with the flyover to the Oxford line and a fine array of semaphores in the background.** *F. Hornby*

Below left **Arguably the Class 310 EMUs looked their best during the blue-grey period between the rather drab 'Rail Blue' and the garish NSE livery of the present day. Here No 310080 pauses at Watford on an up service on 2 March 1984.** *F. Hornby*

vices out of Euston from late 1987, and by March 1988 there were 20 based at Bletchley, increased by August to 35, which, with the 18 remaining Class 310s, made up the depot's allocation of 53 units. Regular travellers pronounced them less comfortable than their predecessors but, thanks to a maximum speed of 90 mph, better timekeepers. The mix of two classes continued a little longer, with just two 310s still in peak-hour use in April 1989, but within a month yet another new class was destined to appear, which would in due course monopolise all the outer suburban duties.

The first unit of Class 321 (irreverently known as the 'Dusty Bins' thanks to a contemporary TV quiz show) emerged from BREL York in 1988, and in May 1989 a new batch - series 321/4 - was allocated to Bletchley. These four-car units are capable of 100 mph, and Bletchley's full complement of 42 units covers 38 daily diagrams.

Over the years the branches have seen as much motive power variety as the main line. Both the Harrow-Stanmore and Watford-St Albans branches were among the last preserves of ex-LNWR Webb '1P' 2-4-2Ts as late as 1948, though the regular engines were Fowler '3P' 2-6-2Ts and Stanier '2P' 0-4-4Ts, all based at Watford shed. Incidentally, the 0-4-4Ts were the first new class to appear during the Stanier regime and were no more than updates of a 50-year-old Midland Railway design.

On the Stanmore line the trains consisted of two-coach push-and-pull sets, with two trains in action at peak hours when as many as 100 passengers per set would be carried.

mum speed of 75 mph and remained in service until early 1989, when they were gradually transferred away with the advent of their successors of Class 317.

Meanwhile, other classes appeared from time to time; in March 1975 a maintenance staff dispute resulted in cancellations and shorter trains and the substitution of a few of the older AM4 (Class 304) 800 hp four-car sets, normally based further north. In June 1980 a Class 312 unit, similar to the 310s but rated at 90 mph, helped alleviate a stock shortage, and in December of the same year, when the 310 units were experiencing problems with disc brakes, a Class 86/3 Bo-Bo electric locomotive with nine coaches gave commuters a taste of 'InterCity' comfort. The ASLEF dispute of 1982 saw 12-car formations of 310s for the first time, creating problems at intermediate stations with short platforms.

The Class 317 units of 1981 vintage, already familiar on the Midland division, were drafted to the ser-

Class	Year introduced (builder)	Traction motors	Max speed (mph)	Weight per four-car unit (tons)	Seating (1st/2nd)
AM10/310	1965 (BR Derby)	4 x 270 hp EE	75	158.0	25/293
317	1981 (BR Derby/York)	4 x 332 hp GEC	90	137.4	22/269
321/4	1989 (BREL/York)	4 x 332 hp Brush	100	137.9	28/291

By 1951 the Ivatt '2P' 2-6-2Ts were also regular performers, and between 1952 and 1959 an experimental ACV diesel unit of three lightweight bus-bodied four-wheel vehicles was active in the area, firstly on the St Albans branch and from 1954 between Harrow and Belmont. Cracked frames caused problems in 1959, possibly to the relief of many travellers, as the unit had earned an unenviable reputation for rough riding. A BR Class '2' 2-6-2T on loan from Bletchley also did a stint on the Belmont 'shuttle' in March 1958. In later steam days a BR class '4' 2-6-4T was used on the Watford-St Albans line, somewhat disproportionate to its two-coach train, and a 'Derby lightweight' DMU in the M79XXX series with two 150 hp engines was also a regular performer. Later on, diesel units of Classes 104, 105 and 108 played their part, in four-car multiples at busy times as traffic continued to grow.

The branch was electrified from 11 July 1988, with Class 313 units - working on 25kV power as a change from their usual 700V DC duties - in place of the diesels. They in turn were displaced by the superior Class 321/4 when suffi- cient units were available, though the 313s reappeared for a short while in the summer of 1990.

Motive power for the Aylesbury and Dunstable branches had been provided by Bletchley shed, Class '2P' 2-6-2Ts being the usual performers, but as a nice touch of nostalgia on the day that the Aylesbury branch closed to passengers (2 February 1953) Webb '1P' 2-4-2T No 46601 officiated, to the delight of the enthusiasts.

Above right Seen from South Kenton DC line station on 29 November 1989, a Class 321/4 EMU hurries past on the down slow en route to Milton Keynes. These units consist of two Driving Trailers, a Trailer and a Motor Coach (with pantograph). *F. Hornby*

Right Many a branch might possibly have been saved had BR persevered with such cost-effective alternatives as this experimental ACV bus-bodied diesel unit No 1. Consisting of three four-wheeled vehicles, it is seen at Watford Junction on 23 August 1952 when on trial on the St Albans branch. *F. Hornby*

4

LINES FROM ST PANCRAS

St Pancras/Moorgate/Blackfriars-Bedford
Kentish Town/Gospel Oak-East Ham and Barking

The Midland Railway came to Town from the north - setting an example followed by the Great Central 30 years later - and opened its own imposing terminus at St Pancras on 1 October 1868.

Completion of the 49¾-mile extension from Bedford put an end to the arrangement whereby, for the previous 10 years, the Midland had shared Great Northern metals from Hitchin into King's Cross. The high tolls charged by the GNR and growing congestion along the line created an intolerable situation, forcing the Midland to press ahead with its own right-of-way into London.

As with the other trunk lines to the north-west and west of the capital, suburban traffic was slow to develop, although six stations were provided in the first 4 miles from St Pancras, five of which eventually succumbed to tube and bus competition. Beyond the built-up area there were few places of consequence south of Bedford - even the cathedral city of St Albans was then of no great size. In early years most local trains served Moorgate rather than St Pancras, via tunnels from St Pauls Road Junction linking with the Metropolitan 'Widened Lines'. By the turn of the century, however, when communities such as Hendon

were expanding, the tide turned in favour of St Pancras; in 1903 there were 38 local trains in and out daily, while Moorgate's share gradually declined. Some 80 years later history was to repeat itself with the introduction of the full electric service in July 1983, when Moorgate once again featured prominently in the timetable. Then, just five years later, with the inauguration of 'Thameslink', the great majority of suburban trains were re-routed via Blackfriars into Kent, Surrey and Sussex, even reaching the coast at Brighton!

The service from Kentish Town to East Ham and Barking resulted first from the opening of the Tottenham & Hampstead Junction Railway in 1868, then from its extension of 1894, the Tottenham & Forest Gate Railway, linking with the London, Tilbury & Southend at Woodgrange Park. The T&HJR became joint Midland and Great Eastern property in 1902 and thus LMS and LNER joint in 1923, while from nationalisation the boundary between the LMR and ER was located west of Crouch Hill.

Midland passenger services over the line commenced in October 1876, though not reaching the eastern extremities until 1894. The line was also used by Great Eastern trains between St Pancras and Cambridge, by Southend excursions until 1961 and by boat trains between St Pancras and Tilbury right up to 1963. In 1939 there were 19 trains from St Pancras and eight from Moorgate along the line, which also carried a heavy freight traffic.

Ready for departure with a full head of steam, Fowler Class '4P' 2-6-4T No 42300 heads a local for St Albans at St Pancras on 15 February 1958. The first of a class of 125 locomotives, No 42300 was built at Derby in 1928 and was withdrawn in December 1960. *F. Hornby*

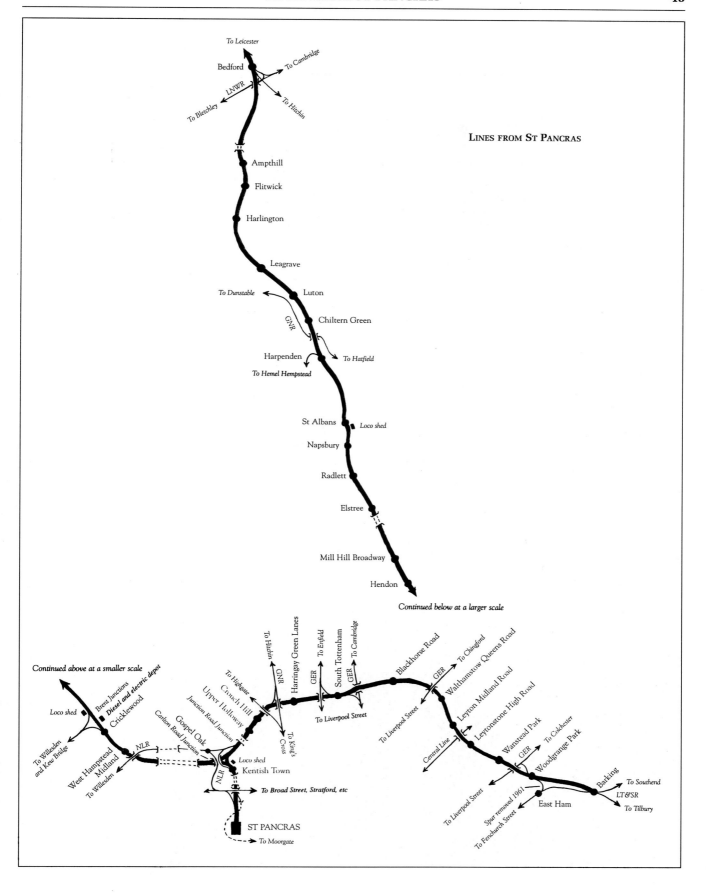

LINES FROM ST PANCRAS

To Leicester

Bedford

To Cambridge

LNWR

To Bletchley

To Hitchin

Ampthill

Flitwick

Harlington

Leagrave

To Dunstable

Luton

Chiltern Green

GNR

Harpenden

To Hatfield

To Hemel Hempstead

St Albans

Loco shed

Napsbury

Radlett

Elstree

Mill Hill Broadway

Hendon

Continued below at a larger scale

Continued above at a smaller scale

Brent Junctions

Diesel and electric depot

Loco shed

Cricklewood

To Willesden and Kew Bridge

West Hampstead Midland

NLR

To Willesden

Carlton Road Junction

Gospel Oak

Junction Road Junction

Upper Holloway

To Highgate

Crouch Hill

To Hitchin

GNR

Harringay Green Lanes

GER

South Tottenham

GER

To Cambridge

To Enfield

Blackhorse Road

To Chingford

GER

Walthamstow Queens Road

Leyton Midland Road

Leytonstone High Road

To Liverpool Street

Central Line

To Liverpool Street

Wanstead Park

GER

To Colchester

Woodgrange Park

To King's Cross

To Liverpool Street

NLR

Loco shed

Kentish Town

To Broad Street, Stratford, etc

ST PANCRAS

To Moorgate

Spur removed 1961

East Ham

To Liverpool Street

To Fenchurch Street

Barking

To Southend

LT&SR

To Tilbury

When the Bedford-London extension opened, a class of 25 double-framed 0-4-4Ts of Kirtley's design was provided for local trains, replaced some years later by Johnson's slightly larger inside-framed variation. From 1907 onwards some ungainly 0-6-4Ts with 6-foot driving wheels appeared, but were unsuccessful and were banished elsewhere. During LMS years ex-L&Y and Caledonian types made brief appearances, but it was Fowler's 2-6-4Ts and 2-6-2Ts that supplanted the smaller Midland engines, and they continued to be so employed by BR until dieselisation.

ROUTES AND INFRASTRUCTURE

St Pancras, notwithstanding its impressive roof with a single 240-foot span, is by no means one of London's largest termini, with only seven platforms. No 1 on the west side is the shortest, used exclusively for suburban trains, with Nos 2-4 also so used as and when required.

Thanks to the whole station being well above street level - with what for many years were beer vaults below - no steep gradient is required to clear the Regent's Canal, which passes beneath the tracks a few hundred yards out, though cuttings and tunnels are much in evidence for the ensuing 3 miles.

At Kentish Town, 1½ miles out, the old locomotive shed has survived on the up side of the tracks, though no longer in railway use. The line to Barking diverged here via a triangular junction and spur, as well as once by a 'flyover', round to Junction Road Junction; only the west-north chord of the triangle survives and now sees little use. The main line turns west through Haverstock Hill Tunnel (1 m 73 yd), then north-west. Quadrupling took place many years ago in stages, necessitated by the heavy coal traffic rumbling south to Cricklewood. Additional freight lines from the

yards there - now reduced to a handful of sidings - cross by a flyover to join the up and down slow lines at Silkstream Junction, north of Hendon. Hereabouts the railway crosses the River Brent on a 19-arch viaduct, with the M1 close by until road and rail part company where the latter plunges into the 1,050-yard-long Elstree tunnel. Beyond Elstree there are stretches of countryside even today, interrupted by Radlett and St Albans - now a thriving centre of 77,000 inhabitants - followed by Harpenden (pop 30,000) and Luton (165,000), a manufacturing town with a nearby airport.

Concurrently with dieselisation and electrification, all the intermediate stations were modernised with the loss of nearly all traces of the characteristic 'Midland' architecture, and a proposal to close St Pancras and divert the traffic into Euston and Moorgate was announced in 1967, but later reconsidered. The three stations remaining between Luton and Bedford were remodelled with platforms serving all four running lines, and a major rebuilding of St Albans City was completed in March 1973. Alterations took place at Luton in 1978 and a new station was opened at Bedford on 9 October of the same year. Normally stopping trains, with the few remaining freights, are confided to the 'slow' roads - something of a misnomer now they are passed for speeds of up to 90 mph!

Luton is the northern extremity of about one in three of today's 'Thameslink' services, and the 19½ miles thence to Bedford are quite thinly populated, although Flitwick has seen some development of late. There are no longer any branches with passenger services south of Bedford, and the only junctions are the former triangular one at Kentish Town with the Tottenham & Hampstead, and the surviving triangular one at Cricklewood with the line to Kew Bridge via Acton Wells Junction. A branch from Harpenden to Hemel Hempstead lost its sparse passenger service in June 1947, but remained open for freight traffic until 1964.

Gradients between St Pancras and Bedford, though undulating, are no steeper than 1 in 176, generally favouring southbound trains, with a summit of 323 feet above sea level at milepost 28¼ and a

In 1961, prior to extensive rebuilding, Kentish Town station still displayed evidence of its Midland Railway origins. A Bedford-bound Derby/Rolls-Royce diesel unit in the original green livery with 'whiskers' pauses at the down platform.
Lens of Sutton

steady descent northwards from milepost 34 - certainly no serious impediment to modern traction.

The line from Kentish Town to Barking, 13 miles in length and double-tracked save for the last half-mile, forms a wide arc through Tottenham, Walthamstow and Leyton. At the east end the spur from Woodgrange Park to East Ham was closed in 1961, all trains having been routed to and from Barking since 1958. At the west end the service was diverted from Kentish Town to Gospel Oak in

Suburban lines from St Pancras, Blackfriars and Moorgate to Bedford, and Kentish Town/Gospel Oak to East Ham and Barking

Miles	Name	Opened	Closed	Notes
From Blackfriars				
	London Blackfriars	5/1988		
½	City Thameslink	5/1990	'Thameslink' dates	Opened as 'St Pauls Thameslink'
1¼	Farringdon	5/1988		
2¼	King's Cross Thameslink	5/1988		Opened as 'King's Cross Midland City'
	Moorgate, Aldersgate and Barbican	1865		
From St Pancras				
	St Pancras	10/1868		
1½	Kentish Town	7/1868		
4	West Hampstead Thameslink	1871		West Hampstead to 9/1950; West Hampstead Midland to 5/1988
5¼	Cricklewood	5/1870		Originally 'Child's Hill'
7	Hendon	7/1868		
9½	Mill Hill Broadway	7/1868		'Mill Hill' to 25/9/1950
12¼	Elstree & Boreham Wood	7/1868		'Elstree' to 5/1988
15¼	Radlett	7/1868		
18¼	Napsbury	6/1905	9/1959	
20	St Albans	7/1868		'St Albans City' to 5/1988
24¾	Harpenden	7/1868		
27¼	Chiltern Green	7/1868	4/1952	
30¼	Luton	7/1868		
32¾	Leagrave	7/1868		
37¼	Harlington	7/1868		
40¼	Flitwick	5/1870		
41¾	Ampthill	7/1868	14/1959	
49¾	Bedford	2/1859		'Bedford Midland Rd' to 5/1988
From Kentish Town/Gospel Oak				
	Kentish Town	7/1868		
	Gospel Oak	5/1888		Present platform opened 5/1/1981
1½	Upper Holloway	7/1868		
2½	Crouch Hill	7/1868		
3¼	Harringay Green Lanes	1880		'Harringay Park' to 27/10/1958, then 'Harringay Stadium'
4½	South Tottenham	5/1871		
6	Blackhorse Road	7/1894		Resited 12/1981
6¾	Walthamstow Queens Road	7/1894		'Walthamstow' to 6/5/1958
7¾	Leyton Midland Road	7/1894		'Leyton' to 1/5/1949
8½	Leytonstone High Road	7/1894		'Leytonstone' to 1/5/1949
9¾	Wanstead Park	7/1894		
10½	Woodgrange Park	7/1894		
11¾	East Ham	3/1858	9/1958	
13	Barking	3/1858		

Blackhorse Road station, on the Tottenham & Forest Gate section of the Kentish Town-Barking route, still displays solid and traditional architecture in this view looking west on 1 April 1961. An upper quadrant signal and the LMR 'lozenges' help to date the picture. *B. W. Brooksbank*

January 1981, connecting there with the North London line. There are substantial engineering works along the way, with a mile-long tunnel between Junction Road Junction and Upper Holloway.

Much of the line is either in cuttings or on brick-arched viaducts, and crosses the reservoirs east of Tottenham by a causeway alongside the main road. Numerous other routes are crossed, including the main line from King's Cross and - until its closure - the Alexandra Palace branch. Further east, the lines from Liverpool Street to Enfield Town, Cambridge, Chingford and Colchester are crossed in that order, not forgetting the LT Central Line near Leytonstone; there are connecting spurs to all the BR lines save for the Chingford branch. The sections between the junctions at either end of South Tottenham station, and between Woodgrange Park and Barking, are now 'under the wires' for the much-reduced freight traffic; in early BR years there were over 30 freight trains daily in each direction. Recently there have been threats of closure and the intermediate stations have been reduced to 'basics', some of them unstaffed. In 1993 lengthy speed restrictions to 15-25 mph highlighted the arrears of maintenance work.

In a ceremony at Blackfriars on 25 April 1988, HRH The Princess Royal inaugurated the Thameslink service of through trains between

the Midland and Southern lines. The north-south route across London is via the spur from St Pauls Road Junction to the Widened Lines, diverging at Farringdon and thence through the reopened Snow Hill Tunnel to Blackfriars, with gradients at the tunnel ends as steep as 1 in 32. Thereafter trains proceed via Elephant & Castle or London Bridge to their destinations in Kent, Surrey and Sussex. Farringdon is the changeover point between the overhead 25kV and third-rail 750V DC current supplies. King's Cross Thameslink station is rather inconveniently sited some distance from the main-line terminus, reached either via the street above ground or through the Underground station below.

Signalling on the main line, which was adequate in the 1940s for a 2-6-2T rattling along at 30 mph - when not checked by a freight in the section ahead - clearly would not suffice for EMUs capable of three times that speed. In 1948 lower and upper-quadrant semaphores were the order of the day, even at St Pancras where it was not until October 1957 that they were replaced by colour-lights, controlled from a new power box in place of three existing installations. The following year the tiny four-level Tunnel box between St Pauls Road Junction and King's Cross (Metropolitan) was also closed.

South Tottenham station is festooned with 25kV catenary between the junctions at either end and still boasts a well-kept signal box on the westbound platform. On 7 July 1993 Class 117 two-coach DMU No L413 departs en route from Gospel Oak to Barking. *F. Hornby*

In May 1965 all 50 route miles from Bedford to London were protected by AWS (Automatic Warning System), and the diesel multiple units were equipped with the appropriate receiving apparatus.

In preparation for electrification, work commenced in 1977 on a power signalling box at West Hampstead to control colour-lights and points over 70 route miles, replacing 29 old boxes. Resignalling was divided into seven stages, working from north to south, for completion in the autumn of 1981. In actuality the last mechanical box (Engine Shed Junction, at Kentish Town) closed in December 1981, and the final stage was completed with the closure of St Pancras power box in July 1982. Meanwhile track layout alterations resulted in the fast and slow lines exchanging functions for the first 1¼ miles out of the terminus, while further out the slow lines were suitably upgraded. Electric current was switched on into St Pancras on 27 September 1982, but the first public run in March 1983 was well behind schedule.

No such all-embracing modernisation has yet spread to the former Tottenham & Hampstead and Tottenham & Forest Gate line, along which several signal cabins still regulate train movements with a mixture of colour-light and semaphore signalling. Examples of the latter survive at the time of writing in the Crouch Hill-Harringay area, while at South Tottenham the junctions are controlled by colour-lights operated from a traditional-style box on the westbound platform. By way of architectural contrast the box west of Upper Holloway station is of wartime 'austerity' design. With the uncertainty hanging over the line, significant changes are unlikely in the foreseeable future.

SERVICES

Table 218 of the London Midland Region 1948 timetable listed 16 stations between St Pancras and Bedford, three of which have since closed - Chiltern Green in 1952, then Napsbury and Ampthill in 1959. There were 31 weekday down stopping trains, of which details are shown in the accompanying table.

Additionally there were three trains from Moorgate - two to St Albans and one to Harpenden - and three short runs connecting with faster trains - one from St Albans to Luton and two from Luton to Bedford. Of the longer-distance trains from St Pancras, 11 stopped at Bedford, several of them calling at one or more intermediate stations; the fastest was non-stop to Bedford in 1 hour. Up trains closely replicated those out of London. The Saturday service was similar in total to that on weekdays, but on Sundays 12 stopping trains were deemed sufficient (five to Luton and seven to Bedford), plus nine fast trains, the up service being slightly better.

On the Kentish Town to Barking line there are ten stations averaging 1¼ miles apart, none having closed since nationalisation. Of 24 weekday eastbound trains 11 started from St Pancras and 13 from Kentish Town, four terminating at East Ham and the remainder at Barking. Journey time from St Pancras to either destination was on average 50 minutes, a somewhat sedate 17 mph! In the summer there were through trains to Southend, one of which started from Cricklewood - one could imagine a '4F' 0-6-0 enjoying a trip to the 'seaside'. A fairly good Sunday service of 15 trains, all to Barking, was supplemented by summer extras to Southend serving all stations along the line, including one from St Albans. All trains were '3rd Class only'.

During the next decade main-line stopping services improved, more so as regards frequency than speed, with a regular-interval service off-peak. In 1959 there were 17 weekday trains to Bedford and 10 to Luton - both well up on 1948 - but it was the advent of the diesel multiple units that heralded a significant change. They first appeared on 28 September 1959 running to steam schedules, and a full-scale service commenced on 11 January 1960, but it was some time before teething troubles were eradicated. Thereafter the benefits were substantial, and introductory cheap day return fares helped ensure success for the new service. Patronage was quickly boosted by 20 per cent or

			Slowest			Fastest		
From St Pancras to:	**Distance (miles)**	**Trains terminating**	**Time (mins)**	**Stops**	**Average (mph)**	**Time (mins)**	**Stops**	**Average (mph)**
St Albans	20.0	7	55	7	21.8	34	1	35.3
Harpenden	24.75	6	66	9	22.5	40	1	37.1
Luton	30.25	7	78	10	23.25	47	1	39.55
Bedford	49.75	11	125	14	23.9	76	3	39.25

TRAIN SERVICE FROM ST PANCRAS TO BEDFORD, 1958

Seen from one of Barking's District Line platforms, Stanier '3P' 2-6-2T No 40167 and a three-coach train for Kentish Town occupy the terminal track on 11 October 1958. No 40167 was one of the six Stanier tanks rebuilt with a larger boiler, a modification which might well have benefited the rest of this rather underpowered class. *F. Hornby*

more, and in due course St Albans alone was dispatching over 60,000 commuters to London every week.

The off-peak service from St Pancras consisted of an hourly train on the hour, all stations to Luton, and another fast to Elstree then all stations to Bedford. Journey time for the latter was 70 minutes with eight stops (42.6 mph), lopping 6 minutes off the steam schedule with only three stops. Moorgate passengers fared particularly well, with peak-hour trains non-stop between King's Cross (Underground) and Elstree, 16 minutes faster then their steam predecessors. The fastest times were in the up direction, for example, 21 minutes from St Albans and 26 from Harpenden, not far off 'even time'. These initial schedules must have proved slightly optimistic, however, as they were subsequently eased by 2 minutes or so.

As for frequency, Elstree was served by 45 daily trains instead of 30, St Albans by 100 instead of 79 and Luton by 88 instead of 50 - the two latter exclusive of long-distance expresses. At the same time diesel units took over on the Kentish Town-Barking line with an hourly off-peak frequency and some reduction in journey times, though there were complaints about poor connections at Kentish Town; just one up and two down trains served St Pancras with a running time of 38 minutes.

An apparently deserted Moorgate station is the setting for 'Bed-Pan' EMU No 317340, seen after arrival there on 5 May 1984. These 90 mph units revolutionised the Midland line service by comparison with their more staid diesel predecessors. *F. Hornby*

Subject to minor alterations, with the Moorgate service reduced to two trains each way prior to complete withdrawal in May 1979, the diesel service remained in operation for over 20 years until the Bedford-St Pancras section was electrified. On 17 May 1982, with much work in progress along the line, an emergency timetable was instigated, with some trains starting or terminating at Kentish Town. The first appearance of the new Class 317 electric multiple units at St Pancras was on 28 March 1983, and from 18 April they took over six daily runs, working to the DMU timings and restricted to 75 mph. The full service on what became popularly known as the 'Bed-Pan line' was delayed due to protracted negotiations over 'one-man operation', and eventually commenced on 11 July 1983 with Moorgate once again playing a major role. Indeed, the basic timetable provided for half-hourly stopping trains from Moorgate to Luton and half-hourly semi-fasts from St Pancras to Bedford. Some of the additional peak-hour trains were non-stop to St Albans.

Inevitably there were problems to be ironed out before the service settled down - the power cars in particular proved to be rough riding - and EMUs of Classes 313 and 315 loaned from the Eastern Region

Mill Hill Broadway as portrayed on 19 May 1993 is typical of the 'modern age' suburban station with a minimum of shelter for northbound passengers. A pair of Class 319 EMUs forms a Luton-Sevenoaks train on 'Thameslink' service 'S1'. *F. Hornby*

together with Class 127 DMUs had to be substituted for a time. There could be no doubts, however, as to the vastly superior performance of the Class 317s with their 90 mph maximum speed; the standard timing from King's Cross (LT) to St Albans was 20 minutes start to stop, as was that from St Albans into St Pancras. Even over so short a distance as from Harpenden to St Albans (4.8 miles) the maximum speed could be attained.

Relatively speaking, therefore, the next development, the launching of 'Thameslink' on 1 December 1987, heralded rather less spectacular improvements, albeit that the top speed of the new dual-voltage Class 319 EMUs is 100 mph. Even so, the north-south service represents a radical advance, although in reality reviving what was commonplace before the turn of the century, using the same reincarnated Snow Hill Tunnel. None of the weekday trains serves St Pancras, there being 29 northbound from Moorgate and a further 104 through the Snow Hill Tunnel to St Albans, Luton and Bedford. The accompanying analysis (below) makes an interesting comparison with that for 1948.

Thus, inclusive of 29 trains from Moorgate, there are 133 trains as far as St Albans and over 100 thereafter - over four times as many as in 1948. On Sundays there is just one early morning stopping train out of St Pancras plus 36 through Snow Hill Tunnel. With the introduction of the full service on 16 May 1988 came the almost obligatory 'teething troubles', some failures being attributed to water seeping into the traction motors. These problems, combined with a massive upsurge in custom, resulted in overcrowding, but there is no doubting the popularity of the service, which could be further expanded but for the limited number of paths through the tunnel for a maximum of six trains each way per hour.

The long-standing link between the Midland line and Barking was severed when, from 5 January 1981, Kentish Town ceased to be the western terminus in favour of Gospel Oak. One of the last outposts of the 'Heritage' DMUs, the service frequency was reduced to hourly from 4 October 1993 and Sunday trains were withdrawn, running time being 34 minutes eastbound and 35 minutes westbound. Off-peak patronage is patchy, with the two-car units providing adequate capacity.

TRACTION AND TRAINS

Steam suburban motive power was based at Kentish Town (14B), where one of the three roundhouses was frequented by tank locomotives, at a two-road shed at St Albans (14C), and at Bedford (15D). At nationalisation Kentish Town and St Albans fielded between

---

TRAIN SERVICE FROM LONDON TO BEDFORD, WINTER 1993/94

From King's Cross (LT) to:	Distance (miles)	Trains terminating	Standard times and speeds		
			Time (mins)	Stops	Average (mph)
St Albans	20.25	5	30	7	40.5
Luton	30.5	35	45	9	47.33
Bedford	50.0	64	59	6	50.85

(Excludes trains from Moorgate)

them some 15 Fowler and Stanier 2-6-4Ts, while Bedford maintained a stud of compound 4-4-0s for the semi-fasts, which were soon displaced by a further nine 2-6-4Ts. Additionally there was a fleet of some 36 '3P' 2-6-2Ts, mostly at Kentish Town and Cricklewood (14A), employed on the less demanding turns. Other classes occasionally seen on local passenger work included Kentish Town's brace of Ivatt '2P' 2-6-2Ts and even '3F' 0-6-0s on the short runs such as St Albans-Luton.

Early in the 1950s BR Standard classes displaced older engines. Kentish Town received four of the efficient 2-6-4Ts and Bedford five, together with Class '4' 4-6-0s Nos 75040-4 when new in 1953. These latter were transferred away for a while, but returned to displace the 2-6-4Ts in January 1955. Compound 4-4-0s from 'foreign' sheds made a brief reappearance in 1957, and the following year the less powerful '2P' 4-4-0s revived an old tradition by working Bedford semi-fasts. Just prior to dieselisation ex-LMS 2-6-4Ts gave com-

Top left The crew of Stanier '4P' 2-6-4T No 42453 appear eager for the 'right away' from St Albans with a Luton stopping train on 4 August 1958. The station has not yet been rebuilt and there are coal wagons in the sidings, now long gone. *F. Hornby*

Middle left Possibly one of St Albans's stud of 2-6-2Ts had failed on 17 August 1957, which would explain the unlikely presence of ex-MR '3F' 0-6-0 No 43565 on the 13.10 Harpenden-St Pancras stopping train. The elderly goods locomotive makes a clean getaway from Elstree with a lightweight rake, including a centre-gangway coach as 'swinger'. *F. Hornby*

Left 'Super power' for a Bedford-St Pancras stopping train, awaiting the road at Luton on 1 August 1959. Doubtless Fairburn 2-6-4T No 42133 is the rostered engine, while Class '5' 4-6-0 No 45274 is returning to London in the most convenient way after an unbalanced northbound run. *F. Hornby*

muters a thrill by working up to 80 mph with nine-coach trains, perhaps by way of a last fling!

Coaching stock consisted mainly of LMS-built 57-foot compartment vehicles, although flat-roofed carriages of Midland origin were not uncommon in earlier years.

On the Kentish Town-Barking and East Ham line the '3P' 2-6-2Ts held sway, though the Southend trains could produce a variety of more powerful locomotives. Similarly the Moorgate services were monopolised by 2-6-2Ts, in this case by the Fowler engines, which were condenser-fitted for working through the tunnels.

The author's own early Midland Division experiences included a lively run to St Albans in January 1949 behind '4P' Compound 4-4-0 No 41034 with six coaches, while by contrast '3P' 2-6-2T No 40112 made heavy going on the return trip with a stopping train of equal load. My first encounter with the 'Tottenham & Hampstead' was in May 1948 when a 2-6-2T - still with its LMS No 36 - handled a St

Top right This scene was recorded at Elstree on 27 March 1954 and is typical of the period when BR Standard Class '4' 2-6-4Ts were much in evidence on the Midland Division. No 80060 of Bedford shed, half-shrouded in steam, heads a train of LMS-built 57-foot compartment stock. *B. W. Brooksbank*

Middle right Condenser-fitted Fowler Class '3P' 2-6-2T No 40022 scurries along near Radlett with a three-coach local on 30 August 1958. No 40022 was one of four such machines maintained at St Albans for less exacting turns, and became a casualty of dieselisation, being withdrawn at the end of 1962. *B. W. Brooksbank*

Right At Luton on 1 August 1959 it is nearly the end of one era and the beginning of another. The brand-new Derby/Rolls-Royce diesel-hydraulic units are at the beginning of a 22-year tour of duty, while the sands of time are running out for 2-6-4Ts like the one at the far platform. *F. Hornby*

Pancras to East Ham train of five ex-Midland Railway bogie coaches. I noticed that there were few passengers and that, even then, some stations looked 'unkempt'. In September 1951 a through train to Southend, calling at all stations, produced a '4F' 0-6-0 on nine well-filled coaches. The return trip was also on a through train, this time with a Fowler 2-6-4T in charge and badly delayed by a preceding freight.

Late 1959 saw the first of the Derby-built four-car diesel-hydraulic units appearing on the Bedford services. They weighed 139 tons, with four Rolls-Royce engines producing 952 hp and with a maximum speed of 70 mph. Later classified 127, they were of similar 'High Density' design to their Western Region contemporaries, with an all-2nd Class seating capacity of 352. Thirty units were allocated, but they were prone to breakdowns in the early stages, and substitutes ranged from the superannuated 2-6-2Ts to Class 2 diesel-electric locomotives. In the winter of 1961/62 the big Class 4 'Peak' diesels lent a hand, and in the even more severe weather of 1962/63 steam made a brief comeback, with BR Class '5' 4-6-0s noted on stopping trains.

The Moorgate services were worked by Type 2 diesels with compartment stock, but a brief trial was made from 6 May 1968 with two-car Craven units, terminated abruptly after one caught fire near St Albans on 12 June. With these exceptions DMUs bore the brunt of the suburban services for 22 years, and in 1970 Cricklewood depot's allocation stood at 51 Motor and 66 Trailer cars forming Derby three- and four-car units. They were eventually phased out as the 'Bed-Pan' Class 317 EMUs came on stream in the early 1980s.

Details of these appeared in the preceding chapter on the lines out of Euston, to which they were transferred on the introduction of the 'Thameslink' service. Their stay on the Midland was thus relatively short, from their first appearance at Cricklewood depot in November 1981, and their first public run in March 1983, until the last two units left in August 1988. They were no less immune from the effects of Arctic conditions than their diesel predecessors and, in the heavy snow of 1984/85, only 20 of the full allocation of 48 units were available. This time inner-suburban Class 313 EMUs came to the rescue and - ironically - the withdrawal of the diesel units was deferred until the emergency was over!

History repeated itself when the Class 319 'Thameslink' EMUs made their debut in December 1987, as not only were there numerous failures, but, while on trial, they were 'blacked' when a cab footstep collapsed, injuring a driver. In consequence, in October 1989 some of the Class 317s reappeared on their old stamping-ground for a while, though not being dual-voltage-fitted they were not able to proceed beyond Moorgate. Problems besetting the 319s persisted throughout 1990, but with 86 units available in due course, the situation gradually improved. They consist of two Driving Trailer Standards, Motor Standard and a Trailer Standard, totalling 136.3 tonnes and seating 316. Maximum speed is 100 mph and each unit is powered by four 332 hp GEC motors.

The Kentish Town-Barking service, dieselised concurrently with that on the main line, was worked initially by four-car Class 127 units, subsequently reduced to three- and then two-car formations during 1983. In 1984 Birmingham RCW Class 104 units with 300 hp Leyland engines took over, and in 1986 Craven Class 105s from Stratford depot replaced the Cricklewood-based sets. To add to the variety the 'Crosstown Linkline', as it became known, has also seen Classes 101, 104 and even Class 121 single cars from Old Oak Common. These in turn gave way to Class 115s, made available from the Chiltern Line in February 1992 and which remain on the service at the time of writing.

'Thameslink' dual-voltage EMU No 319036, in Network SouthEast livery, rests in the sunshine at Luton on 11 August 1990 before its next foray through the tunnels into 'Southern' territory. With over 100 trains daily to and from London, Luton residents now enjoy a service four times that of 1948!
F. Hornby

5

LINES FROM KING'S CROSS

KING'S CROSS/MOORGATE/BROAD STREET-HITCHIN
FINSBURY PARK-ALEXANDRA PALACE
WOOD GREEN-STEVENAGE VIA HERTFORD NORTH
BRANCHES FROM HATFIELD (HERTFORD EAST, ST ALBANS AND DUNSTABLE)

The Great Northern Railway's first London terminus opened at Maiden Lane on 7 August 1850 and was relocated at King's Cross from 14 October 1852, by which time four stations were open along the 17¾ miles to Hatfield. Three more had opened by 1861, and a service via spurs from either side of King's Cross station, through the tunnels and on to the Metropolitan to Farringdon Street, commenced in October 1863. This was extended across the river and over the London Chatham & Dover Railway into Victoria in July 1866, with trains provided by both the GNR and LCDR. To deal with this traffic the 'Widened Lines' were opened alongside the Metropolitan tracks in 1868.

Thereafter suburban traffic grew apace - on a far greater scale than on the lines to the north-west and west of London - with the building of the 'Northern Heights' branches from Finsbury Park to Edgware, High Barnet and Alexandra Palace. These, and the line from Wood Green to Enfield, opened in the 1860s and '70s. As with the Midland Railway a high proportion of the early suburban trains served the City, and in 1893 three times as many did so as used the main-line terminus. Finsbury Park became the focus of activity, eventually with five island platforms serving seven through tracks. In 1912 it dealt with 550 trains daily, including many operated by the North London Railway to and from Broad Street via a spur from Canonbury. This practice dated back to 1875 and was perpetuated by the LMS (still using four-wheeled carriages well into the 1930s!), and in BR days by the Eastern Region.

The first GNR engines built for the London suburban traffic were Sturrock's 0-4-2 well tanks of 1865, condenser-fitted for working over the Widened Lines, and these were followed successively by 0-4-4Ts, 4-4-2Ts and 0-6-2Ts of Stirling and Ivatt designs. The latter also introduced a class of massive 0-8-2Ts, which, less than successful, were banished to the north.

Some inroads were made into this intensive traffic as early as 1904 when the Great Northern & City tube line, built to main-line dimensions, was opened as a more direct route between Finsbury Park and Moorgate. It was never linked with the main system as intended, but nevertheless the GNR, and subsequently LNER, steam service to and from the City was much reduced outside peak hours. As laid the GN&C line had negative and positive conductor rails outside the running rails, but in 1939, when the original vehicles were replaced by smaller 'tube' stock, the current supply was converted to London Transport's standard fourth-rail system.

Because of the bottlenecks and congestion caused by the tunnels outside King's Cross it was realised that the 'Northern Heights' traffic could be more expeditiously handled by extending London Transport's Northern Line from Highgate Archway through East Finchley and thence over the LNER tracks to High Barnet. This project was completed in April 1940, and the Edgware branch was so treated as far as Mill Hill East in May 1941. Work then ceased due to wartime pressures, and the Alexandra Palace branch continued to be steam operated until closure in 1954.

The tube service on the High Barnet line was far more frequent than in steam days and boosted originating journeys from 3.5 to 12 million in a year. Thus the volume of traffic inherited by BR in 1948, though by no means insignificant, was considerably less than in the pre-war years.

ROUTES AND INFRASTRUCTURE

By virtue of gradients and bottlenecks, the steam-worked suburban services on the Great Northern section were as difficult to operate as any in the London area, and the infrastructure in 1948 was little changed from that which had come into LNER ownership 25 years previously.

SUBURBAN LINES FROM KING'S CROSS/MOORGATE TO HITCHIN (MAIN LINE) AND BRANCHES

Miles	Name	Opened	Closed	Notes
From King's Cross				
	King's Cross	10/1852		Terminus at Maiden Lane 8/1850-10/1852
2½	Finsbury Park	7/1861		'Seven Sisters Road' to 1869
	Finsbury Park-Canonbury spur opened for passenger services 1/1875; ceased 1976			
3½	Harringay	1885		'Harringay West' from 5/1950
4	Hornsey	8/1850		
5	Alexandra Palace	1859		'Wood Green' to 3/1971; 'Wood Green (Alexandra Palace)' 3/1971-5/1982
6½	New Southgate	8/1850		'& Friern Barnet' to 3/1871
8½	Oakleigh Park	1873		
9¼	New Barnet	8/1850		
10¼	Hadley Wood	1885		
12¾	Potters Bar	8/1850		
14½	Brookmans Park	1926		
15½	Welham Green	9/1986		
17¾	Hatfield	8/1850		
22	Welwyn North	8/1850		'Welwyn' to 7/1926
25	Knebworth	2/1884		
27½	Stevenage	8/1850		Original closed 7/1973; new opened 9/1973
31¼	Hitchin	8/1850		
'Widened lines'				
	Moorgate	2/1868		Opening date for GN trains
½	Aldersgate & Barbican	1865		
¾	Farringdon Street	1865		
1½	King's Cross York Road	6/1866	3/1977	
Former Great Northern & City line				
	Moorgate			
½	Old Street	1904		
1¾	Essex Road	1904		'Canonbury & Essex Road' to 7/48
2¼	Highbury & Islington	1904		
2¾	Drayton Park	1904		
Alexandra Palace branch				
	Finsbury Park			
¾	Stroud Green	4/1881		
1¼	Crouch End	8/1867		
2¼	Highgate	8/1867	7/1954	
3	Cranley Gardens	8/1902		
3¾	Muswell Hill	5/1873		
4¼	Alexandra Palace	5/1873		

King's Cross station layout and its approaches were remodelled and simplified early in 1977, prior to which time there were five suburban terminal platforms, Nos 11-15 (renumbered 9-13 from 1972) on the west side of the station, all long enough to accommodate eight coaches with a tank locomotive at either end. Additionally No 16 (renumbered 14 from 1972) was a through platform on a 1 in 37 gradient for trains emerging from the Widened Lines via the notorious 7½-chain-radius 'Hotel Curve'. An unnumbered platform on the opposite side of the station, accessible from York Road, served their City-bound counterparts. All these platforms were closed on Sundays when local trains used the main-line platforms, as did some outer-suburbans at peak times during the week. The two through platforms became

Miles	Name	Opened	Closed	Notes
Hertford loop				
	Moorgate			
6¾	Bowes Park	1871		
7¾	Palmers Green	1871		'& Southgate' to 3/1971
8¾	Winchmore Hill	1871		
9½	Grange Park	4/1910		
10¼	Enfield Chase	4/1910		Replacing Enfield, opened 1871
11	Gordon Hill	4/1910		
12½	Crews Hill	4/1910		
14¼	Cuffley	4/1910		
17¾	Bayford	6/1924		
20¾	Hertford North	6/1924		Original station opened 3/1858, closed 6/1924
25	Watton-at-Stone	6/1924		Closed 9/1939, re-opened 5/1982
St Albans branch				
	Hatfield			
2	Nast Hyde Halt	1910		
2¾	Smallford (for Colney Heath)	11/1866		
4	Hill End	1899	10/1951	
5¾	St Albans London Road	11/1866		
6½	St Albans (Abbey)	5/1858		Opened by LNWR; closure date for ER service
Dunstable branch				
	Hatfield			
4½	Ayot	1877	1949	Destroyed by fire
7¼	Wheathampstead	1860		
9½	Harpenden East	1860		
12	Luton Hoo	1860	4/1965	
15	Luton (Bute Street)	1858		
19¼	Dunstable Town	1860		
20¼	Dunstable North	1866		Joint with LMR
Hetford North branch				
	Hatfield			
4	Cole Green	3/1858	5/1951	
5½	Hertingfordbury	3/1858	5/1951	
6½	Hertford North	3/1858		

redundant when the electrified line from Moorgate to Finsbury Park became operational in November 1976, and from the following year, with the elimination of locomotive-hauled trains, two terminal platforms, Nos 9 and 10, were deemed sufficient. Later, as traffic increased, a third, No 11, was reinstated in October 1988. The suburban platforms are little more than a road's width away from St Pancras, and thus both King's Cross and St Pancras share a common Underground station served by the Northern, Victoria, Piccadilly, Metropolitan and Circle lines. The sub-surface 'Thameslink' station is also close by.

Trains leaving King's Cross are faced immediately with a 1½-mile climb at 1 in 107, much of it in tun-nels, with a further 8 miles at 1 in 200 from Alexandra Palace (formerly Wood Green). After the summit at Potters Bar there are undulations varying from 1 in 200 to 1 in 300 thence to Hitchin. Until 1959 there were two bottlenecks south of Stevenage caused by tunnels through which the suburban trains had to share two tracks with all other traffic. The first extended from Greenwood signal box, 10 miles out, for 2¾ miles through three tunnels to Potters Bar. This was eliminated by extensive engineering works commenced in 1955 and completed four years later. The second, extending for just over 2 miles across the 500-yard Digswell Viaduct and through two short tunnels to Woolmer Green, remains with us to this

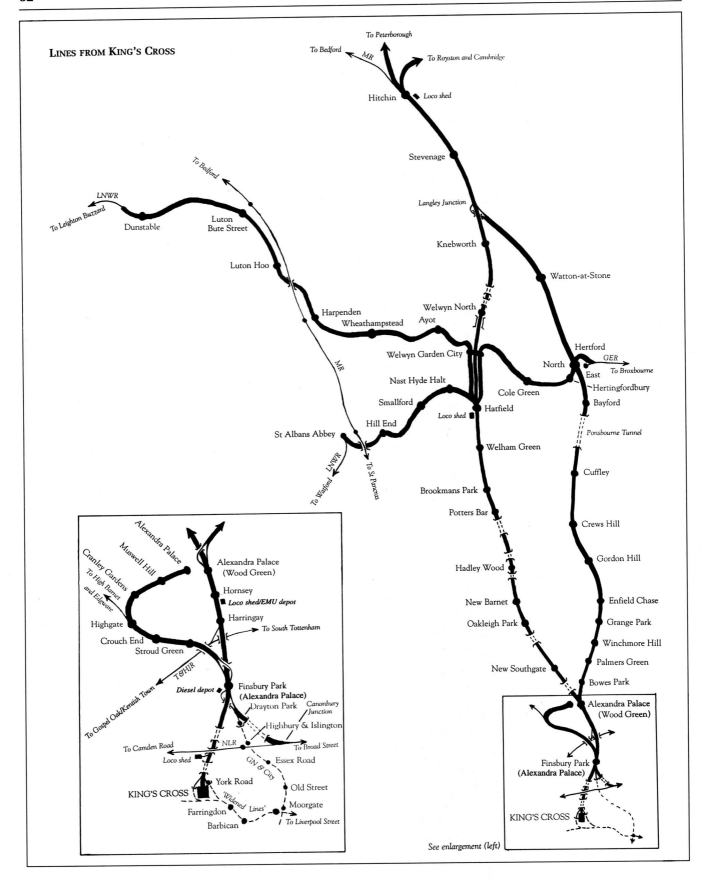

LINES FROM KING'S CROSS

To Peterborough

To Bedford

To Royston and Cambridge

MR

Hitchin

Loco shed

Stevenage

Langley Junction

To Bedford

LNWR

Knebworth

To Leighton Buzzard

Dunstable

Luton
Bute Street

Watton-at-Stone

Luton Hoo

Welwyn North

Ayot

Hertford

Harpenden

Wheathampstead

GER

Welwyn Garden City

North

To Broxbourne

MR

East

Hertingfordbury

Nast Hyde Halt

Cole Green

Bayford

Smallford

Hatfield

Loco shed

St Albans Abbey

Hill End

Welham Green

Ponsbourne Tunnel

To Watford

LNWR

To St Pancras

Brookmans Park

Cuffley

Potters Bar

Crews Hill

Gordon Hill

Hadley Wood

New Barnet

Enfield Chase

Oakleigh Park

Grange Park

Winchmore Hill

New Southgate

Palmers Green

Bowes Park

Alexandra Palace
(Wood Green)

Alexandra Palace

Muswell Hill

Cranley Gardens

To High Barnet
and Edgware

Alexandra Palace
(Wood Green)

Hornsey

Loco shed/EMU depot

Highgate

Harringay

To South Tottenham

Crouch End

Stroud Green

Finsbury Park
(Alexandra Palace)

Finsbury Park
(Alexandra Palace)

T&HJR

Diesel depot

Drayton Park

Canonbury
Junction

To Gospel Oak/Kentish Town

Highbury & Islington

To Camden Road

NLR

To Broad Street

Loco shed

GN & City

Essex Road

KING'S CROSS

KING'S CROSS

York Road

Old Street

'Widened Lines'

Moorgate

Farringdon

To Liverpool Street

Barbican

See enlargement (left)

Right Although the 'Northern Heights' lines passed from LNER into London Transport hands as long ago as 1940, it is pleasing to see how the stations have retained their Steam Age character. In this view at Totteridge on 27 March 1985 a train of Northern Line 1959 stock is about to leave for High Barnet. *F. Hornby*

Middle right A peaceful scene in King's Cross suburban station on 11 May 1974 with a pair of Class 105 Craven two-car DMUs in 'Rail Blue' resting between duties. At this stage only two terminal platforms were deemed necessary as compared with five formerly. *F. Hornby*

Bottom right A Craven two-car diesel unit pauses at King's Cross (York Road) platform on 27 February 1976 on a Welwyn Garden City-Moorgate service. This route was abandoned in November of that year when the inner suburban electrified service commenced, using the old Great Northern & City route via Highbury. *F. Hornby*

day. The removal of the first gives 21 miles of continuous four tracks from King's Cross, with the slow lines flanking the fast pair; this arrangement is resumed northwards from Woolmer Green.

Most suburban stations on the main line, save those in the bottlenecks, consisted of two island platforms serving all four running lines, but there were exceptions to the rule and the five 'islands' at Finsbury Park have already been mentioned; these have now been reduced to three, serving five tracks. Hatfield has staggered platforms with an island for down trains and a single platform on the up side. In the course of modernising, the tracks were realigned and a bay platform on the up side was removed, as were the sidings and engine shed. Hadley Wood and Potters Bar were rebuilt during the widening operations to conform to the 'two islands' pattern, and more recently a new station has been opened at Welham Green, 2½ miles south of Hatfield, with local line platforms only. This brings the number of stations on

Left Hatfield shed, though small, played a vital role in providing motive power for main-line and branch-line local passenger traffic with an allocation of some 25 0-6-2Ts. The station is just visible on the right in this view looking north on 23 May 1959. *F. Hornby*

Middle left The 1973-built station at Stevenage is one of the busiest in the Great Northern suburban area, served by long-distance expresses as well as by stopping trains via the main line and Hertford loop. A 90 mph EMU, No 317363, awaits the road before leaving for King's Cross on 29 July 1988. *F. Hornby*

Bottom left Considerable realignment of tracks and rebuilding of stations preceded the suburban electrification of November 1976. Three-car EMU No 313034 is seen here pausing at a modernised Hornsey, en route to Moorgate on 4 February 1977. *F. Hornby*

the main line between King's Cross and Hitchin to 16 in the 32 miles.

At Welwyn Garden City the station entrance is now incorporated in a shipping mall completed in October 1990. A flyover was provided south of the station in 1975 to facilitate the reversal of electric trains terminating there. Drastic measures were needed at Stevenage due to the dramatic expansion of the New Town - the population has grown from 6,000 to 75,000 in three decades - and the old station has been replaced by a new one a mile to the south with two long island platforms, opened in 1973. Hitchin, with platforms for the slow lines only - lengthened in 1989 - retains something of its pre-BR atmosphere, save of course for the disappearance of the adjacent locomotive shed and sidings.

Closer to London, Harringay and Hornsey were modernised with the loss of their main-line platforms and with the local tracks realigned preparatory for the suburban electrification of 1976, while Wood Green (since renamed

Alexandra Palace) was updated in 1973, losing its gas lighting in the process!

The Alexandra Palace branch, having narrowly escaped incorporation into London Transport, continued to function spasmodically until final closure on 5 July 1954. As far as Park Junction, beyond Highgate, the route had been shared with the other 'Northern Heights' services to High Barnet and Edgware until 1940. Beyond this junction there were two more stations in the remaining 1¾ miles to the terminus. The station there, 310 feet above sea level, consisted of a wide island platform overshadowed by the Palace, which had attracted great crowds in earlier years; latterly the trains were almost deserted outside peak hours. The maximum gradient was 1 in 80, with tunnels at either end of Highgate station and with a 17-arch viaduct between Cranley Gardens and Muswell Hill. In its declining years it was hard to imagine that, years before, there had been through services to and from Victoria and Woolwich.

The present Alexandra Palace is the junction for the 24-mile loop line to Langley Junction, south of Stevenage, double track throughout and accessed by flying junctions at both ends. It opened in stages between 1871 and 1924, Hertford North being the terminus for suburban services for many years. There was once a connection to Hertford East on the GE section, though not used by passenger services; it was severed in October 1965.

When the loop was completed it formed a valuable diversionary route at times when the main line was blocked, although various restrictions limited the maximum speed along it to 50 mph. Engineering work involving single-line working at peak hours and off-peak bus substitutions enabled the limit to be raised to 70 mph by the summer of 1960. Most stations have the conventional two platforms, though the southernmost one, Bowes Park, has an island platform, and in steam days Hertford North - then also the terminus of a branch from Hatfield - had two of them. There are two tunnels of which Ponsbourne, between Cuffley and Bayford, is 1 m 924 yd long. The northern portal marks the summit of a 7-mile climb followed by a steeper (1 in 198) descent to the

second, short tunnel just beyond Hertford North. There are currently 11 intermediate stations, and traffic has greatly increased since electrification, although beyond Enfield the only town of consequence is Hertford, with a population of 22,000 and with another station served from Liverpool Street.

All the branches from Hatfield were cross-country lines terminating at places with more direct routes from London. The St Albans branch (1866-1951) was 6½ miles long with four intermediate stations; it shared St Albans Abbey station with the ex-LMS line from Watford. The Hertford North branch (1858-1951) was of identical length but with only two stations en route. The longest branch, via Luton to Dunstable, was of 1860 vintage with six stations along its 20¼ miles and made an end-on connection with another ex-LMS branch, from Leighton Buzzard. It lasted into the diesel era, closing in April 1965. Though practically all trains on the Hertford and Dunstable branches worked through from and to Hatfield, they diverted from the main line, to the east and the west respectively, one station north at Welwyn Garden City. Between those two stations there was a single track for the Dunstable trains, on the down side of the main lines.

The conversion of the former Great Northern & City tube into a BR electrified line from Moorgate to Finsbury Park in 1976 enabled the old route via the Widened Lines to be abandoned. The line surfaces at Drayton Park, whence the down track burrows beneath the main lines from King's Cross. There is cross-platform connection with the Victoria Line at Highbury, with further access to the latter, and to the Piccadilly Line, at Finsbury Park. Coincidental with the closure of the old route, the peak-hour service to and from Broad Street via the Finsbury Park-

Two compartment coaches suffice for this off-peak train at Alexandra Palace on 6 March 1954. 'N2' 0-6-2T No 69519 is about to leave bunker-first for Finsbury Park, doubtless enjoying the respite from its more onerous main-line duties. N. L. Browne

On 14 May 1960, in the early months of dieselised suburban services, three Craven two-car units form a King's Cross-bound stopping train at Harringay. Note the flyover spanning the main line and the impressive array of semaphore signals. *F. Hornby*

crossing from the east to west side of the main lines. At the same time the hitherto 'slow' lines were passed for 75 mph instead of 50 mph maximum speeds. For outer suburban trains using the fast tracks the permissible maximum rose to 100 mph beyond Alexandra Palace! A public address system was installed in the power box to relay information to passengers at any of 35 suburban stations, although 'regulars' would claim that the information was not always infallible!

Canonbury spur was also discontinued; the spur remains open for freight traffic.

The replacement of steam by diesel traction from 1959 onward and electrification some 17 years later enabled a more intensive service to be worked over a greatly simplified track layout, which in turn depended on a modernised signalling system. As of 1948 only the short section from King's Cross to Belle Isle was controlled by colour-lights, dating from 1932. Elsewhere upper quadrant semaphore signals were in vogue, with even a few somersault signals of GNR origin; a gantry of them at Finsbury Park was replaced by colour-lights in 1950.

Further out, save for a few distant signals, colour-lights were confined to the 3½ miles from New Barnet to Potters Bar, installed during the widening works. In 1970 approval was given to re-equip the main line and the Hertford loop, and work proceeded in stages until April 1977, when King's Cross power box, controlling 830 trains daily, replaced 57 manual boxes. The slow lines were equipped with three-aspect colour-lights, save at the southern end of the Hertford loop where the close proximity of stations necessitated four-aspect signals.

In conjunction with track alterations the flyover at Holloway was upgraded from 15 to 30 mph for use by inbound suburban trains

Hertford North no longer needs a water tank, and the semaphore signals are long gone since this scene was recorded on 20 September 1958. The fireman is clambering down from the bunker before 'N2' 0-6-2T No 69572 leaves with the 1.31 pm to King's Cross. *F. Hornby*

SERVICES

In the first years of BR's stewardship the rather complex GN line suburban services were virtually unchanged from those operated post-war by the LNER, with trains between Moorgate, Broad Street, King's Cross, Finsbury Park and a variety of stations on the main line and Hertford loop.

Exclusive of the Cambridge buffet car expresses, which called at Hitchin (and in most cases at Welwyn Garden City), the 1949 winter timetable listed 100 weekday suburban departures with destinations as shown in the upper table opposite.

These were spread over a long day; the first departure from King's Cross (Mondays excepted) was at

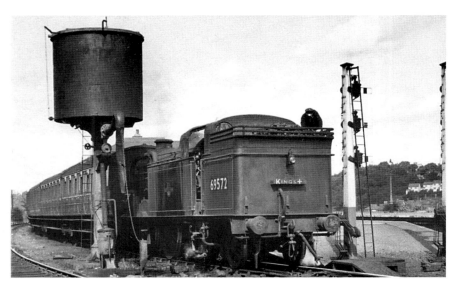

GN LINE DOWN SUBURBAN SERVICES, 1949

From: To:		King's Cross	Finsbury Park	Moorgate	Broad Street	Total
	Gordon Hill	3	4	-	2	9
	Cuffley	-	-	1	1	2
	Hertford North	19	6	5	3	33
	New Barnet	2	1	2	1	6
	Potters Bar	-	-	1	-	1
	Hatfield	7	-	2	-	9
	Welwyn Garden City	9	1	1	1	12
	Hitchin and beyond*	28	-	-	-	28
	Total	68	12	12	8	100

* Mostly Baldock or Royston

GN LINE SUBURBAN TRAIN TIMINGS, 1949

	Distance (miles)	Stops	Time (mins)	Average (mph)
King's Cross-Hertford North	19¾	13	57	20¾
King's Cross-Hitchin	32	8	72	26¾
Moorgate-New Barnet	10¼	6	36	18
Broad Street-Gordon Hill	12¼	9	44	16¾

1.00 am and the last at 12 midnight. Typical journey times are shown in the second table.

There were 50 departures on Sundays - all from King's Cross save for two from Finsbury Park to Hertford North. These included some distinctly leisurely timings - for example, 81 minutes to Hitchin with 15 stops. The favourite Sunday destinations were Hertford North, Hatfield and Welwyn Garden City. On summer Saturdays, incidentally, all suburban trains were routed to Moorgate to ease the strain on an over-taxed King's Cross. The Broad Street services, inherited from the LMS, were worked after nationalisation by ER locomotives and stock and confined to peak hours.

As reported in the contemporary *Railway Observer*, the 5.34 pm departure from Moorgate made post-war history by being scheduled to run through King's Cross without stopping, on an 11-minute 'sprint' from Farringdon Street to Finsbury Park, where it was then one of three northbound trains leaving within 2 minutes!

The Alexandra Palace branch was well served by 24 'weekdays only' trains from Finsbury Park, of which all but two made good connections from King's Cross. The first morning train terminated at Highgate, the remainder running through to the Palace in 17 minutes for the 4¾ miles inclusive of six stops; this 15 mph average reflected the steep gradients and short distances between stations.

The service on all three branches from Hatfield was sparse as per the 1949 timetable reproduced overleaf. However, save for the first train of the day to Hertford North, all the others made connections to or from King's Cross, and the through train from Luton will be noted.

In 1951 service cuts gave rise to many complaints, as is not surprising when - to quote an extreme example - there was no train from King's Cross to New Barnet, a mere 9 miles away, between 6.59 pm and 9.21 pm. The Alexandra Palace service was withdrawn on 27 October but, with most of the cancelled trains on the main line, was restored on 7 January 1952. The Hatfield to Hertford North branch lost its passenger service -permanently - on 14 June 1951, followed in October by closure of the St Albans branch. Workmen's tickets, as on other lines, were replaced after 30 September 1950 by early morning returns.

By 1953 marginal improvements were made in the main-line and Hertford North stopping services, though journey times were unchanged. At least the residents of New Barnet now had two trains in the evening between 7 and 9 pm! The Alexandra Palace branch saw its last trains on 5 July 1954 after an eventful existence of 81 years.

It was not until late 1958, however, that significant changes were implemented, thanks to the completion

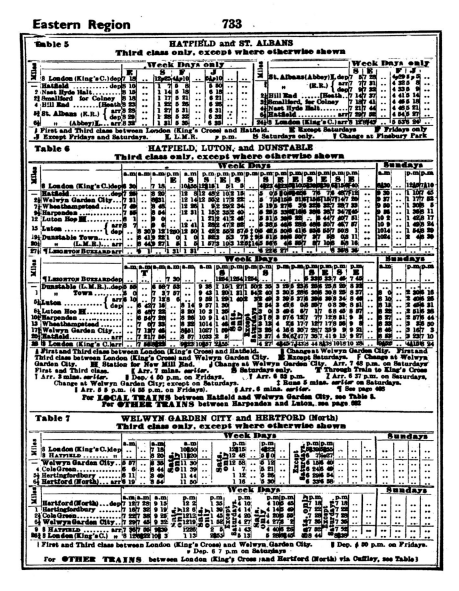

Services on the branches from Hatfield, from the 1949 Eastern Region timetable.

There followed a period of relative stability while diesel traction was consolidated, one innovation being the restoration on 5 March 1962 of services between Hertford North and Hitchin - worked pre-war by a Sentinel railcar but now by a diesel unit - with seven trains each way daily.

During the 1960s the off-peak timetable listed two stopping trains per hour between King's Cross and Hertford North, one between King's Cross and Welwyn Garden City, omitting some stops, and one between Finsbury Park and Hatfield or Welwyn Garden City. The other suburban customers were catered for by an hourly train between King's Cross and either Baldock or Royston, non-stop south of Hatfield. Cambridge had an (approximately) hourly service, also fast south of Hatfield or Welwyn Garden City. Enforced economies resulted in some highly unpopular cuts in evening peak-hour services in October 1971.

Electrification came later in the 1970s in two stages, the first covering the inner suburban services from Moorgate over the former GN & City line, thence to Hertford North and Welwyn Garden City; good connections with the diesel outer-suburbans were provided at Finsbury Park. This service commenced on 8 November 1976 and was augmented by the second stage from 3 October 1977, from Welwyn Garden City northwards through Hitchin to Royston. The full timetable came into effect on 6 February 1978, marking a temporary cessation of the long-standing through trains between King's Cross and Cambridge until the Royston-Cambridge section was energised a decade later, in the summer of 1988. Meantime electrification had been extended northwards along the main line, as far as Huntingdon from 3 November 1986 and then to Peterborough and beyond; an hourly semi-fast service between King's Cross and Peterborough commenced on 11 May 1987. The catenary was also in place at the northern end of the loop line, from Hertford North to Langley

of the widening works at Potters Bar and the introduction of diesel traction. The last 'all steam' timetable was that for Summer 1958, though a considerable period elapsed before steam was finally ousted, but by the early 1960s the advantages of the new motive power were becoming evident. In Summer 1961 there were 130 weekday stopping trains arriving in London, including 73 designated for diesel traction, from 13 points of origin. The accompanying table shows that diversity was still high. Journey times showed improvements ranging from 10 minutes (Hitchin-King's Cross) to 5 minutes (Gordon Hill-Broad Street).

Services along the sole remaining branch, between Dunstable and Hatfield, were little changed from 1949, still with the Luton-Dunstable short workings and a through train from Luton to King's Cross.

GN LINE UP SUBURBAN SERVICES, 1961

To:	King's Cross	Finsbury Park	Moorgate	Broad Street	Total
Arrivals from: Gordon Hill	4	-	3	2	9
Cuffley	-	1	1	3	5
Hertford North	18	13	3	5	39
Wood Green	1	-	-	-	1
New Barnet	-	-	1	1	2
Potters Bar	2	-	2	-	4
Hatfield	13	1	1	1	16
Welwyn Garden City	16	3	2	1	22
Luton	1	-	-	-	1
Hitchin and beyond*	31	-	-	-	31

* Including 24 from Baldock, Royston and Cambridge (stopping trains)

Junction, enabling the re-routing of the Huntingdon service via Hertford from the start of the 1990 summer timetable.

Initially the inner suburban off-peak service ran from and to Moorgate at 10-minute intervals, but from Winter 1987 it was reduced to four per hour, alternately serving Hertford North and Welwyn Garden City. Moorgate station's opening hours were curtailed with all early morning, late evening and weekend trains using King's Cross. The Winter 1993/94 timetable provided for 80 departures from Moorgate, of which 10 terminated at Finsbury Park and 10 went through to Stevenage via Hertford North. From King's Cross the off-peak service consisted of hourly trains to Peterborough, Letchworth, Royston and Cambridge, all running fast through the inner suburban area. Journey times by electric traction are of course less than in steam or diesel days, as shown for example in the accompanying table.

GN LINE DOWN SUBURBAN SERVICES: COMPARATIVE JOURNEY TIMES

From London to:	Steam	Diesel	Electric
Hertford North	57 mins	51 mins	45 mins (M)
Hatfield	46 mins	40 mins	39 mins (M)
Hitchin	72 mins	53 mins	42 mins (K)

M - from Moorgate; K - from King's Cross

TRACTION AND TRAINS

From the early 1920s to the coming of the diesels, Gresley's Class 'N2' 0-6-2Ts were the backbone of the inner suburban motive power. Of the 107 locomotives built between 1920 and 1929, all but one were still at work in 1948. At that time the majority were stationed in the London area, with 57 at King's Cross shed, 10 at Hornsey, 14 at Hatfield and two at Hitchin. Most were condenser-fitted for working through the tunnels on the Widened Lines, virtually monopolising the traffic for which they were designed. The only exceptions were occasional turns worked by their Ivatt 'N1' predecessors, especially on Sundays, though even this was rare by 1950. Traditionally the 'N2s' worked chimney-first northbound, though this was uncomfortable for the crews on the sulphurous climb round the Hotel Curve into King's Cross. They worked long hours, frequently double-manned, some rosters including eight journeys spread over 14 hours. Their home at King's Cross was the seven-road 'Met shed' where some with regular crews were commendably well-kept. Withdrawal began in 1957 and their last regular duties were in 1960, though it was May 1962 before the last of the class left the London area.

In 1949 King's Cross shed received its first 'L1' 2-6-4T, of which nine were also allocated to Hitchin for outer-suburban duties. By the end of 1954 there were eight at 'Top Shed', and they ousted 'N2s' from some inner-suburban turns, although they were not permitted to work to Moorgate or, until 1958, to Broad Street. Their career, inevitably, was much shorter than that of the 'N2s' although they still deputised for failed diesels up to 1961. By the end of 1960 the sole remaining turn rostered for steam was a peak-hour train from Broad Street to Potters Bar.

If Sir Nigel Gresley's name is honoured for his famous 'Pacifics' it may have been regarded with less

giving way in turn to ex-GCR engines of Classes 'F2' (2-4-2T), 'C13' (4-4-2T) and 'N5' (0-6-2T). Also used on the branch before closure in 1954 were 'N7' 0-6-2Ts transferred from Neasden. This class was also the normal motive power on the branches from Hatfield, where up to 15 were stationed; the Dunstable branch in particular was the preserve of these engines. The two-road shed at Hatfield (34C) closed in January 1961, followed by Hitchin (34D) in June.

Travellers by semi-fast trains experienced a wide variety of steam power over the years, even including, for a short time after nationalisation, the chance of a run behind one of the last surviving Ivatt 'C1' 'Atlantics' based at Hitchin. Eleven of their successors, the 'B1' 4-6-0s, were already established at that shed before 1948, working Cambridge line trains, and in 1950 one of them regularly double-headed with an 'A2/2' 4-6-2 on the 5.55 pm stopping train from King's Cross - 'super power' indeed!

Other classes participating in outer-suburban duties ranged from 'A4' streamlined 'Pacifics' and 'V2' 2-6-2s to the 'L1' 2-6-4Ts and a Fowler 2-6-4T loaned from the LM Region. Later, various engines were called on to substitute for diesels, until King's Cross 'Top Shed' (34A) closed in July 1963. *The Railway Observer* quoted, as

reverence by the thousands who endured their daily travels in his 'Quad-art' sets, whose lifespan approximated to that of the 'N2s' that hauled them. First introduced on the GNR with accommodation in three classes and gas lighting, over 100 sets were built by 1929, the post-Grouping examples being electrically lit. The four coach bodies were articulated on five bogies with a substantial saving in weight, and a pair of 'Quad-arts' with 700 people on board weighed 182 tons tare, and thus around 235 tons gross. Overall length of a pair was 337 ft 5½ in, which, with locomotives, just fitted the terminal platforms at Moorgate. Although withdrawal in favour of BR standard compartment coaches began in 1955, they remained in service on peak-hour trains for a further 10 years, as five of the new BR coaches, seating only 468, was the maximum that Moorgate could accommodate. Hence the new vehicles, although more comfortable, provided far fewer seats, as did also their diesel unit replacements! From early BR days the 'Quad-arts' forsook their varnished teak livery for maroon, but the lineage, to the end, was unmistakably 'Great Northern'.

On the steeply graded Alexandra Palace branch the peak-hour trains required the tractive power of an 'N2', but off-peak, with a two-coach set, ex-GNR 'C12' 4-4-2Ts sufficed,

Soon after the introduction of five-coach rakes of BR standard suburban stock, 'N2' 0-6-2T No 69498 hurries past near Potters Bar on 17 March 1956 with northbound 'empties'. Misleadingly the locomotive still carries a 'New Barnet' destination board across the smokebox. *F. Hornby*

examples in early 1963, a Class 'A3' on a Hatfield-King's Cross stopping train, a 'B1' on a morning train from Baldock, and a Class '4' 2-6-0 from Cuffley to Broad Street. Remarkably even in April 1964, a 'B1' from Peterborough was recorded on a morning train from Hatfield.

Diesel traction first appeared late in 1958 in the shape of both locomotives and multiple units. Servicing facilities for the locomotives were temporarily provided at the steam sheds until a six-road depot was ready at Finsbury Park in the spring of 1960, with a two-road sub depot at Hitchin.

Initially the locomotives were of three classes in the Type 2 power group, of which the first to arrive were 20 Birmingham RCW D53XXs, followed shortly by 10 North British Loco Co D61XXs and 10 English Electric 'Baby Deltic' D59XXs. The intention was to combine suburban and empty stock duties with overnight freight trips to and from the Southern Region, but the Civil Engineer banned all three types from the latter function. In consequence the D53XX and D61XX Classes were exchanged for Derby/Sulzer D50XXs and the more powerful Brush D55XXs, while the D59XXs were outstationed at Hitchin. Sadly the latter gave a great deal of trouble and were withdrawn for overhaul in July 1963, returning to traffic the following year and used sporadically until retirement between 1968 and 1971.

Additionally two classes in the Type 1 category - English Electric D80XXs and BTH-built D82XXs - also saw service on the GN lines in small numbers. Neither were equipped for steam heating so were unpopular when deputising for other classes on suburban duties during the winter. They saw service on the Dunstable branch, with Hatfield's 'N7s' deputising during the winter until the shed closed, whereafter the Brush D55XXs took over during the branch's final years.

As in steam days, passengers using the outer-suburban services were treated to unusual haulage on occasions, even including the experimental locomotives DP2 and *Lion*, which, with 'Deltics' and 'Peaks', were recorded on Cambridge trains in 1964. At least once a 3,300 hp 'Deltic' gravitated to a Hertford North 'stopper' - presumably keeping time with ease! All the seven evening departures from Broad Street in the late 1960s were locomotive-hauled, the majority by the Class '31s'.

The first multiple units consisted of a fleet of 28 Class 105 Craven two-car diesel-mechanicals powered by 300 hp AEC engines and capable of 70 mph. They provided 12 1st and 103 2nd Class seats per unit and weighed 53 tons. Moorgate could only accommodate three units in multiple, with scarcely more than half the seats provided by a pair of

Birmingham RCW 1,160 hp Bo-Bo diesel-electric No D5307 was only a few months old when entrusted with a Cambridge-King's Cross stopping train, seen here approaching Hatfield on 23 May 1959. Colour-light signalling is in evidence and the locomotive of a southbound freight can just be seen waiting in the loop. *F. Hornby*

	'TOPS' Class	Built	Year introduced	Wheel arrangement	Horse-power	Weight (tons cwt)	Max speed (mph)	Finsbury Park allocation 1965
DIESEL-ELECTRIC LOCOMOTIVE TYPES EMPLOYED ON SUBURBAN DUTIES								
Type 2								
D5000	24	Crewe/Derby	1958	Bo-Bo	1160	75 0	75	25
D5300	26	BRCW	1957	Bo-Bo	1160	77 10	75	-
D5500	31	Brush	1957	AIA-AIA	1365	104 0	75	49
D5900	23	English Electric	1959	Bo-Bo	1100	73 17	75	10
D6100	21	NBL Co	1958	Bo-Bo	1100	72 10	75	-
Type 1								
D8000	20	English Electric	1957	Bo-Bo	1000	72 0	75	10
D8200	15	BTH	1957	Bo-Bo	800	68 0	60	7

the much-maligned 'Quad-arts'. Although the Cravens remained in a majority they were joined by Derby/BUT three-car units in the later 1960s and also by Derby/Rolls-Royce diesel-hydraulics. The 1970 allocation at Finsbury Park was made up of 46 Cravens, four Derby three-cars and 20 Derby/Rolls-Royce units. They were stabled and inspected at Finsbury Park Western Sidings, with the Rolls-Royce units visiting Stratford and the others Cambridge for periodical maintenance. By 1970 most had exchanged their original green livery for 'Rail Blue'.

At the commencement of the inner-suburban electrified services in November 1976 the Derby/Rolls-Royce units went into store and the Cravens' diagrams were reduced from 31 to 16 daily, but the three diagrams for the Derby three-car units were retained. There was a further reduction in the requirement for DMUs when the Hertford North-Stevenage section was electrified from 14 May 1979, and their last regular duties on GN lines were on the Hitchin and Huntingdon and Royston-Cambridge sections until

these also came under the catenary in 1988 and 1989 respectively. For these two services a small fleet of Metro-Cammell 'Low Density' two-car units (Class 101) was assigned.

For the inner-suburban electrification BREL at York built 64 three-car multiple units, Nos 313001-64, in 1976. Each unit weighed 103 tons, seated 230 and was powered by eight 110 hp GEC motors. As the 2.73 miles in tunnel from Moorgate to Drayton Park is electrified on the 750V DC third-rail system, while the surface mileage is on 25kV from overhead catenary, they are equipped with shoe gear on the outer bogies and a pantograph on the middle coaches. Changeover is made during the Drayton Park stop and the respective maximum speeds are 30 mph in the tunnel and 75 mph on the surface. Power for the 25kV section is drawn from the National Grid at Wood Green and Welwyn Garden City.

The units are based at Hornsey where a six-road main shed and sidings are situated on the site of the old steam depot, with stabling sidings at Hertford North and Welwyn Garden City. When the services began 150 drivers were retrained from DMUs and there were 22 daily diagrams. Of the 64 units originally deployed, 44 remain on GN line duties, the remainder having been reallocated to the North London line.

Viewed from the buffers at Moorgate on 3 April 1969, the near-empty platforms are deceptive as the 'evening peak' is in progress! On the left Brush Type 2 No D5641 has arrived with the stock to form the 17.31 to Potters Bar, while on the right Derby three-car diesel units make up the 17.41 to Hatfield. *J. M. Tolson*

Right On 9 March 1993 a Class 313 EMU approaches Drayton Park, en route for Moorgate. During the stop the driver will lower the pantograph as 750V DC current will be collected from the third rail for the rest of the journey. The northbound track on the left burrows under the main lines in the background. *F. Hornby*

Middle right A Moorgate-Stevenage via Hertford North train sets down a few passengers at Palmers Green station on 4 October 1989. The 30-mile journey is allowed 58 minutes with 19 stops, making full use of the accelerative powers of graffiti-daubed EMU No 313050. *F. Hornby*

Bottom right A Royston train comprised of Class 312 EMUs, with the first of the class, No 312001, leading, awaits departure from King's Cross main-line station on 27 May 1978. Similar in appearance to the pioneer Class 310s, they were built at York from 1975 and later renumbered in the 312700 series. *F. Hornby*

The outer suburban service to Royston commenced in October 1977, worked by a batch of 26 new four-car Class 312 units modelled on the LM Region Class 310 prototypes. Built at BREL York in 1975-77, they tip the scales at 151 tons, and their 1,080 hp motors give them a maximum speed of 90 mph. Seating capacity is for 297 in Standard and 25 in 1st Class accommodation. The full service came into effect in February 1978 and was operated by these units until 1986, when replacements from the LMR, in the shape of 100 mph Class 317s of 1981 design, first arrived at Hornsey depot. In March of that year Hornsey's roster included 23 Class 312 and seven Class 317 units, but in due course 72 units of sub-Classes 317/1 and 317/2 have completely ousted the 312s and have extended their activities to Peterborough and Cambridge. Interestingly, they also covered inner-suburban duties at weekends, when the Moorgate line was closed, for a 12-month period in 1989/90.

6

NORTH LONDON LINES

BROAD STREET-RICHMOND AND NORTH WOOLWICH

The North London Railway, small in size but big in enterprise, was sponsored from its inception by the mighty London & North Western, and after entering into an even closer working arrangement in 1909, it was eventually absorbed by that company in 1922.

Although conceived with freight traffic in mind, as a link between the LNWR and the East London docks, it soon proved its value as a cross-London line for passenger traffic, and even by the 1860s was an archetypal suburban railway, running frequent trains at regular intervals long before that sensible principle was widely adopted elsewhere.

From early days its little 4-4-0Ts and four-wheeled carriages ranged far and wide well beyond the NLR, and at one time or another reached such diverse destinations as Windsor, Enfield and Plaistow. Some of these services were short-lived, but the trains continued to run on the Great Northern line throughout the Grouping era and, though discontinued during the Second World War, resumed in 1945 until the electrified service from Moorgate commenced in November 1976.

By nationalisation, however, much had changed and North London line services proper had been reduced to those initiated by the LNWR electric trains, first to Richmond in 1916, then to Watford in 1922. The service eastward to Poplar had ceased to run in May 1944 and it was largely thanks to GLC initiatives that stations were reopened and trains resumed running in 1979 - under the 'Crosstown Link' banner - with diesel multiple units between Camden Road and North Woolwich. Sufficient custom was attracted to warrant extension of the third rail to the new eastern terminus, reversing the relentless fall in patronage over many years, with the introduction of a North Woolwich to Richmond service - the 'North London Link' - from 13 May 1985.

It could be said, with the closure of Broad Street and the lack of success of the diversion into Liverpool Street, that the wheel had turned full circle, since the North London Railway's first services in the 1850s were along the east-west axis, just as are those of today.

ROUTES AND INFRASTRUCTURE

The 'City Extension' to Broad Street, southwards for 2 miles from a triangular junction at Dalston, opened on 1 November 1865, climbing at 1 in 60 from Dalston Junction station on to a continuous viaduct alongside Kingsland Road and Shoreditch. Broad Street at its zenith was London's third busiest terminus, handling over 700 trains daily at its eight platforms by 1906, and over 40,000 passengers during the morning rush hours. Practically all the trains were strictly suburban, the only exceptions in BR years being some diversions from the GN main line during holiday weekends in 1951 and 1952 to relieve congestion at King's Cross.

By the 1920s five platform roads

A Class 105 Craven two-car DMU has just arrived at Camden Road on its 'Crosstown Link' run from North Woolwich on 19 August 1981. The freight lines under the 25kV catenary and the remains of the old platforms can be seen on the far left. *F. Hornby*

Right Even the unsightly arcade of shops fails to conceal the architectural style of Broad Street station as completed in 1865. With nine platforms and 700 trains daily in its prime, the situation was very different at the time of this photograph in May 1974 when, outside business hours, few would-be passengers disturbed the peace. *F. Hornby*

Middle right On a wet day at Broad Street in May 1974 there is no protection for passengers beyond the first two coaches after the rest of the roof has been dismantled. A Class 501 EMU on a Richmond service is just visible on the left, while Craven DMUs on the right will form a peak-hour train for Hertford North. *F. Hornby*

Bottom right Dalston Kingsland station opened in May 1983 in anticipation of the closure of the nearby Junction station on the 'City Extension' to Broad Street. On 5 May 1993 it is host to dual-voltage unit No 313003 en route from North Woolwich to Richmond. *F. Hornby*

were equipped with conductor rails for the electric services, as were two of the four running lines to Dalston Junction; the two intermediate stations on this section were closed in 1940. During early BR years there was a steady decline in traffic, and in the late 1950s facilities at the terminus were reduced by closing the main block and substituting a small booking office on the concourse.

The decline continued to such an extent that by 1968, outside the peak hours, two men on duty sufficed to issue and collect tickets. Most of the train shed roof was removed and platforms 6 to 8 were closed in 1971. The remaining electrified line to Dalston Junction was lifted, one having already been dispensed with in 1966. The terminus proper fell into disuse in June 1985 and a single platform was substituted some 600 yards north, until final closure on 27 June 1986. The six-platform Dalston Junction closed simultaneously, an alternative station having opened some 2½ years previously on the east-west line at nearby Kingsland, at the same location as the original one of 1850!

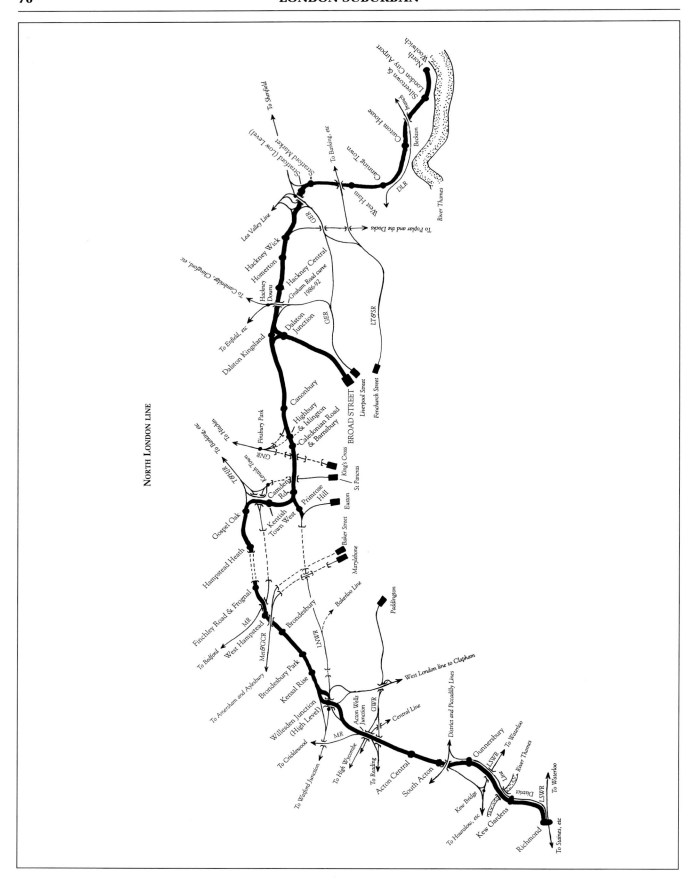

North London lines from Broad Street to Dalston Junction, North Woolwich to Richmond, and Camden Road to Primrose Hill

Miles	Name	Opened	Closed	Notes
From Broad Street				
	Broad Street	11/1865	6/1985	
¼	(temporary station)	6/1985	6/1986	
2	Dalston Junction	11/1865	6/1986	
	Graham Road curve (to GE section)	6/1986-9/1992		
From North Woolwich				
	North Woolwich	6/1847		
¾	Silvertown & London City Airport	6/1847		'Silvertown' to 1987
1¾	Custom House	1855		
3	Canning Town	4/1846		Originally 'Barking Road'
3¾	West Ham	5/1979		
4½	Stratford Market	6/1847	5/1957	'Stratford Bridge' to 11/1880
4¾	Stratford (low level)	8/1854		
5¾	Hackney Wick	6/1850		Originally 'Hackney'; new station from 5/1980, original closed 4/1945
6½	Homerton	10/1868		New station from 5/1985; original closed 4/1945
7¼	Hackney Central	9/1850		New station from 5/1980
8	Dalston Kingsland	5/1983		Date for resited station; original open 11/1850 to 11/1865
9	Canonbury	12/1870		Resited station; 'Newington Road & Balls Pond' from 9/1858
9½	Highbury & Islington	9/1850		'Islington' to 1872
10	Caledonian Road & Barnsbury	6/1852		'Barnsbury' 1870-93
11	Camden Road	12/1850		'Camden Town' to 5/1950
11¾	Primrose Hill	6/1851	9/1992	Originally 'Hampstead Road' then 'Chalk Farm' to 9/1950
11¾	Kentish Town West	1/1860		Closed 4/1971-10/1982 following fire; 'West' from 1924
12¼	Gospel Oak	1/1860		'Kentish Town' to 2/1867
12¾	Hampstead Heath	1/1860		
13¾	Finchley Road & Frognal	1/1860		
14¼	West Hampstead	3/1888		'West End Lane' to 5/1975
14¾	Brondesbury	1/1860		
15	Brondesbury Park	6/1908		
15¾	Kensal Rise	11/1861		'Kensal Green' to 1890; second station opened 1873
16¾	Willesden Junction	9/1866		
18¼	Acton Central	8/1853		'Acton' to 1925
19¼	South Acton	1/1880		
20	Gunnersbury	1/1869		'Brentford Road' to 11/1871
21	Kew Gardens	1/1869		
22¼	Richmond	1/1869		

Left Highbury & Islington station provides an unsightly contrast of old and new architectural styles, with some remains of the original buildings on the right and the catenary for the freight lines visible beyond the fence on the left. This view is looking east on 20 April 1993. *F. Hornby*

Middle left Kentish Town West has had a chequered history as the old station was destroyed by fire in April 1971 and it was 11 years before a replacement was opened. A Richmond-bound Class 313 EMU departs on the left as another arrives en route to North Woolwich on 20 April 1993. *F. Hornby*

Bottom left EMU No 313006 sets out from leafy West Hampstead station on 7 July 1993. The North London line can hardly be described as 'scenic', but the Hampstead area provides a small oasis in the otherwise unbroken vista of housing and industry east of Willesden Junction. *F. Hornby*

Westwards from Dalston Junction four tracks were provided from 1871 as far as Camden Road Junction, all originally having platforms at the intermediate stations, although the northernmost pair were not electrified and so were for many years used exclusively for freight traffic. This was very heavy until the decline of the docks, whereafter one track has been lifted from Canonbury for over a mile through Caledonian Road & Barnsbury. From 18 April 1988 catenary at 25kV was energised from Camden Road over the freight lines and eastwards to Stratford, facilitating the replacement of diesel by electric locomotives on some freight trains. Thus the 4-mile section to the east of Canonbury is shared by 750V DC and 25kV AC traction.

Just east of Highbury & Islington the connection used by Great Northern line services until November 1976 diverges northwards, passing through a quarter-mile tunnel en route to Finsbury Park. Between Caledonian Road & Barnsbury and Camden Road stations the North London crosses the main lines out of King's Cross and St Pancras on a high brick-arched viaduct. At Camden Road Junction one route, now used only by freight but formerly also by the Broad Street-Watford trains, continues straight ahead to join the DC lines from Euston at Primrose Hill. The Richmond route curves north, crossing the Midland again beyond Kentish Town West, then swings west at Gospel Oak, the junction with the Tottenham & Hampstead line from Barking. The line then skirts Hampstead Heath, making a pleasant change from bricks and mortar, but immediately after the station of that name a three-quarter-mile tunnel penetrates the high ground of Finchley.

Soon after emerging from the tunnel there is a third crossing over the Midland main line near West Hampstead, where the North London, Thameslink and Jubilee Line stations are conveniently close for interchange, and shortly afterwards the Chiltern Line and Metropolitan tracks pass overhead. The last major change of direction, to the south, is 2 miles further on at Willesden Junction high level, where the island platform is above and at right-angles to the station for the Euston-Watford and Bakerloo Line trains; an electrified spur connects the high- and low-level lines, once used by an occasional Broad Street-Watford train. Then follows a veritable tangle of junctions where the North London crosses the main lines from Euston and Paddington together with the Central Line to West Ruislip.

The North & South Western Junction line from Cricklewood is joined at Acton Wells Junction and followed through the two Actons - Central and South - until it branches away to Kew Bridge. Then the District Line, on tracks of LSWR origin, is joined at Gunnersbury and North London and District Line trains share the remainder of the route to Richmond. They cross over the South Western Lines Hounslow loop and the River Thames at Kew before turning westwards for the final quarter-mile into Richmond. The station here has two terminal platforms for each of the two services, alongside the Windsor line through platforms. At this end of the line the stations are somewhat further apart and the aspect from

the train is rather more pleasant than that eastwards from Willesden.

Retracing our steps to Dalston Kingsland, there are now eight intermediate stations in the 8 miles to North Woolwich, four of which were reopened in the 1980s for the 'Crosstown Link'. Half a mile east of Kingsland the Graham Road curve for the short-lived service between Watford and Liverpool Street diverges to the right, to join the line into the latter near London Fields. Two miles further on the convolutions at Stratford are negotiated into the low-level station, at right-angles to the busy main station above. A mile to the south, the London, Tilbury & Southend route and District Line cross overhead at West Ham, with a footbridge linking the two stations. In traversing the still highly industrialised purlieus of Canning Town the tracks of the Docklands Light Railway Beckton branch (opened in April 1994) run parallel for a while. London City Airport is conveniently close to Silvertown station, though, by stark contrast to Gatwick, one doubts if much revenue is generated thereby!

The North Woolwich terminus, now reduced to a single platform, is close to the River; its fine old station building is now home to a museum dedicated to the Great Eastern Railway, as witness a 'plinthed' saddle tank outside.

The original North London Railway stations were quite impressive with tall if rather gaunt buildings in the mid-Victorian style. Little remains of these, though some stations do retain their protective awnings while others are reduced to steel-framed glass shelters. At the western end of the line several stations retain buildings at least partially intact - in particular Kew Gardens, which still displays evidence of its LSWR origins - while the genuine North London station house at Acton Central has survived as a pub!

The tracks at South Acton on 3 August 1993 could have benefited from a visit by the weed-killing train. Note the contrast in platform shelters at this unmanned station. The route-indicating signal on the right controls the junction of the lines to Richmond and to Kew Bridge, the latter for freight only. *F. Hornby*

Left It is a rainy scene at North Woolwich on 24 January 1985 as a Class 105 Craven DMU prepares to leave for Camden Road. The station building houses a museum dedicated to the GER, and a saddle tank locomotive undergoing restoration can be glimpsed on the left. *F. Hornby*

Middle left The erstwhile station building at Acton Central has at least escaped demolition in its new guise as a hostelry. Passengers have to be content with the narrow entrance on the left, but the eastbound platform still retains its sheltering roof. *F. Hornby*

Bottom left This view of Brondesbury station looking east in February 1961 shows the fourth-rail system and, at the far end of the station, one of the then few colour-light signals. The viaduct in the distance carries the 'GC & Met' lines, while the signal box in the foreground, complete with fire buckets, is of vintage LNWR design. *B. W. Brooksbank*

In this age of high-tech signalling one must pay homage to the way the once numerous manual boxes coped with the intensive flow of passenger and freight traffic, the latter still entirely steam-hauled until the late 1950s. By the 1960s there were pockets of colour-lights - notably along the 2-mile section east of Kensal Rise - with isolated automatic signals elsewhere. Special bell-codes were used to differentiate between the various routes, but by 1971 colour-lights had been installed in the Camden Road area and on the 'City Extension' to Broad Street. In recent years they have become universal and most boxes have closed, although some distinctive 'North London' boxes have survived, as at Dalston Kingsland and Camden Road.

As a footnote, at the time of writing plans are under consideration for the extension of 25kV electrification from Camden Road to Acton Wells Junction, together with the spur to Acton Main Line. The existing service is to be increased to four trains per hour and two new stations are to be provided between Willesden and Gunnersbury, together with platforms on the main slow lines at Willesden Junction. It would seem therefore that, at last, the North London line has effectively cast off its reputation of being one of the 'Cinderellas' of London's rail network!

SERVICES

Notwithstanding early electrification, the North London has always been a difficult line to work, particularly on the double-track sections shared with a sometimes unpredictable volume of freight traffic, while between Gunnersbury and Richmond there are the District Line trains to contend with. These days the problems have diminished with the freight traffic, which, thanks to diesel and electric traction, can dovetail in more easily with the EMUs.

Due attention was given to the Broad Street to Watford service when dealing with the DC line out of Euston, since both shared common trackage beyond Primrose Hill. Suffice it to recapitulate that in 1948 there were 33 weekday trains plus one to Rickmansworth, with a 5-hour gap from mid-morning onwards. The number increased to 44 on Saturdays with at least a half-hourly frequency until late evening, while on Sundays there were 17 trains each way during the afternoon and evening. Some trains omitted one or two stops, while a few - greatly daring - managed sprints, such as the weekday 4.50 pm, non-stop from Dalston Junction to Stonebridge Park!

The Richmond line notched up 50 trains each way on weekdays with an off-peak half-hourly frequency, and 55 on Saturdays, while on Sundays the attractions of Hampstead Heath and Kew Gardens were acknowledged by the provision of a 20-minute-interval service throughout most of the day. Hampstead Heath station in particular coped with large crowds on Bank Holidays in the pre-motor age. Save that Brondesbury Park was closed on weekday evenings and Sundays, the majority of trains were 'all stations'.

Additionally to the two electrified services, Broad Street received two steam trains from Tring and seven from Great Northern line stations on weekday mornings, and dispatched the same number in the afternoons. By the following year, 1949, Sunday services

to Watford had been withdrawn, while on Saturdays some trains ventured no further than Willesden Junction.

Moving on to 1957, the overall picture had not greatly changed. Between 10 am and 2.30 pm there was a half-hourly service to and from Willesden, connecting with the Euston line for Watford, while on the Richmond line the 20-minute service on Sundays was still in place. Annual bookings at all North London line stations at this time were 4½ million and falling - one tenth of the 1896 figure - so it is hardly surprising that it was earmarked for closure under the Beeching plan a few years later.

In 1963 the 20-minute interval was applied to the weekday services and the overall journey time was reduced by 4 to 8 minutes, though late evening trains were withdrawn. By 1966 the Sunday service was down to half-hourly and operated between 10.32 and 21.32 only, though with the introduction of the summer timetable the 20-minute frequency was restored throughout the day.

Management attitudes towards the line changed from time to time; for example, in 1952 fares were adjusted - upwards - so as to reflect more closely the distance travelled, resulting in a severe drop in patronage, but in 1972, faced with an annual loss of £367,000, a 'Crosstown' ticket was introduced, priced at 25p between any two stations. Later on, GLC involvement produced a subvention of £150,000 annually to maintain services at the 1975 level.

It was also thanks to GLC initiatives that the dieselised North Woolwich-Camden Road 'Crosstown Link' commenced on 14 May 1979 by diverting the former North Woolwich-Tottenham (Hale) service westwards from Stratford. There were 29 through trains each way daily, on weekdays only, at approximately half-hourly intervals off-peak. Journey time varied from 37 to 42 minutes for 11 miles with 10 intermediate stops. Would-be travellers were lured by introductory free tickets available from 14-18 May, and subsequent results were encouraging enough for a Saturday service to be added from July 1983.

Statistics for 1968 had showed that 9,000 passengers arrived at Broad Street on weekdays and a third as many on Saturdays, and it gradually became obvious that the days of the once-thriving terminus were

NORTH LONDON LINE: 1948 JOURNEY TIMES AND SPEEDS

From Broad Street to:	Distance (miles)	Stops	Time (mins)	Average (mph)
Watford	22	23	60	22
Richmond	16¼	18	50	19½

numbered. In 1984 a start was made in laying conductor rails on the North Woolwich-Dalston Kingsland section in preparation for a through service to Richmond, which was inaugurated on 13 May 1985 under the title 'North London Link'. The honours were done by the former West Ham footballer Trevor Brooking. Meantime completion of the Graham Road curve enabled the remaining Broad Street-Watford trains (five up and six down) to be diverted to Liverpool Street from 30 June 1986. Possibly because of frequent cancellations, this service was never popular and survived only until 25 September 1992, by then reduced to just two trains each way.

So ended the 70-year history of the Broad Street-Watford service, leaving only the Richmond-North Woolwich link, running at 20-minute intervals throughout the day plus a few short workings (for example Willesden-Richmond and North Woolwich-Stratford) in the early and late hours. With 26 stops in 22¼ miles, the overall time is 67 minutes (23½

mph) - a modest improvement, at least, on the 1948 performance!

TRACTION AND TRAINS

For much of the period under review the traction situation on the North London line is identical with that on the DC line from Euston. In 1948 the ex-LNWR Oerlikon and LMS-built compartment stock EMUs operated both the Richmond and Watford services, and continued to do so until replaced by the Eastleigh-built Class 501s in the late 1950s. Until this time two units worked in multiple during peak hours, but enforced economies resulted in all services being worked by single three-car units throughout the day. Thanks to reductions in journey and turnround times, and more regular intervals, it was found possible to reduce the DC fleet from 105 LNWR/LMS units to 57 of the Eastleigh design. On the Richmond line eight trains, each made up of two three-car units, were needed up to 1962, and only five three-car trains thereafter.

The North Woolwich-Camden Road 'Crosstown Link' service of 1979-85 was operated by two-car Craven DMUs of Class 105 provided by Stratford depot, six units being rostered per day.

For the North Woolwich-Richmond 'North London Link' electrified service 15 two-car 2EPB (Class 416) units were transferred from the Southern Region, after bars had been fitted over the droplights because of restricted clearances in tunnels. They went into traffic on 13 May 1985, but it was claimed that their acceleration did not match that of the Class 501s, although their maximum speed of

Above left Two Oerlikon three-car units of LNWR origin await departure time for Richmond beneath Broad Street's lofty roof on 20 August 1955. The fourth-rail system of current collection will be noted - as will also the obligatory oil-lit tail lamp! *F. Hornby*

Left On 26 July 1980 a Class 501 EMU with barred toplights 'awaits the road' at Kew Gardens station before proceeding to Broad Street via Willesden Junction. On the BR and LT joint line, Kew Gardens was originally opened by the LSWR in 1869. *F. Hornby*

75 mph was higher (and well in excess of that required on their new duties!). In consequence late running was not uncommon, when Richmond-bound trains were turned back at Gunnersbury. Their seating capacity was, of course, less than the 501s at 186 as against 242 per unit. Perhaps no tears were shed when the time came for them to be replaced by the 1976-built Class 313 EMUs as also used on the Watford services. Although equipped for dual-voltage operation, their activities on the North London lines are wholly concerned with DC current collection from the third rail. There is no depot on the North Woolwich-Richmond line and they are based at Bletchley for maintenance purposes.

Until 1976 Broad Street station had witnessed a variety of motive power on the locomotive-hauled services to and from the Great Northern line and Tring, as has been touched on in the preceding chapters. 'B1' 4-6-0s and, later, 'L1' 2-6-4Ts were no strangers on the Eastern Region trains, to be supplanted by Type 2 diesels and eventually by Class 105 DMUs. At various times the main-line diesels Nos 10000/01 and 10201-03 appeared on the Tring duties, and on one occasion in August 1956 the pilot engine supplied by Willesden shed was a BR '9F' 2-10-0 - an impressive contrast to the usual diet of electric multiple units!

7

LINES FROM LIVERPOOL STREET

The evolution of Liverpool Street's suburban services from the 1920s onwards could well be summed up by the tabloid-style heading 'From Jazz to Juice!' - the 'Jazz' being the popular name given to the intensive service introduced in 1920, and having nothing to do with the syncopated noises from a multitude of Westinghouse pumps! The 'Juice' came much later as electrification was delayed by the Second World War and did not embrace the whole suburban network until 1969.

But the story began much earlier as, by the time Liverpool Street opened in 1876, the Great Eastern Railway - successor to the Eastern Counties and Northern & Eastern companies - was already handling a thriving traffic generated by the rapid expansion of London's north-eastern suburbs. In 1894 the East Side Extension comprising platforms 11-18 was opened at Liverpool Street, by which time nearly 900 trains were being dealt with daily.

In the aftermath of the Great War this increased still further to 1,350, but while other railways turned to electrification in similar circumstances, the Great Eastern balked at the huge cost of such a project. By resignalling and track realignments it became possible to run a substantially improved service, in rakes of 16 four-wheeled carriages providing 848 seats per train. Almost miraculously this traffic was worked by small tank engines of 2-4-2 and 0-6-0 types, with a few new 0-6-2Ts just coming on stream. In the mid-1920s daily passenger usage fell from 244,000 to 200,000, then remained more or less constant during the LNER era. There was some alleviation immediately after the Second World War when, as with the GN lines, some routes were transferred to London Transport, in this case by eastward extensions of the Central Line. By December 1947 Woodford had been reached, with further developments, as we shall see, in early BR years. Electrification of the remaining BR suburban lines commenced in 1949 and was completed two decades later.

The rebuilding of Liverpool Street started in 1985 with the commensurate resignalling in mid-1988, and the virtually new station was 'opened' by HM The Queen on 5 December 1991. Despite a decline in traffic, partially due to the opening of the Victoria Line to Walthamstow in September 1968, the station still deals with over 1,000 trains daily, with some 60,000 people arriving and departing in the peak hours.

From April 1988 all lines out of Liverpool Street, together with those from Fenchurch Street, came under the jurisdiction of the new Anglia Region, the suburban services of course all being well within the boundaries of Network SouthEast.

WEST ANGLIA LINES

LIVERPOOL STREET-BROXBOURNE VIA TOTTENHAM HALE
BROXBOURNE-HERTFORD EAST AND BUNTINGFORD
HACKNEY DOWNS-CHESHUNT VIA SEVEN SISTERS
EDMONTON GREEN-ENFIELD
CLAPTON-CHINGFORD

ROUTES AND INFRASTRUCTURE

As a legacy from early days the suburban services out of Liverpool Street fall into two distinct groups, using separate sets of platforms on opposite sides of the station.

The West Anglia lines serving the north-eastern suburbs use platforms 1-6 on the west side of the station dating from 1876, and four tracks are available out through Bethnal Green, where they bear away from the Great Eastern lines, and on to Hackney Downs. The

Right At London Fields station, 2½ miles from the terminus, preparations for electrification are well in hand in this early 1960 scene looking south. One of several stations with names deceptively suggestive of a rural setting, London Fields is now served by trains at peak hours only. *Lens of Sutton*

Middle right Rebuilding is in full swing at Tottenham Hale station on 17 September 1991 as 'Stansted Express' EMU No 322483 pauses en route to Liverpool Street. The ultra-modern architectural style emphasises its importance as an interchange station with the Victoria Line and with local bus services. *F. Hornby*

Bottom right Hertford East terminus is graced by a stylish building just visible in the background of this 26 October 1985 scene. Two generations of EMUs occupy the platforms, a '315' on the left and a '305' from two decades earlier on the right. *F. Hornby*

three stations on this stretch have platforms on the slow lines only and services to two of them - London Fields and Cambridge Heath - are confined to peak hours. At Hackney Downs the Enfield and Cambridge lines part company, with the latter veering to the north-east through two tunnels before joining the original route via Stratford at Copper Mill Junction. It then runs due north along the Lea Valley, throwing off a spur on to the Tottenham & Hampstead line at Tottenham South Junction en route. (Until 1964 this was used by the North Woolwich-Palace Gates service, which is discussed in the following 'Great Eastern' section.)

Tottenham Hale, the next station, offers interchange with the northern end of the Victoria Line, and has recently been modernised, being a stopping place for the 'Stansted Express' and Cambridge trains as well as for local services. Cheshunt (population 40,000) has a bay platform for Churchbury loop trains - of which more anon - and Broxbourne has a modern station that was opened in 1960 on a site 100 yards north of its predecessor.

WEST ANGLIA AND GREAT EASTERN SUBURBAN LINES FROM LIVERPOOL STREET

Miles	Name	Opened	Closed	Notes
From Liverpool Street (West Anglia lines)				
	Liverpool Street	2/1874		
1¼	Bethnal Green	5/1872		
1¾	Cambridge Heath	5/1872		
2½	London Fields	5/1872		Closed 11/1981-9/1986 (fire damage)
3	Hackney Downs	5/1872		
3¾	Rectory Road	5/1872		
4¼	Stoke Newington	5/1872		
5	Stamford Hill	7/1872		
5½	Seven Sisters	7/1872		
6¼	Bruce Grove	7/1872		
7¼	White Hart Lane	7/1872		
8	Silver Street	7/1872		
8½	Edmonton Green	7/1872		Originally 'Lower Edmonton'
	Lower Edmonton-Angel Road opened 8/1872; closed to passengers 1939			
Enfield Town branch				
9¾	Bush Hill Park	1880		
10¾	Enfield Town	3/1849		
Southbury (Churchbury) loop				
10½	Southbury	10/1891	10/1909;	'Churchbury' to 11/1960
12¼	Turkey Street	10/1891	re-opened	'Forty Hill' to 11/1960
13½	Theobalds Grove	10/1891	11/1960	
Lea Valley line				
3	Hackney Downs			
4	Clapton	7/1872		
6	Tottenham (Hale)	9/1840		'Tottenham' to 5/1968
7	Northumberland Park	9/1840		Originally 'Marsh Lane'
7¾	Angel Road	9/1840		Originally 'Water Lane'
10	Ponders End	9/1840		
10¾	Brimsdown	1884		
11¾	Enfield Lock	1855		
12¾	Waltham Cross	9/1840		Originally '& Abbey'; second station opened 1885
14½	Cheshunt	1846		New station opened 1891
17¼	Broxbourne & Hoddesdon	9/1840		New station opened 11/1960
Hertford East branch				
17¼	Broxbourne			
19	Rye House	5/1846		
20¼	St Margarets	10/1843		Station enlarged 1864
22¼	Ware	10/1843		
24¼	Hertford East	10/1843		
Chingford branch				
4	Clapton			
5¾	St James Street	4/1870		
6¼	Walthamstow Central	4/1870		'Hoe Street' to 5/1968
7	Wood Street	4/1870		
8½	Highams Park	1873		'Hale End' to 10/1894
10½	Chingford	11/1873		New station from 9/1878

Miles	Name	Opened	Closed	Notes
From Liverpool Street (Great Eastern lines)				
	Liverpool Street (east side)	4/1894		
4	Stratford	6/1839		
4½	Maryland	1873		Originally 'Maryland Point'
5¼	Forest Gate	1840		
6¼	Manor Park	1873		
7¼	Ilford	6/1839		
8½	Seven Kings	1899		
9¼	Goodmayes	1901		
10	Chadwell Heath	1864		
12½	Romford	6/1839		
13½	Gidea Park	12/1910		'& Squirrels Heath' to 2/1969
15	Harold Wood	1868		
18¼	Brentwood	7/1840		
20¼	Shenfield	1850		
From North Woolwich				
	North Woolwich	6/1847		
1	Silvertown	6/1863		
2	Custom House	1/1855		
3	Canning Town	4/1846		
3¾	West Ham	1980		
4¾	Stratford (Market)	10/1854		'Stratford Bridge' to 11/1880
5	Stratford (Low level)	8/1854		
8	Lea Bridge	1840	7/1985	
10	South Tottenham	1871		
10¾	Seven Sisters	7/1872		
Palace Gates branch				
10¾	Seven Sisters			
11	West Green	1/1878	1/1963	
12	Noel Park	1/1878	1/1963	'Green Lanes' to 5/1884, 'Green Lanes & Noel Park' to 1/1902
12½	Palace Gates	10/1878	1/1963	
Central Line from Ilford (Fairlop loop)				
1¾	Newbury Park	1903		
2½	Barkingside	1903		To LT 31/5/48
3¼	Fairlop	1903		
3¾	Hainault	1903		
4¼	Grange Hill	1903		
5¼	Chigwell	1903		To LT 21/11/48
6½	Roding Valley	1936		
Central Line from Stratford				
5	Woodford	1856		To LT 21/11/48
6¼	Buckhurst Hill	1856		
7¼	Loughton	4/1865		
8½	Debden	4/1865		To LT 25/9/49
10¾	Theydon Bois	4/1865		
12¾	Epping	4/1865		
Ongar line				
	Epping			
2½	North Weald	4/1865		To LT 18/11/57
4½	Blake Hall	4/1865		
6¼	Ongar	4/1865		

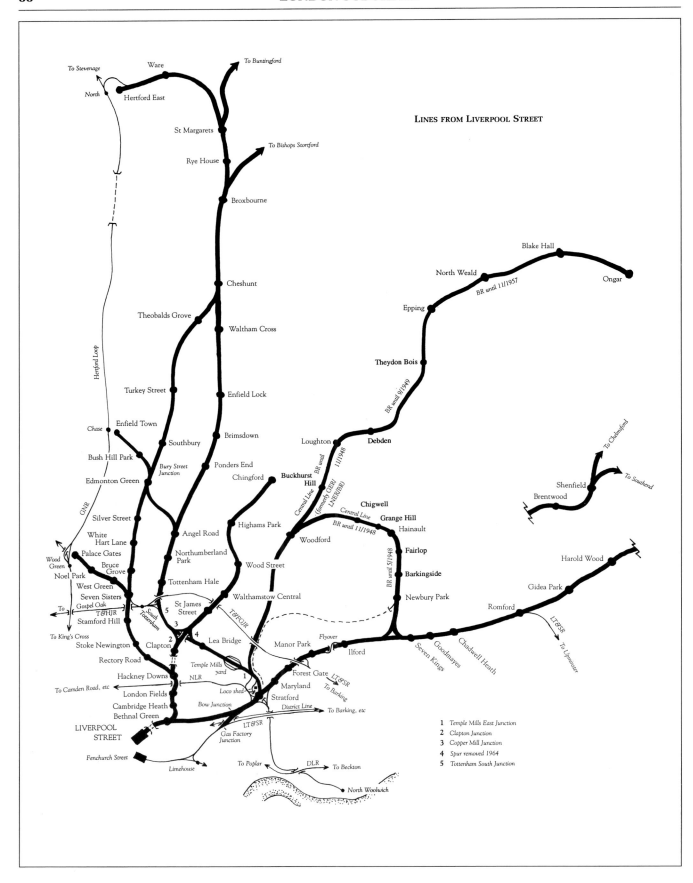

LINES FROM LIVERPOOL STREET

1 Temple Mills East Junction
2 Clapton Junction
3 Copper Mill Junction
4 Spur removed 1964
5 Tottenham South Junction

It consists of two island platforms, facilitating the splitting and joining of the Hertford and Bishops Stortford sections of trains on the outer loops.

Chronologically the Lea Valley line was first in the field, opened in 1840 with branches from Angel Road to Enfield Town dating from 1849, and Broxbourne to Hertford East from 1843. The latter, 7 miles long, has four intermediate stations, the second of which - St Margarets - was until 1964 the junction for the Buntingford branch. This had opened in July 1863 with six small stations along its 13¾ miles, so just survived its century. It was very much on the periphery of the suburban area and Buntingford, with single platform, run-round loop and sidings, epitomised the 'country branch' terminus. Hertford East, by contrast, is still graced by an impressive 'period' station building and, in its heyday, had a spacious yard in addition to its two terminal platforms.

It was not until 1872 that the more direct route to Enfield was opened, northwards from Hackney Downs along gently rising gradients to Lower Edmonton (now Edmonton Green) where it joined the old line from Angel Road. This latter line lost its passenger service in 1939, since when all Enfield trains have been routed via Seven Sisters. Enfield, with a quarter of a million inhabitants, is, of course, also served by Enfield Chase station on the GN Hertford loop, but the ex-GER station is more central and in steam days had four platforms and a locomotive depot - one of Stratford's 'sub-sheds'. The old station buildings were another of the casualties of the modernisation programme.

The Churchbury loop was

opened in 1891 from Bury Street Junction on the Enfield line to Cheshunt, giving three new stations a direct service to London, but it was relatively short-lived, succumbing to tramway competition in 1909. Save for a period during the First World War when trains were run along it for munitions workers, it remained closed until 1960 when electrification gave it a new lease of life, with two of the three stations renamed.

On a parallel with Enfield as one of the West Anglia Lines' most important sources of revenue is the 6-mile Chingford branch, climbing steadily from Clapton Junction at 1 in 78 through four intermediate stations. Opened throughout in 1873, its early claim to fame derived from the vast crowds of day-trippers bound for Epping Forest on high days and holidays. It currently more than earns its keep from commuters and off-peak patronage with interchange at Walthamstow Central for both the

Above right Edmonton Green, better known for most of its days as Lower Edmonton, is the junction station for the Enfield Town branch. On 25 January 1993 EMU No 315840 of 1980 vintage contrasts with the traditional GER style of the station canopies, which have survived on both platforms. *F. Hornby*

Right Enfield Town in steam days maintained a dozen or so 'N7' 0-6-2Ts at the small shed, a 'sub' to the huge depot at Stratford. On 20 September 1958 No 69662 is replenishing its water supply through a rather slender hose, in between journeys to and from Liverpool Street. *F. Hornby*

Chingford is the terminus for arguably the busiest of all 'West Anglia' services, and there are extensive stabling sidings for EMUs when not in use. On 10 April 1989 the scene is dominated by Class 305 units in blue-grey livery. *F. Hornby*

miles) was added from 5 May 1969 using 25kV current, trial running having commenced in March, thus completing what is now the West Anglia suburban network. However, later on standardisation of the 25kV voltage was implemented; carried out in stages, it involved closure of the Clapton tunnels for three weeks, during which time the Hertford East and Bishops Stortford trains ran via Seven Sisters. The work was completed on 21 August 1983.

Victoria Line and an adjacent bus station. Motive power in steam days was provided by a sub-shed at Wood Street, Walthamstow, as well as by Stratford. Chingford terminus originally had four platform faces (of which three are still in use) and is a signing-on point for drivers of the EMUs that stable in the adjacent sidings.

Contracts were placed in 1957 for rolling-stock and equipment in anticipation of electrification to Enfield Town, Hertford East and Bishops Stortford via Seven Sisters, together with the Chingford branch. Work started in 1958 on erecting catenary, and in all 28 stations had their platforms lengthened to take nine cars in the inner and eight cars in the outer suburban areas. Bridges were raised or the trackbed lowered at many places to allow headroom for the catenary. The single-phase AC system was adopted, with a power supply of 6.25kV as far out as just south of Cheshunt - due to clearance problems - and 25kV beyond that point, so the multiple unit fleet was suitably equipped for both currents. Trains began running to steam timings on 14 November 1960 and a full service commenced a week later. In all 45 route and 111 track miles were converted.

The Lea Valley line between Clapton and Cheshunt (9 route

Even in pre-war days the intensive services on the Enfield Town and Chingford branches had warranted the installation of colour-light signals and continuous track-circuiting northwards from Bethnal Green in 1938-39. Post-war, in September 1949, a new box was opened at Liverpool Street, taking over complete control of the station with four-aspect colour-lights overseeing all six tracks. Beyond Bury Street Junction, Edmonton, semaphore signals were replaced by three- or four-aspect colour-lights in readiness for electrification, and the Broxbourne to Hertford East section was similarly equipped in January 1960. New signal boxes at Hackney Downs, in the angle of the junction, and at Ware and Broxbourne replaced most of the older boxes. When it was the turn of the Lea Valley line to follow suit the opportunity was taken also to re-signal the then unelectrified Tottenham-Stratford line, with

The Network SouthEast livery adorns EMU No 315860, heading north from Brimsdown on the Lea Valley line on 19 January 1993. Generally straight and easily graded with the stations not too close together, modern units can show their paces more readily hereabouts than on the difficult sections closer to London. *F. Hornby*

Temple Mills West box taking over control of the Copper Mill Junction to Tottenham Hale section, while Cheshunt and Brimsdown boxes were modernised. Much rationalising of tracks and sidings and improvements to stations was also carried out.

In recognition of its value as a diversionary route, the Stratford-Copper Mill Junction section was electrified in 1989, together with the South Tottenham-Seven Sisters spur. Resignalling in conjunction with the rebuilding of Liverpool Street commenced in mid-1988, but prolonged problems were experienced, and in the following spring there was such serious disruption that regular commuters were offered free rides by way of compensation! The 1949 box and the one at Bethnal Green were replaced by a new panel box, and by the end of May 1989 things began to settle down and all was functioning smoothly.

SERVICES

In the early years of nationalisation both the Chingford and Enfield Town services were sufficiently intensive for *Bradshaw* not to consider it necessary to show detailed timetables. In 1949, for example, only the early morning and late evening trains were listed, those from Chingford commencing at 12.55 am and finishing at 11.50 pm with 'frequent intervals' covering the greater part of the day. There was no separate table for Saturdays, while Sunday trains ran at half-hourly intervals over a 16-hour period. Enfield Town fared slightly less well, as the first and last departures were at 4.11 am and 11.35 pm respectively, with a half-hourly frequency outside peak hours and on Sundays.

Hertford East and Broxbourne services did warrant a detailed timetable as some trains used the direct route to Liverpool Street via Clapton (20 from Hertford East and two from Broxbourne on weekdays), while others were routed via Stratford, where some terminated. One train ran through from Hertford East to North Woolwich, while there were also two short workings from Hertford East to Broxbourne and one from Tottenham to Stratford.

Generally services remained at similar levels during the steam era,

In the early days following electrification a pair of green-liveried Class 305/1 EMUs pause at Bush Hill Park on the Enfield Town branch in April 1961. Equipped for dual voltage, the train is collecting current from the catenary at 6.25kV on this section. *B. W. Brooksbank*

but in the 1954 summer timetable the Enfield Town off-peak frequency was stepped up to three per hour, one of which was semi-fast.

Electrification brought great improvements and a special timetable was issued commencing 21 November 1960 after a week of trial running to steam timings. In it the Chingford and Enfield Town services were combined; Chingford was endowed with no fewer than 126 weekday up trains, even the off-peak service being six per hour. Enfield Town also enjoyed the same frequency, inclusive of two trains per hour making all 13 stops and providing the only service for London Fields and Cambridge Heath. On Sundays both branches had quarter-hourly services between 9 am and 9 pm with earlier and later trains half-hourly.

In the table for Hertford East and Bishops Stortford we find that 5 minutes was allowed at Broxbourne for trains to divide or combine. From the first weekday up train at 4.18 am until the last at 11.18 pm there were 44 scheduled - more than twice as many as in steam days and appreciably faster, albeit with fewer stops. Note that these were now routed via the re-opened Southbury (former 'Churchbury') loop, leaving diesel stopping trains to serve the Lea Valley line. These comprised 40 southbound services, of which 14 - including two from Brimsdown - terminated at Stratford, with the remainder going to Liverpool Street via Clapton. The diesel timings were approximately 25 per cent faster than with steam traction.

While electrification work was in progress there had been some disruption, particularly at weekends, with, for example in March 1958, DMUs shuttling between Lower Edmonton and Enfield Town on Sundays in place of through trains. Then, needless to say, there were 'teething troubles' with the new equipment, causing cancellations when the units were

		SUMMARY OF WEST ANGLIA SUBURBAN SERVICES					
Year	Line	Route via	Distance (miles)	Stops	Time (mins)	Average (mph)	Traction
1949	Hertford East	Lea Valley	24¼	15	75	19.4	Steam
	Enfield Town	Seven Sisters	10¾	13	34	19.0	Steam
	Chingford	Clapton	10½	11	33	19.1	Steam
1960	Hertford East	Churchbury (Southbury) loop	24½	13	51	28.8	Electric
	Enfield Town	Seven Sisters	10¾	13	29	22.4	Electric
	Chingford	Clapton	10½	7	23	27.4	Electric
1966	Broxbourne	Lea Valley	17¼	9	36	28.75	Diesel
1993	Hertford East	Lea Valley	24¼	13	51	28.5	Electric
	Enfield Town	Seven Sisters	10¾	8	26	24.7	Electric
	Chingford	Clapton	10½	7	26	24.2	Electric
	Cheshunt	Churchbury (Southbury) loop	14½	13	38	23.0	Electric

withdrawn for modifications. Eventually a full service was restored on 17 June 1963 with strengthened trains providing extra seats, and that year in the afternoon peak there were no fewer than 67 departures scheduled hourly from Liverpool Street.

Over the ensuing years there has been some retrenchment from the lavish level of the early 1960s, a 'low spot' being at the end of 1981 when some timetable revisions coincided with a spate of train and signalling failures. More successful was the restoration of a 10-minute off-peak frequency to the Enfield line in 1983 (four per hour to Enfield Town plus two to Broxbourne or beyond). Harking back to the 1920s, the Class 305/1 EMUs were decorated with a colourful 'Jazz' label!

In the final BR timetable of 1993/94, weekday off-peak services on the Chingford and Enfield Town branches ran at 20- and 30-minute intervals respectively, while on the Lea Valley line electric stopping trains were allowed 1 minute longer than their diesel predecessors, but with more calls en route. The basic frequency to and from Hertford East was half-hourly, with the same number of Cambridge semi-fasts calling only at Tottenham Hale south of Cheshunt.

When inaugurated in 1969 the diesel service between North Woolwich and Tottenham Hale consisted of a dozen or so weekday trains in each direction, reduced to just four by 1981. In 1990, after the line between Copper Mill Junction and Stratford was electrified, an attempt was made to revive the service with a half-hourly 'shuttle' between Broxbourne and the new platforms 11 and 12 at Stratford; instead of reversing there, the trains were routed round the loop via the Channelsea and Fork junctions. Presumably due to lack of support, this venture lasted only two years before withdrawal.

TRACTION AND TRAINS

See page 96.

GREAT EASTERN LINES

LIVERPOOL STREET-SHENFIELD AND
NORTH WOOLWICH-PALACE GATES VIA STRATFORD
STRATFORD-ONGAR AND NEWBURY PARK

ROUTES AND INFRASTRUCTURE

By contrast with the West Anglia network, the only 'Great Eastern' service remaining operative is that along the main line through Shenfield. The Palace Gates branch from Seven Sisters closed in 1963, the remainder of the line to Ongar and the Fairlop loop have been absorbed by the Central Line, and a

Stratford-Broxbourne service introduced in October 1990 was discontinued in less than two years.

At Liverpool Street all Great Eastern suburban trains use the east side platforms Nos 11-18, which, in the course of rebuilding, have been covered by a low roof supporting a raft of offices, whereas the remainder of the station enjoys the splendour of the restored train shed.

The Eastern Counties main line, originally of 5-foot gauge, opened to Romford in 1839 and on to Colchester in 1841, and was converted to standard gauge in 1844. It became part of the Great Eastern Railway in 1862.

Local trains use the southernmost pair of tracks up the 1 in 70 Bethnal Green bank and out through Stratford to Ilford, where the flyover constructed in readiness for the post-war electrification carries them to the opposite side of the main lines. There is a steady climb for 14 miles from just beyond Stratford, steepening for the final 3 miles on average to 1 in 100 - presenting in steam days quite a challenge to game little tank engines with a pair of crowded 'Quint-arts' in tow.

Since December 1946, when Coborn Road closed, Stratford has been the first station out of Liverpool Street on the line under discussion. It has become progressively more important as an interchange station, with the Central Line emerging briefly on to the surface giving cross-platform connection and - more recently - the Docklands Light Railway having a bay in the up island platform. Two new platforms, Nos 11 and 12, were provided for the Broxbourne

shuttle service, and now, regrettably, stand disused. As given due notice in the previous chapter, there are two platforms below and at right-angles for the North London line.

Of the 11 stations in the 16¼ miles on to Shenfield, with platforms for all four running lines, the most important are Ilford and Romford (pop 75,000), the latter being served by Colchester semi-fast trains as well as by the 'locals'. Harold Wood and Forest Gate stations were modernised in 1985/86 as a joint GLC/BR venture. Shenfield, where some services terminate, is the junction for the line to Southend and Southminster, which parts company from the Colchester main line just beyond the station by means of a burrowing junction.

The Stratford-Palace Gates service was a magnet for enthusiasts, not only because of the motive power used at various times, but also because it

Above right Stratford's interchange facilities are emphasised by this scene on 5 March 1980 as a Central Line train of 1960 stock bound for Epping emerges from the tunnel. Alongside, en route for Liverpool Street, is Class 306 'Shenfield' EMU No 071. Built for the 1,500V DC electrification of 1949, the unit has since been modified for AC current collection. *F. Hornby*

Right This view at Ilford looking north on 5 May 1993 gives some idea of the generous proportions of Shenfield line suburban stations. Class 315 unit No 838, bound for Gidea Park, is one of the 64 of this type based and maintained at the nearby depot. *F. Hornby*

On 15 October 1956 at Palace Gates, 'N7' 0-6-2T No 69613, with a 'Quintart' set in tow, forms the 12.31 to North Woolwich. The branch closed to passenger traffic in 1963, and the substantial station with its tall chimney stacks is now but a memory. *F. Hornby*

under the waterway linking the Royal Victoria with the newly opened Royal Albert dock; a journey along it in steam days was fascinating as, not only was there a heavy freight traffic, but Port of London Authority tank locomotives could also be seen. The line remained an outpost of semaphore signalling when colour-lights were the norm elsewhere, and because

passed close to the locomotive sheds, then through the extensive and busy Temple Mills yards. Sadly only a few weed-grown sidings remain where once a small army of shunting engines worked round the clock. The line crosses the Hackney and Walthamstow marshes and the Warwick reservoirs, then a sharply curved spur leads to the 'Tottenham & Hampstead', which was followed through South Tottenham station before taking another 90-degree curve into Seven Sisters.

Here the Palace Gates branch proper began, with its own two platforms where it swung away to the north-west. It was 2¾ miles long with two intermediate stations, and had an active life of 85 years, from 1878 to 1963, with freight traffic lingering until October 1964. A direct connection to the GN Hertford loop, installed in 1944 in place of a less convenient shunt spur, was useful for transferring stock (and was covered by the author on a memorable railtour, hauled by an ex-GER 'E4' 2-4-0!).

The line south of Stratford was a good deal older and was opened throughout to North Woolwich, close to the Royal group of docks, in June 1847 with connections for ferries and steamers. In 1880 the line was diverted into a tunnel

of sharp curvature was renowned for the wear and tear inflicted on rolling-stock. The terminus, once generously laid out with two island platforms and a centre engine release road, now consists of but a single platform.

During 1948 and 1949 the Central Line was further extended along former BR tracks through Loughton to Epping. A new line in tunnel from Leytonstone to Newbury Park, connecting with the Fairlop loop, had opened in December 1947 and the remainder of the loop was converted the following year. The old GER line, northwards to Newbury Park from a triangle junction east of Ilford, was abandoned on 30 November 1947 and a bus service substituted until the work was completed. All this left the 6¼-mile Epping-Ongar section isolated from the rest of BR, and it remained steam worked until electrified in November 1957. Since then the tube stock has looked slightly incongruous, scuttling along the sin-

Barkingside on the Fairlop loop remained in BR hands until May 1948, but the London Transport 'bullseyes' confirm that this photograph is of later origin. Taken on 1 April 1961 it is a pleasing reminder that the Central Line has, in many cases, retained the old pre-Grouping railway station buildings in good order. *B. W. L. Brooksbank*

Epping station on 20 October 1956 provides a contrast between the old and the 'not quite so old'. Class 'F5' 2-4-2T No. 67200 is a rebuild of a GER Worsdell creation of 1904, heading a two-coach 'auto' set from Ongar. The Central Line train, about to undertake a lengthy cross-London journey to West Ruislip, is of pre-war 1936 stock. *F. Hornby*

gle-track line through open countryside with two intermediate stations. In steam days the terminus at Ongar had a small engine shed and goods yard alongside the single platform.

The LNER, having operated one of the world's most intensive steam-worked services since its formation, decided in 1936 to electrify the main line out as far as Shenfield, but the work was interrupted by the outbreak of war and was eventually completed by BR on 26 September 1949. All four running lines over the 20¼ miles were equipped with overhead catenary for 1,500V DC current, as were platforms 11-18 at Liverpool Street and also the two tracks from Bow Junction into Fenchurch Street. Preparatory work included layout rearrangements, extensive rebuilding of Stratford station, and the flyover between Manor Park and Ilford. Four-aspect colour-light signals were installed out to Gidea Park, beyond which point they were already in place to Chelmsford. Nine new and three modernised signal boxes replaced 33 old mechanical ones; the new signalling permitted 1½-minute headways and a maximum speed of 75 mph. A depot with repair facilities for the new trains was opened at Ilford, and subsequently enlarged in 1959 to cope with additional stock.

The 1,500V DC catenary was extended to Chelmsford in June 1956 and to Southend by the end of the year, but in November 1960 the power supply was changed to 6.25kV AC between Liverpool Street and Shenfield, and to 25kV AC eastwards to Chelmsford, with services maintained by a mixture of diesel and electric trains and buses during the changeover weekend. Electrification was further extended to Colchester in mid-1962, where it linked up with the existing 25kV lines to Clacton and Walton, which had been energised for trial purposes in April 1959. In the opposite direction the conversion to 25kV advanced towards London from Shenfield in stages, commencing in January 1976 and completed into Liverpool Street on 12 October 1980, with the Shenfield-Southend line similarly converted in January 1979.

SERVICES

Steam timings out to Shenfield in the late 1940s fluctuated between 48 minutes and 1 hour depending on the number of stops. Trains ran at 'frequent intervals' throughout the day (stopping trains were every 20 minutes off-peak) and the principal stations - Stratford, Ilford and Romford - also benefited from calls made by semi-fasts for destinations as far down the line as Ipswich or Clacton.

Nevertheless the 1949 electrified service provided more and faster trains even if the new units could hardly compete with the old steam stock in the matter of seating the maximum number of bodies in the minimum of space! The first electric train to Shenfield ran on 26 September and the full service commenced on 7 November - only to be disrupted during the first morning rush hour when the catenary was brought down at Seven Kings! On the same day the peak-hour service between Fenchurch Street and Ilford was withdrawn, although the connecting line from Bow Junction was electrified and made use of during emergencies - as when floods blocked the LT&S Southend line in February 1953.

The first timetable featuring the full service listed 62 weekday electric trains to Shenfield, with three per hour off-peak, semi-fast as far as Romford and all stations thereafter. Gidea Park was the outer terminus for 65 more trains, running every 20 minutes and calling at all stations. The earliest and latest trains out of Liverpool Street were still steam-hauled, as was of course the Southend service, which provided Shenfield with a further 37 weekday down trains - a grand total of 101 in 24 hours! On Sundays four electrics left the terminus hourly - two each to Shenfield and Gidea Park. Journey time to Shenfield was down from 55-60 minutes in steam days to 38 minutes.

Fourteen steam trains each way covered the 12½ miles between Palace Gates and North Woolwich (11 on Saturdays), averaging 48 minutes en route with 10 stops, with two others between North Woolwich and Lea Bridge and one in the opposite direction; these trains were valuable for those living in the northern suburbs and working in the docks. A shuttle service along the branch from Seven Sisters supplemented the through trains and, unlike them, operated on Sundays. At the other end of the line 26 trains plied between North Woolwich and Stratford, including two that continued northwards along the Lea Valley line, balanced only by one southbound working. As the author discovered purely by chance, at least one train was extended northwards from Stratford, unadvertised, when 'Spurs' were at home on Saturday afternoons!

The Palace Gates branch closed in 1951 due to fuel shortages, and though it reopened later on, the shuttle service from Seven Sisters was not resumed.

Electrification to Southend and Chelmsford resulted in double the number of passengers within a year, and in consequence fewer trains terminated at or started from Shenfield. In the summer of 1961 that town was served by 120 weekday trains daily from Liverpool Street, of which only 20 terminated there - generous indeed as the population was then no more than 5,000! By then the Gidea Park stopping service was only half-hourly, with three other trains calling there hourly to and from Southend.

In 1962 there were still six through trains between Palace Gates and North Woolwich plus 30 southwards from Stratford, but the branch from Seven Sisters closed to passengers and the gradual move towards a five-day week saw the withdrawal of Saturday trains between Stratford and North Woolwich in January 1969.

In 1949 the Epping-Ongar section boasted a shuttle-service of 35 weekday and Saturday trains each way and 26 on Sundays. Journey time for the 6¼ miles was 16 minutes with two intermediate stops. The connecting Central Line trains gave a frequent service, taking 40 minutes to and from Liverpool Street. When electrification reached Ongar in November 1957 there were initially more trains, but in recent years only a sparse peak-hour service penetrated beyond Epping, and a 1980 census revealed that a mere 650 passengers were using the trains daily. In the present climate, in which London Underground Lines are constantly seeking to reduce costs, it is not surprising that this service was withdrawn from 30 September 1994.

TRACTION AND TRAINS (BOTH LINES)

The backbone of suburban operations out of Liverpool Street - all steam-worked at nationalisation - was the Class 'N7' 0-6-2T, of which the first 12 had appeared in 1921 in GER colours. Another 122 were in service by 1928, slightly smaller than their 'N2' counterparts of GNR origin and with smaller driving wheels. They were, however, sturdy machines and a distinct improvement over the Edwardian 'F5' and 'F6' 2-4-2Ts, of which a number were still at work in the London area into the 1950s.

The Shenfield electrification in 1949 brought some relief to the hard-pressed motive power department, confining the older engines to such relative backwaters as the North Woolwich and Epping-Ongar lines. Nevertheless an 'F5' made a 'comeback' on a Chingford train in August 1952, and as late as 1954 two 2-4-2Ts were noted on early Sunday morning through trains from Epping to Liverpool Street.

While all engines were nominally allocated to the huge shed at Stratford (30A), in practice the sub-sheds had fairly permanent studs of 'N7s' - 14 at Wood Street, Walthamstow, 10 at Hertford East and 12 at Enfield Town. By 1950 Stratford had also acquired a fleet of 33 recently built 'L1' 2-6-4Ts, which were employed on outer suburban duties such as to

One of the stalwarts of the London suburban services, Class 'N7' 0-6-2T No 69720 comes off the line from Clapton at Hackney Downs with a stopping train from Hertford East on 20 September 1958. The stock consists of compartment coaches somewhat 'up market' from the traditional articulated sets. *F. Hornby*

Bishops Stortford and Hertford East, also working further afield on extra trains at summer weekends. Their numbers at Stratford were later reduced and remained constant at around 20 for several years thereafter. Similarly the 'N7' allocation diminished thanks to electrification and the introduction of DMUs on the Lea Valley line.

Nine engines were maintained at the two-road shed at Palace Gates, inclusive of three 'G5' 0-4-4Ts from the North Eastern area, which worked the two-coach 'push-pulls' until transferred away in 1951. On a visit made by the author in November 1949 an 'F5' powered an articulated set out to Palace Gates and a 'G5' worked a two-coach train in the opposite direction. The return fare from Liverpool Street was 1 shilling (5p)!

With the departure of the 'G5s' and the withdrawal of the 'F5s', the 'N7' tanks were left in sole charge, as was also the case during the last years of steam working between Epping and Ongar. By 1961, when most 'N7s' had joined the sad procession to the scrapyard, the 'L1' 2-6-4Ts were 'regulars' on the North Woolwich trains.

With Stratford's vast and varied allocation it is hardly surprising that other classes deputised for failed engines, and in February 1953 Class 'J15' 0-6-0s were noted on early morning Hertford East trains. On the same line a rare stranger in 1957 was an ex-LT&S '3P' 4-4-2T, while in September 1959 a 'J69' 0-6-0T abandoned its Liverpool Street pilot duties for a foray on to the Chingford branch. Early in 1960 a locomotive shortage saw ex-LMS '3F' 'Jinty' 0-6-0Ts filling in on Hertford East trains - to the detriment of punctuality, one must assume. August 1956 had seen the equally unusual appearance of an 'N2' 0-6-2T and a BR Class '4' 2-6-0 on the Epping-Ongar 'shuttle'. Both were fitted with trip-cocks as required for working over LT tracks, but not with the push-pull gear of the regular motive power.

As for coaching stock, the GE section of the LNER went one better than the GN with 'Quint-art' sets - five coach bodies articulated on six bogies - as introduced by Gresley in 1924 to replace older bogie coaches of GER design. There were, however, also 'Quad-arts' of 1929 vintage for the longer-distance Hertford East trains, while the Bishops Stortford semi-fasts were graced with LNER-built compartment and part-corridor stock. When first built the 'Quint-arts' catered for three classes of accommodation, seating 872 in a 10-coach formation, but ultimately became 'all 3rd'. So, with standees aboard, our game little 65-ton 'N7' tanks would be tackling Bethnal Green bank with some 280 tons in tow.

Steam traction was finally abolished in September 1962, prior to which 'L1s' and surviving 'N7s' still worked a few turns on the North Woolwich branch, by then with outer-suburban coaches in place of articulated sets.

Since the Shenfield electrification there has been a considerable variety in the ever-growing fleet of electric multiple units, of which the first were the 92 dark green 1,500V DC three-car sets that became Class AM6 and later 306. With open saloons, push-button sliding doors and ample provision for 'straphangers', they were more akin to London Transport stock than to the steam trains they replaced, and a nine-car train could seat 528 with another 660 standing. They were converted for AC current in 1960, but rarely strayed from the Shenfield main line and gave over 30 years of yeoman service, their last day on normal duties being 15 September 1981.

When the 1,500V DC catenary was extended beyond Shenfield in 1956, 32 units of Class AM7 (later 307) were delivered from Eastleigh, not surprisingly having an affinity with contemporary Southern Region flat-fronted designs. They were similarly converted for AC power supply in 1960-62 and have since been refurbished. They later diversified their activities by visits to the Hertford East line, and continued in service on the GE section until June 1990.

For the west-side suburban electrification - today's

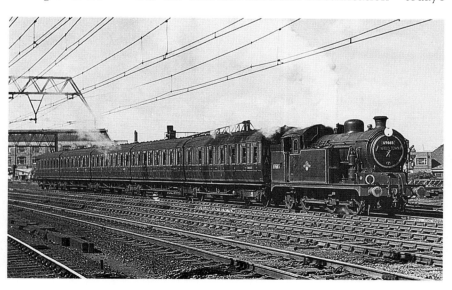

On 7 June 1959 smart 'N7' 0-6-2T No 69665 wheels a 'Quint-art' set past Stratford on an Enfield Town train, diverted because of engineering works. It will regain its route via the line through Lea Bridge, thence via the 'Tottenham & Hampstead' and the curve into Seven Sisters. *F. Hornby*

Goodmayes is traditionally the terminus for inner-suburban stopping trains, but this one is continuing to Shenfield. Led by No 041, a trio of Class 306 units in 'Rail Blue' livery are seen on 14 April 1979. It would be interesting to know how many miles they had clocked up on this same stretch in the previous 30 years! *F. Hornby*

West Anglia lines - 72 units were delivered in 1960 from BR York and Doncaster with English Electric equipment, comprising 52 three-car units (Class AM5/1 - later 305/1) and 19 four-car (Class AM5/2 - later 305/2), the latter being intended for Hertford East and Bishops Stortford services, with some 1st Class seating. They differed considerably from the Shenfield units, with sloping ends and slam-doors to each seating bay. While the 75 mph maximum of both sub-classes might be of advantage on the longer runs, it would be more than adequate on the sharply curved and steeply graded Chingford branch!

As mentioned, problems were experienced when they first went into service, and other units were loaned from the LTS section during late 1960. Also seen, around 1962, were AM4 units loaned from the LMR with 'Crewe' on their destination blinds! Again, in 1965/6, when the AM5/2 series had a high failure rate, they were transferred to the LTS section in

exchange for nine AM8/1 units, built at York in 1961, similar in appearance and also with dual-voltage capability. Another LTS-based type, the flat-fronted AM2 four-car units of 1959 vintage, made their appearance on the Lea Valley line after it was electrified in May 1969.

By mid-1973 Ilford depot's allocation consisted of 236 EMUs embracing Classes 302, 305/1, 305/2, 306, 307 and 308. The gradual elimination of 1960s designs was given impetus by the arrival of 19 new outer-suburban Class 312 four-car sets in 1979, all based at Clacton and employed on Colchester and Southend line services, joined in due course by the similar Hornsey-based '317s', which are used indiscriminately on inner- and outer-suburban duties.

The year 1980 ushered in a new era when the first of 61 four-car units of Class 315 came off the production line at BREL York and took up their duties on the Shenfield line as replacements for the aging Class 306. These all-Standard Class units were designed solely for 25kV power collection, with push-button-operated doors and inter-coach gangways, and extended their activities to all lines when conversion to the higher voltage was completed. In 1981 there were 44 weekday diagrams for the 315s, supplemented by 18 for Class 306s

EASTERN REGION EMU DIMENSIONS

Class	Introduced/ builder	Traction motors	Voltage	Max speed (mph)	Weight (tons)/ cars per unit	Seating (1st/2nd)
AM2 (302)	1959 BR Doncaster/York	4 x 192 hp EE	6.25kV, 25kV	75	155/4	19/344
AM5/1 (305/1)	1960 BR York	4 x 200 hp GEC	6.25kV, 25kV	75	119/3	-/272
AM5/2 (305/2)	1960 BR Doncaster	4 x 205 hp GEC	6.25kV, 25kV	75	153/4	19/344
AM6 (306)	1949 Metro-Cammell/BR	4 x 207 hp Crompton Parkinson	1,500V DC, 6.25kV, 25kV	70	104/3	-/168
AM7 (307)	1956 (reb't 1960) BR Eastleigh	4 x 175 hp GEC	1,500V DC, 6.25kV, 25kV	75	155/4	19/344
AM8 (308)	1961 BR York	4 x 192 hp English Electric	6.25kV, 25kV	75	154/4	19/344
315	1980 BREL York	8 x 110 hp Brush	25kV	75	102/3	-/318

Right In this September 1991 view of Liverpool Street prior to rebuilding, two distinct designs of EMU stand side by side in the West Side suburban platforms. On the left, flat-fronted four-car unit No 302 505 is of type AM2 introduced in 1959 for the Tilbury section. On the right, Class 305/1 No 437 was a product of BR York in 1960 for the Chingford and Enfield lines. *F. Hornby*

Middle right With four-digit headcode blind prominent, four-car unit No 302201 leads a Southend semi-fast past Bethnal Green on 13 September 1981. The platforms at this station have since lost their canopies, and serve only the West Anglia local lines. *F. Hornby*

Bottom right In 1977 BREL at York outshopped a batch of 19 EMUs of Class 312, as previously employed on the GN section, for residential services on the Great Eastern lines. No 313790, seen here at Shenfield on 25 September 1980, is on a Colchester-Liverpool Street working, and will call only at Romford on a smartly timed sprint up to Town. *F. Hornby*

until the latter were retired later in the year; Class 308 units were transferred back to the LTS section from whence they had come.

In the present decade the 1990-design Class 321 units have taken a major share of the longer runs, with 66 of series 321/3 and a few of series 321/4 stationed at Ilford, so that most of the fleet now dates from the late 1970s onwards.

The role of the diesel unit on GE suburban duties was comparatively low-key, and the main sphere of operations was on the Lea Valley line and - at first alongside steam traction, then in full possession - on the North Woolwich service. The first appearance of DMUs was in the spring of 1956 when the two-car sets made driver-training runs on the Palace Gates branch and elsewhere. Wickham railcars performed briefly on that branch on Whit Monday 1958, but the first serious application was on Hertford East services from January 1959, when Derby/Rolls-Royce three-car suburban sets came into use. From

The 'modern image' with a vengeance at Ilford! Up and down trains of the 100 mph Class 321 EMUs make a brief stop, with an 'inner-suburban' Class 315 unit in the background. *F. Hornby*

1962 they were responsible for most North Woolwich duties and continued to work on this branch before and after diversion along the North London line in 1979. Ex-WR three-car suburban sets were based at Stratford from September 1968, but DMU duties declined with the Lea Valley electrification in 1969. In 1977 there were just three two-car units on the roster for the North Woolwich-Tottenham Hale shuttle.

A further use was found for DMUs while conversion from 6.25 to 25kV power was carried out during October 1980, when they covered Liverpool Street-Hackney Downs runs, supplemented by units from Cricklewood. When they were no longer required for passenger purposes a few units could still be seen in the suburban area converted for express parcels duties, in a dark blue livery with orange stripes.

8

LINES FROM FENCHURCH STREET

FENCHURCH STREET-SHOEBURYNESS VIA UPMINSTER
BARKING-PITSEA VIA TILBURY
ROMFORD-UPMINSTER-GRAYS

In compiling this work the author has become increasingly aware that the term 'London Suburban' covers a wide spectrum, with at one extreme, for example, the Chingford branch with its closely spaced stations, and at the other the Chiltern Line, terminating at Aylesbury, nearly four times as far away. The LT&S section has something in common with the latter, both having comparatively small termini and both being overwhelmingly concerned with 'outer suburban' traffic. However, the territory served by the LT&S could hardly be more different, ranging from the dormitory towns centred on Southend, to the docks and industry around Tilbury and Dagenham. Virtually all trains from Fenchurch Street set out on journeys of between 22 and 45 miles, many being non-stop to Barking, 7½ miles out. Even in steam days, once the District Line had annexed the intermediate stations out to Upminster, most trains could be correctly described as 'semi-fast'.

This was self-evident in the motive power provided from early years, with several classes of 4-4-2Ts, not forgetting Whitelegg's massive 4-6-4Ts of 1912 which were deemed too heavy to work into Fenchurch Street!

As to ownership, we recall that the London terminus was Great Eastern property until the 1923 Grouping and LNER thereafter, although most of the trains using it were those of the London, Tilbury & Southend Railway until that company was absorbed by the Midland Railway in 1913 and in turn by the LMS in 1923. At nationalisation the Tilbury section first became part of the London Midland Region, then was transferred to the Eastern Region in February 1949, and in 1986 became an important constituent of Network SouthEast. Now, as a largely self-contained entity, it could well become one of the first BR lines to be privatised.

Notwithstanding electrification in the early 1960s, the 'Tilbury', with its ageing infrastructure, has unfortunately become a byword for breakdowns, cancellations and delays. One can only hope that at least some of its long-suffering regular users appreciate the valiant efforts of hard-pressed staff who keep the wheels turning in extremely difficult circumstances.

ROUTES AND INFRASTRUCTURE

Fenchurch Street station opened in 1841 as the terminus of the London & Blackwall Railway and was linked to the Eastern Counties Railway in 1854. A new and enlarged station was completed in that year, incorporating the building that has survived to the present day. The first LT&SR trains entered it over a newly laid direct line from Barking in March 1858. Ownership passed into the hands of the GER, as successors to the Eastern Counties Railway, in 1869, with the LT&SR exercising running powers into it from Gas Factory Junction. The direct route to Southend via Upminster was completed in June 1888, prior to which the longer route via Tilbury, dating from 1856, had been used.

A connection with the Metropolitan District Railway at Campbell Road Junction, Bromley-by-Bow, was opened in 1902 and District electric trains took over much of the shorter-distance traffic thereafter, reaching Barking in April 1908. In that year track quadrupling was completed between Bromley and Barking and extended to Upminster in September 1932, when District Line trains made it their outer terminus.

Fenchurch Street, then with five platforms, handled some 300 trains daily in 1930, and was rebuilt between 1932 and 1935 with two island platforms, the longer for LMS and the shorter for LNER trains. Services operated by the latter and its Eastern Region successor were either discontinued or transferred to Liverpool Street during the 1940s, leaving the LT&S trains as sole occupants at last. The station was further rebuilt commencing in December 1983 when the concourse was enlarged, but remains the only London terminus without direct access to the Underground; Tower Hill (Circle Line) and Tower Gateway

LINES FROM FENCHURCH STREET

(Docklands Light Railway) stations are both nearby.

Notwithstanding the generally flat terrain of Essex, the Southend direct line is by no means free from gradients, being generally downhill out to Plaistow. There is a slight hump at Upminster and a more pronounced one at Laindon, approached by gradients of 1 in 110 from either side. A third summit with similar grades is at Southend Central, so in steam days the locomotives had no easy task with their heavy peak-hour loads.

SUBURBAN LINES FROM FENCHURCH STREET (LT&S SECTION) TO SHOEBURYNESS VIA UPMINSTER, PITSEA VIA TILBURY, AND BRANCHES FROM UPMINSTER

Miles	Name	Opened	Closed	Notes
From Fenchurch Street				
	Fenchurch Street	8/1841		
1¼	Limehouse	7/1840		'Stepney East' to 5/1987
3¼	Bromley	1858	To LTE control 1970	Originally 'by Bow' (to 1967)
4½	Plaistow	1858	To LTE control 1970	
5¼	Upton Park	1895	To LTE control 1970	
6¼	East Ham	1858	To LTE control 1970	
7½	Barking	3/1858		
Tilbury loop				
10½	Dagenham Dock	7/1908		
12½	Rainham	1854		
15¼	Purfleet Rifle Range halt	1911	5/1948	
16	Purfleet	1854		
19¾	Grays	1854		
21½	Tilbury Town	1885		'Dock' to 12/1934
22½	Tilbury Riverside	1854	12/1992	'Tilbury' to 7/1936
24¼	Low Street	1861	6/1967	
25¼	East Tilbury	1936		
27¼	Stanford-Le-Hope	1854		
32¼	Pitsea	1855		
Direct Southend line				
9½	Becontree	6/1926	LT stations from 9/1932	Originally 'Gale Street halt'
11¼	Dagenham	5/1885	LT stations from 9/1932	LT station originally 'Heathway'
13¾	Hornchurch	5/1885	LT stations from 9/1932	
15¼	Upminster	5/1885	LT stations from 9/1932	
19¼	West Horndon	5/1886		Originally 'East Horndon'
22¾	Laindon	1888		
24½	Basildon	11/1974		Date for second station
26½	Pitsea	6/1888		
29¼	Benfleet (for Canvey Island)	1855		Rebuilt and resited 8/1921
32½	Leigh-on-Sea	1855		Rebuilt and resited 4/1934
34	Chalkwell	9/1933		
34¾	Westcliff	1895		Originally 'on Sea'
35¾	Southend Central	1856		Originally 'on Sea'
36¾	Southend East	7/1932		
38	Thorpe Bay	7/1910		'Southchurch on Sea' for first 17 days
39½	Shoeburyness	2/1884		
Romford and Ockendon branches				
	Upminster			
1¾	Emerson Park	10/1909 (LT&S)		Originally 'Halt'
3½	Romford	6/1893		
3¼	Ockendon	7/1892		

Left The exit from Fenchurch Street on 22 May 1991, as seen from the adjacent Docklands Light Railway station at Tower Gateway. EMU No 310060, built at Derby in 1965, is leaving for Southend via Upminster. *F. Hornby*

Middle left This is Limehouse, the first station out of Fenchurch Street, better known for many years as Stepney East. The sharply curved platforms, built on a viaduct, are seen in this view looking west on 9 March 1993. *F. Hornby*

Bottom left The true spirit of the 'Tilbury' is captured in this scene at Barking on 11 October 1958. Stanier three-cylinder 2-6-4T No 42516 heads an eight-coach Shoeburyness train, with a District Line 'Metadyne' train in the background. The speed restriction sign on the left is in connection with construction of the flyover just beyond the bridge. *F. Hornby*

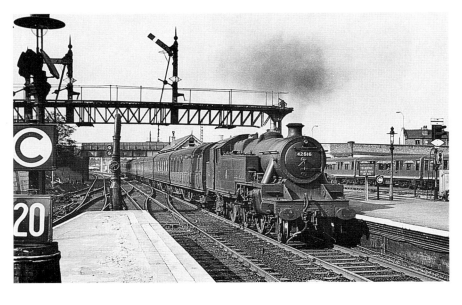

Limehouse station (formerly Stepney East), on a sharp curve just 1¼ miles from the terminus, and with a DLR station alongside, is now the only stop west of Barking, but accounts for only 0.1 per cent of LT&S section revenue. There was once a triangular junction here with the old L&B line to Blackwall and North Greenwich, closed in 1926. The four stations thence to Barking now retain platforms for the District Line tracks only, but 'LT&SR' monograms in the ironwork proclaim the original ownership at several of them. These stations were finally transferred from BR to London Transport Executive control in 1970.

Barking station was comprehensively rebuilt (for the second time) in 1959-62, with three island platforms for six through tracks and two terminal platforms, one each for District and Gospel Oak line trains. Track rearrangements included a dive-under east of the station and a flyover at the west end, facilitating cross-platform interchange between westbound trains on the District and LT&S lines, together with a second flyover for freights between Ripple

Lane yards and Woodgrange Park. The station buildings, spanning the tracks at right-angles, are of an impressive modernistic design with a spacious hall incorporating booking offices and shops.

As mentioned in Chapter 4, some steam trains via the Tottenham & Forest Gate line used to terminate at a bay platform at East Ham until 1958, after which the spur from Woodgrange Park was subsequently removed. The main LT&S depot for electric units is between the up and down lines just east of East Ham, on a site previously occupied by a London Transport depot.

Immediately beyond Barking the Tilbury and Southend routes part company, the latter continuing more or less due east, accompanied on the north side by the District Line tracks, along which five new stations were provided in the 1930s. One main reason for the extension was the building of the LCC Becontree Estate, now with 90,000 residents, adjoining the populous Hornchurch Urban District with Upminster at its eastern extremity. The station here is important, being the first stop east of Barking for LT&S trains, and the junction for the single-track lines north to Romford and south to Grays, as well as being the District Line terminus. There are four through platforms - those for the District Line giving access to the depot east of the station - with terminal platforms for each of the branches.

The Romford-Upminster line opened in 1893, one year after the Upminster-Grays section, and had one intermediate station. Both lines are worked by self-contained shuttle services.

Continuing eastward, the modern town of Basildon, with 150,000 inhabitants, ranks fifth in revenue importance on the LT&S section, although the BR authorities were slow to recognise the need for a station there; one was eventually opened in November 1974. Next comes Pitsea, the junction with the eastern end of the Tilbury loop, and thereafter the railway is in close proximity to the Thames Estuary, serving a succession of resort-cum-residential towns of which Southend itself (pop 156,000) is the largest. Gone are the days when the 'Kursaal' amusement park, the cockle-and-whelk stalls and the mile-long pier (with its own railway) drew vast crowds of daytrippers - your author went there from East Putney on the District Line as a small boy in 1937!

Nowadays most of the revenue is derived from commuters and shoppers, though surprisingly Southend comes no higher than tenth in the revenue chart. The Central station has two terminal platforms facing London as well as the two through lines which continue for a further 3¾ miles to Shoeburyness. The sta-

The once-bustling Tilbury Riverside station looks forlorn and deserted in this February 1986 scene, with EMU No 308152 about to depart for Upminster. The buildings once contained a customs hall and all the amenities required for passengers on cruise ships and the regular Swedish Lloyd sailings. *F. Hornby*

is 60 mph, as compared with 75 mph on favourable sections of the main line via Upminster.

Electrification first came to Fenchurch Street in 1949 when it was intended to run a 1,500V DC shuttle service to and from Stratford via Bow Junction. The scheme proved abortive, but the connection came into its own in February 1953 when the LT&S line was flooded east of Benfleet and a service between the Great Eastern section and Fenchurch Street was organised for the benefit of Southend passengers. It also proved useful, after conversion to 6.25kV DC current, for transferring stock between the two sections. This was after electrification of LT&S lines in 1961-62, when two different voltages were adopted for clearance reasons. The power supply out of Fenchurch Street was at 6.25kV AC to points about half a mile beyond Barking on both lines, and eastwards from just beyond Leigh-on-Sea. The intermediate mileage, including the Upminster-Grays line, was at 25kV AC. The Romford-Upminster line was excluded and did not find itself 'under the wires' for another 25 years, but by mid-1989 the higher voltage had been standardised throughout the LT&S section.

Resignalling in preparation for the new traction was completed in August 1961, extending colour-

tion there is simple, with wooden buildings, but there are extensive stabling sidings for electric multiple units. All traces of the four-road steam shed have disappeared.

The Tilbury loop is of a very different nature, at least for the first 14 miles, past what remains of Ripple Lane yards and the environs of Dagenham, with the huge rail-connected Ford Motor Works to the south of the line and the town to the north. After Rainham and Purfleet the branch from Upminster comes in at West Thurrock Junction, three-quarters of a mile short of Grays station.

Tilbury Town, hard by the container port, is unimpressive with its two through platforms, by contrast with the Riverside terminus, which closed in November 1992. Connected to the loop line by a triangle junction, it had six platform faces and dealt with boat trains from St Pancras until 1963 as well as the Fenchurch Street and Southend services; nowadays rail passengers for the adjacent Tilbury-Gravesend ferry must use a bus connection from the Town station. In steam days a busy motive power depot occupied a site within the triangle.

The Tilbury-Pitsea section dates from 1846 and skirts sand and gravel pits before passing to the west of Stanford-le-Hope town, 5 miles short of the junction at Pitsea. The maximum permissible speed throughout the Tilbury loop

This BR Class '4P' 2-6-4T, recorded at Benfleet on 12 May 1961, has only a few months more of active service ahead on the Tilbury section, as witness the catenary already in position. The station, 29¼ miles from London, opened in July 1855. *B. W. Brooksbank*

lights and track circuiting along the whole of the Shoeburyness main line and the Tilbury loop. The freight-only Thames Haven branch retained absolute block working, and the electric token blocks on the Romford-Upminster line remained in use until colour-lights were installed in November 1978.

At Fenchurch Street, the 1935-built electro-mechanical box spanning the tracks outside the station originally had 140 levers controlling four-aspect colour-lights at the platforms and approaches. In 1961 a push-button panel was installed, for remote control of Stepney East and Gas Factory Junctions, and after track rationalising the number of levers was reduced to 33.

On the direct route via Upminster 41 signal boxes were replaced by nine, including new power-operated installations at Barking, Pitsea and Southend Central. On the Tilbury loop 21 boxes were reduced to 12, with a new power cabin opened at Tilbury. The new installations permitted 2-minute headways along the direct route, while at the same time a start was made to replace the Hudd system of Automatic Train Control dating from 1947 with the BR standard Automatic Warning System. Another innovation, then unique on BR, was the provision of electric train description apparatus in 12 signal boxes, automatically linked to a control office at Fenchurch Street.

The 3½-mile Romford-Upminster line was electrified at 25kV AC during 1985/86 at a cost of £303,000, and free rides were given when the first electric trains ran on 12 May 1986. The terminal platform at Romford was duly lengthened to accommodate a four-coach unit.

Looking to the future, under a new resignalling project it is intended to replace all 17 remaining signal boxes, including that at Fenchurch Street, by a new centre at Upminster, in conjunction with track alterations to permit reversible running on all lines.

SERVICES

In the Summer 1948 timetable there were 74 departures from Fenchurch Street on weekdays, of which 47 were routed via Upminster and 27 via the Tilbury loop. Forty of the former and seven of the latter were through trains to Shoeburyness, involving of course a reversal at Riverside station for those via Tilbury. Six terminated at Riverside and 14 continued to Pitsea, Southend or Thorpe Bay. On Saturdays the half-day was catered for by no fewer then 23 departures between 11.25 am and 2.00 pm. Even on Sundays the departure total stood at a respectable 44, though one could well visualise how peaceful it would be at Fenchurch Street on the Sabbath!

Although hard work with heavy loads and smart running was required, overall average speeds fell mostly within the range of 20-38 mph, as demonstrated by the examples in the table below.

The Romford-Upminster-Grays link saw 22 trains each way between Romford and Upminster, plus three continuing to Grays and one through to Tilbury. There were ten from Upminster to Tilbury and three from Grays to Tilbury, plus two return trips between Upminster and Ockendon. On Sundays six trains ran through each way between Tilbury and Romford, allowed between 49 and 66 minutes for the 14¼ miles.

The following year (1949) saw the introduction of regular-interval services on both the main line and Tilbury loop, which were adhered to with minor changes until electrification. Off peak there were hourly fast and slow trains via Upminster to Southend and beyond, and one to Southend via Tilbury, with variations of intermediate stops. The slow trains to Shoeburyness via Upminster took 92 minutes (25.75 mph), but the fast trains made some smart running, with the palm going to the 4 pm from Fenchurch Street, non-stop to Westcliff in 44 minutes (47.5 mph). At rush hours and at Bank Holiday weekends some Tilbury trains started or terminated at Barking, while one early morning up train from Pitsea via Tilbury avoided Riverside, running direct via the north curve.

When electric working commenced in late 1961 it

EXAMPLE JOURNEYS ON LT&S LINES, 1948

Journey	Distance (miles)	Stops	Time (min)	Average (mph)
Fenchurch St-Shoeburyness (via Upminster)	39½	19	111	21.35
Fenchurch St-Shoeburyness (via Upminster)	39½	10	84	27.5
Fenchurch St-Southend (via Upminster)	35¾	6	56	37.3
Fenchurch St-Shoeburyness (via Tilbury Riverside)	45¼	23	133	20.41
Fenchurch St-Tilbury Riverside	22½	10	71	19.0
Fenchurch St-Tilbury Riverside	22½	8	56	24.1

With numerous 1960-vintage units still in service, one wonders why a comparatively modern 90 mph Class 312 has been diagrammed for the 3-mile trip from Upminster to Ockendon! Possibly it is on a 'running in' turn after a visit to the works for the EMU's equivalent of a '10,000-mile service'! *F. Hornby*

was not at first possible to implement the full service, thanks to the temporary retention of some units on the GE section. Once the full fleet was available the weekday departures from Fenchurch Street totalled 134 - an 80 per cent increase over 1948. Six trains left hourly off-peak, four for Shoeburyness via Upminster and two via Tilbury. Faster trains at peak hours produced times such as 37 minutes to Leigh-on-Sea with one stop (52.75 mph). However, as is often the case, some 'pruning' took place in due course; from 7 November 1966 the service via Upminster was reduced to three per hour with additional stops, though a few weeks later one train hourly was speeded up again. Nevertheless, patronage was up by 60 per cent in 1968 as compared with 1959, with over 67,000 passengers using Fenchurch Street every weekday.

In 1970 there was a spate of cancellations due to staff shortages and equipment failures, but in the May timetable for that year improvements were made in the services to the Estuary towns, with some trains terminating short of Southend Central. Again, in May 1973, the 'regular-interval' principle was applied to peak hours, so that in the down direction six trains left Fenchurch Street in each of four consecutive 15-minute periods, giving fast services to a variety of stations.

Present-day frequencies fall slightly short of those in the first heady days of full electrification, with 117 weekday departures from Fenchurch Street in the 1993/94 timetable, plus three in the small hours of Mondays only. There are five hourly off-peak departures from Fenchurch Street, of which two serve the Tilbury loop, terminating at Southend Central, while the three via Upminster all go through to Shoeburyness. The fastest time to Leigh-on-Sea is 39 minutes with two stops, the corresponding up train

being 3 minutes slower. Late at night four trains out of Liverpool Street serve LT&S destinations, via Forest Gate Junction and Barking.

The Romford-Upminster line has a half-hourly service - first introduced when diesel units took over in 1956 - while the longer section thence to Grays has to be content with an hourly through train, plus another shuttling between Upminster and Ockendon.

TRACTION AND TRAINS

In 1948 the LT&S section was 100 per cent steam operated, with depots at Plaistow (13A), Tilbury (13C), Shoeburyness (13D) and Upminster (13E), which, after transfer to the Eastern Region in 1949, became 33A, B and C, Upminster being relegated to sub-shed status. The combined allocation was around 140 locomotives, of which the majority were passenger tanks of the 2-6-4 and 4-4-2 types. The prime movers were Stanier's '4P' three-cylinder 2-6-4Ts Nos 42500-36, built in 1934 and humorously dubbed 'Tugboat Annies' thanks to their ship's-siren-style hooters. Most were based at Shoeburyness, with the remainder at Plaistow. There were also 25 Fowler, Stanier and Fairburn two-cylinder variants of the same wheel arrangement at Plaistow and Tilbury. They were supported by 39 '3P' 4-4-2Ts of LT&S design, some of them Derby-built as recently as 1930. Others of the class dated back to the late 1890s but had been substantially rebuilt, while a few surviving '2P' 4-4-2Ts of 1900 construction still languished at Plaistow or nearby Devons Road.

The '3Ps' did useful secondary work, particularly on the Tilbury loop, including those trains that, at busy weekends, started or terminated at Barking. Many were withdrawn or dispersed further afield when displaced by 28 BR Standard Class '4' 2-6-4Ts, newly built from 1953-56. By this time the Fowler engines had left the section and the assorted fleet of some 81 ex-LMS and BR 2-6-4Ts held the fort until electrification. After the Eastern Region took control a proposal to draft in 'L1' 2-6-4Ts was considered and rejected, possibly because of the expense of fitting

Right In this busy scene at Tilbury on 2 April 1960 Class '4P' 2-6-4T No 42511 heads a stopping train of Eastern Region stock from Fenchurch Street to Riverside station. Among the locomotives in the shed yard, a 'WD' '8F' 2-8-0 and a Class '4' Ivatt 'Mogul' are visible. *F. Hornby*

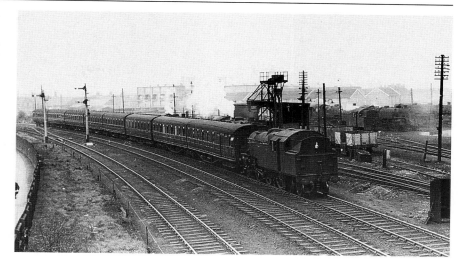

Middle right In April 1951 ex-MR Johnson '1P' 0-4-4T No 58045 stands alongside the wooden terminal platform at Romford prior to departure for Upminster. At this juncture the 1884-built locomotive has a life expectancy of barely seven months. The GE section Colchester main line is in the background. *F. Hornby*

Bottom right A train of Class AM2 units in green livery with No 246 leading arrives at Barking on 11 April 1964 en route to Shoeburyness. The District Line track climbing steeply on to the flyover can just be glimpsed on the extreme left. *F. Hornby*

ATC gear. One wonders how they would have coped with 13-coach trains grossing 350 tons over a difficult road?

During the summer there were numerous through workings off the Midland and Western Divisions of the LMR, for which purpose 4-6-0s, 2-6-0s and 0-6-0s from the London sheds were fitted with the ATC apparatus.

The small shed at Upminster maintained five ex-MR '1P' 0-4-4Ts equipped for push-pull working on the lines to Romford and Grays, including one of 1876 vintage that was withdrawn in 1954. However, the '3P' 4-4-2Ts were no strangers to these lines in earlier years, as for example in November 1949 when the author travelled behind one in a six-coach train from Tilbury Riverside to Upminster. On the demise of the 0-4-4Ts their replacements were auto-fitted 'N7' 0-6-2Ts from Stratford shed, one of which made the last steam-hauled run before DMUs took over on 17 September

1956. The Grays line remained the preserve of steam traction until January 1958, with a short appearance thereon by ex-GNR 'C12' 4-4-2Ts and by a pair of

'3F' 'Jinty' 0-6-0Ts, a menial duty shared at times by non-auto-fitted 2-6-4Ts.

Plaistow shed closed in June 1962 and in the same

month Tilbury lost its passenger engines and became a 'sub' to Stratford for freight work only. One of the last steam workings was a down rush-hour train on 15 June of that year hauled by No 42501, which, by coincidence, was the last engine to leave Shoeburyness for scrapping. The footplate staff retrained as motormen, working from the new depot at East Ham, while their former steeds were dumped at Plaistow and Shoeburyness, where both shed buildings were eventually demolished.

Steam-hauled coaching stock included ex-LT&SR, MR, LMS, LNER and eventually BR standard vehicles. At nationalisation there were 17 sets of 11 close-coupled 54-foot carriages of LMS origin, each including two lavatory composites, of 1924-34 construction. Ex-MR set trains were made up of elliptical-roofed 48-foot and 50-foot carriages with both Westinghouse and vacuum brakes, while ex-LT&SR vehicles, mostly eight-compartment 3rds, survived until 1956.

The first post-war additions comprised six four-coach sets with bodies of early Eastern Region design mounted on ex-GER 54-foot frames; some had centre gangways and toilets. There were also 30 coaches of post-war LNER suburban design, replacing ex-MR 13-coach rakes, and from 1954 onwards four variations of BR standard vehicles appeared. Latterly more ER and BR stock arrived, formed into 8- and 11-coach trains, releasing early LMS wooden-bodied coaches for scrapping. Thus by the late 1950s many trains consisted of ex-LNER/ER stock, hauled by ex-LMS engines!

The first electric multiple units were four-car sets of Class AM2 (later 302), of which 112 were built for the LT&S section by BR at Doncaster and York. After trials in June 1961 they took over some services on steam schedules in November. A full service was running by March 1962 after 24 units had returned from loan to the GE section. Some 30 units are still on LT&S duties in the 1990s after refurbishing with fluorescent lighting and a public address system.

For nearly 30 years, with some interchange between East Ham and Ilford (GE) depots, the LT&S fleet consisted entirely of EMUs of 1960 vintage, all dual voltage and of 'High Density' designs with slam-doors to each seating bay. Early on the scene were five sloping-fronted four-car Class AM8 (308/2) units, uniquely incorporating a Motor Luggage Van. These were rebuilt in 1971 and reclassified 308/4, with the MLVs converted to Motor Brake Seconds, and in 1984 were again modified as parcel units, now withdrawn. Also used on the stopping services have been Classes 305/1, 305/2 and 308/1; the 1974 allocation at East Ham consisted of 96 units, reduced slightly by 1986 to 85 of Classes 302 and 308.

By the end of the 1980s the whole section was taking current at 25kV AC, thus eliminating the need for units equipped for dual voltage, and it became possible to draft in 38 Class 310 four-coach sets, originally built in 1965 for outer-suburban services from Euston. With a better power-to-weight ratio than the 'High Density' designs and with bodies based on Mk II coaching stock, they are still currently responsible for many of the faster duties.

A crisis arose in 1991 when 35 units were taken out of service after overheating of cooling oil in transformers had started fires. As a precautionary measure all motor coaches were locked until the faults were rectified, drastically reducing seating capacity. Fortunately, by this time 17 of the 90 mph Class 312s of 1976 design were on LT&S metals and were not similarly affected.

In October 1993 the Class 308 units, by now refurbished, were transferred away, leaving Classes 302, 310 and 312 to cover all duties, the peak-hour requirement being for 80 units with maximum 12-coach formations. Additionally, Ilford-based Class 315 three-car suburban units work the Romford-Upminster service.

Thanks to the transition directly from steam to electric traction, diesels have played only a minor role in the LT&S section story. In early BR years the less than successful experimental Bo-Bo locomotive No 10800 ran trials for a few months, and in 1958 an ML2 Bo-Bo of the D61XX series equally failed to distinguish itself on Barking-Tilbury duties. More successful were the Brush Type 2 A1A-A1A D55XX machines, which filled in on passenger work at weekends when released from freight traffic.

Diesel multiple units have largely been confined to the Romford-Upminster-Grays routes; Derby twin units took over from the 'N7s' between Romford and Upminster in September 1956, and appeared on the Upminster-Grays line from January 1958. They were ultimately replaced by Craven Class 105s, which remained on the former line until electrification in 1986. For a time from the end of 1958 diesel units also worked a shuttle service between Tilbury and Pitsea, connecting with steam-hauled trains at either end.

Although there have been rumours of Class 321 units being drafted to the LT&S section, none has yet appeared at the time of writing, so for the immediate future the 310s, 312s and even the remaining 302s look set fair to continue to shoulder the burden!

9

'SOUTHERN ELECTRIC' STOCK

Now that our clockwise progress around London has brought us south of the Thames, we encounter the 'Southern Electric' network, which bequeathed to BR at nationalisation 706 route and 1,760 track miles, embracing not only the suburban area but reaching to the South Coast, the Medway towns and Reading. During 1958 the three Sections of the Southern Region - the Western, Central and Eastern - were redesignated as the South Western, Central and South Eastern Divisions, destined to be absorbed into Network SouthEast in June 1986.

The origins of this great undertaking go back to 1909 when high tension 6,700V AC current was first fed into the overhead catenary along the LB&SCR Victoria-London Bridge loop line, in a move to win back lost traffic. Its success led to extensions, publicised as the 'Elevated Electric', and the final section, to Coulsdon North, was completed under Southern Railway auspices in 1925.

Meanwhile the LSWR, also facing road competition, had embarked on third rail electrification at 600V DC of lines to Kingston, Shepperton, Hampton Court and Claygate in 1915-16. This system was adopted as standard by the Southern Railway after amalgamation and extended thereafter on all three Sections; conversion of the former LB&SC routes was completed in 1929. The voltage has since been increased to 750 DC.

As the result of all this activity an impressive fleet of multiple units came into BR ownership in 1948, and it will be convenient to survey the suburban types before examining the routes and services on which they operate.

Ex-LSWR unit No 4150, leading this eight-coach formation near Shepperton on 11 April 1955, began life as one of the E1-84 series, renumbered from 1201 upwards by the SR. Further renumbering took place post-war when an extra trailer was inserted. 'Wrong line' working is in progress as the up line is blocked by Kempton Park race specials.
F. Hornby

INHERITED STOCK

The stock as inherited included 81 of the 84 original LSWR 'torpedo-ended' units, together with many built in successive batches in SR years, incorporating coach bodies and frames from redundant steam stock as well as those from the LB&SC AC sets. Thus far the trains consisted of three-coach units, each of two motor coaches flanking a trailer, run in pairs at peak times separated by two additional trailers to make up an eight-car formation. During and after the war they were reformed as four-car units and all the two-car trailer sets were withdrawn by September 1948. The strengthening coaches for the four-car units were either converted steam stock, or new steel-bodied vehicles then coming on stream.

There were additionally 12 two-car units, Nos 1801-12, provided specially for the South London and Wimbledon-West Croydon lines in 1929. Eight of these were made up from 16 ex-LB&SC side-gangway motor coaches, half of which were adapted as driving trailers. These were all replaced by new construction of 2EPBs in 1954.

In 1934-36 a fleet of 78 2NOL outer-suburban units went into service, initially on the Windsor Lines (the '2NOL' designation ominously indicated an absence of toilet facilities!). They were joined in 1936-38 by 152 2BILs and in 1938-40 by 76 2HALs (both better

provided in this important respect), the former for the Western and Central Sections and the latter for Eastern Section semi-fast services. They were numbered in the 2000-2100 and 2600 series respectively.

A new era began in 1941 with the introduction of four-car sets with flush steel-panelled sides with six-a-side seating. Only two, Nos 4101-2, were built in that year, but more appeared in 1946 of which Nos 4103-10, equipped with 11-compartment trailers, became somewhat obscurely known as the 'Queen of Shebas'. The next batch from No 4111 onwards adopted the flat fronts, which became the hallmark of the Bulleid

---

SOUTHERN REGION EMUs, 1949-1994

Date introduced	BR Class ('TOPS' Class)	No of vehicles per unit	Passenger Classes	Motors per unit	Weight per unit (tons)	Length per unit (ft in)	Max speed (mph)	Year withdrawn	Notes
1915 (LSWR)	3SUB	3	1st/3rd	4 x 275hp	95	157 5 - 159 5	54	see below*	Rebuilt 1934 with 62-ft bodies
Representative SR pre-war classes									
1925 (SR)	3SUB	3	1st/3rd	4 x 300hp	109	193 8	?	All by 1962	
1928 (SR)	3SUB	3	1st/3rd	4 x 275hp	104	193 5	?	All by 1962	
1929 (SR)	2SL	2	1st/3rd	2 x 275hp	78	127 2	?	9/1954	For South London line
1929 (SR)	2WIM	2	1st/3rd	2 x 275hp	76	127 4	?	9/1954	For Wimbledon-West Croydon line conversions
1934 (SR)	2NOL	2	1st/3rd	2 x 275hp	71-73	129 6	?	8/1959	
1935 (SR)	2BIL	2	1st/3rd	2 x 275hp	74-76	129 6	?	9/1971	
1938-9 (SR)	2HAL	2	1st/3rd	2 x 275hp	74-76	129 6	?	1971	6 sets built 1948 and 1 built 1955
Wartime classes									
1941 (SR)	4SUB	4	3rd	4 x 275hp	144	257 4½	?	1972	Series 4101-10
1942 (SR)	4SUB	4	3rd	4 x 275hp	139	256 8 - 257 5	?	6/1956	*Ex-LSWR 3SUBS as rebuilt
Post-war									
1946 (SR)	4SUB (405)	4	3rd	4 x 250hp	134	257 5	75	9/1983	Variations in subsequent batches
1949 (BR)	4DD	4	3rd	4 x 275hp	134	257 5	75	10/1971	Double-deckers, 552 seats per unit
1951 (BR)	4EPB (415)	4	3rd	4 x 250hp	136	264 - 275 5	75	**	
1953 (BR)	2EPB (416)	2	3rd	2 x 250hp	70-71	129 6 - 32 8½	75	**	
1957 (BR)	2HAP (414)	2	1st/2nd	2 x 250hp	70	132 8½	90	12/1994	Second batch 72 tons, 129 ft 6½ in
1974 (BR)	2SAP (418)	2	2nd	2 x 250hp	72	129 6	75	-	Converted from 2HAP and back to 2HAP
1982 (BR)	4CAP (413)	4	1st/2nd	4 x 250hp	149	265 5	90	**	2HAPs paired permanently
'High Density' units									
1972 (BR)	4PEP (461)	4	2nd	16 x 100hp	142	267 2	75	1976	To Derby Research Centre 1979
1979 (BR)	('TOPS') 508	4	2nd	8 x 110hp	122	264 10	75	**	To Merseyrail 1985, Nos 508101-43
1982 (BR)	455	4	2nd	4 x 250hp	(tonnes) 146.2	(metres) 79.68	75	**	Nos 5701-50, 5800-74, 5901-20
'Thameslink'									
1987 (BR)	319	4	Std	4 x 332hp	136.3	79.50	100	**	Nos 319001-60, 161-86
1990 (BR)	456	2	Std	2 x 185kW	72.5	39.46	75	**	Nos 456001-24
'Networkers'									
1991	465	4	Std	8 = 1,875kW	138.56	81.90	75	**	Nos 465001-50, 151-97, 201-50
1992	466	2	Std	4 = 940kW	72.33	41.60	75	**	Nos 466001-43

NB Last pre-war two-car trailer units withdrawn 9/1948   ** in service 1994

Right This undated photograph at Wimbledon shows two-car unit No 1812 of 1929 on a West Croydon service. The coaches were built originally for the LB&SCR South London line electrification and thereafter did a spell as main-line steam-hauled stock before conversion as shown. *F. Hornby collection*

Middle right This unit, No 4110, is one of the steel-bodied batch of 1945 construction that paved the way for the mass-produced '4SUBS' introduced in 1946. The sets included an 11-compartment trailer and acquired the soubriquet 'Queen of Shebas'. No 4110 is seen trailing a down train at Wimbledon in October 1963. *A. J. Pike*

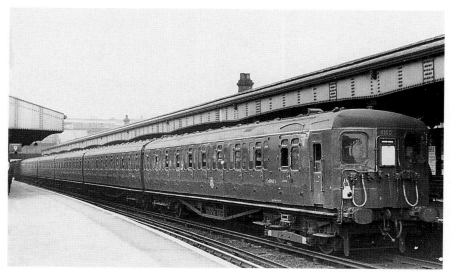

Bottom right Widely used throughout the Southern suburban network, the flat-fronted Bulleid 4SUBS notched up phenomenal mileages during 35 years of hard service. No 4636 in 'Rail Blue' livery pauses at Earlsfield on 21 June 1980 en route to Chessington South. *F. Hornby*

4SUBS, while those from No 4121 had centre gangways in some compartments. This practice was extended so that in new construction from 1948 onwards only one trailer in each unit retained compartments. Altogether, including a few 'hybrids' using redundant trailers, 209 Bulleid units were built between 1946 and 1951, and they had a long and honourable career terminating in September 1983. Meanwhile the last of the LSWR sets had been withdrawn in June 1956 and all those with pre-war wooden bodies had gone by 1962.

THE 1950s AND '60s

In the face of increasing overcrowding on the Eastern Section Bulleid tried the bold experiment of contriving double-decked stock within the British loading gauge, two four-car units being built in 1949. They were used on Dartford services until withdrawal in 1971, but in spite of seating 1,104 in the eight-coach train, they were handicapped by the comparative slowness of loading and unloading. In

Left The double-decker 4DD units represented a bold but unsuccessful attempt to cram more passengers into a train of conventional length. Unit 4902 (originally 4002) languishes in temporary preservation at Ashford Steam Centre on 13 May 1973. *F. Hornby*

Middle left Class 415/1 4EPB unit No 5276 is pictured towards the end of its long career at Elephant & Castle station en route for Blackfriars on 17 April 1991. It is in blue-grey livery and bears the 'Kent Link' logo alongside the luggage compartment. *F. Hornby*

Bottom left Back in 1909 Wandsworth Road station found itself 'under the catenary' on the first section of the LB&SCR's 'Elevated Electric' network. Decades later a Class 416/1 2EPB unit of 1953 design calls there on 21 March 1981 on a Victoria-London Bridge service. *F. Hornby*

consequence, the platforms had to be lengthened to enable conventional 10-coach trains to be run.

As successors to the 4SUBS came the 4EPB units - 'EPB' signifying electro-pneumatic brakes - introduced in 1951 and numbered from 5001 upwards until 283 were in service by 1963. Neither the braking system nor the buckeye couplers of the EPBs were compatible with the air-operated brakes and screw-couplings of the 4SUBs, preventing the two types from running in multiple. The last batch of 68 4EPBs were on BR standard underframes and recognisable by their roofs, which protrude slightly at the ends. Thanks to successive refurbishing, a diminishing number have soldiered on into the 1990s on the South Eastern Division, embellished with the 'Kent Link' logo.

Simultaneously in 1951 came the first two-car units of classes 2EPB and 2HAP. Of the former, 128 were built between 1951 and 1956, numbered in the 5600 and 5700 series, including 15 for the South Tyneside services of the North Eastern Region. They returned to the Southern Region when the Tyneside lines were 'de-electrified' in 1963, and could be distinguished by their smaller headcode panels and larger brake compartments. On the South Eastern routes 2EPBs and 4EPBs ran in multiple to form 10-car trains after platforms had been lengthened.

The 2HAPs, of which 205 were outshopped between 1951 and 1958, catered for 1st and 2nd Class passengers, being intended for semi-fast duties as replacements for the 2HALs. Originally numbered 6001-6173 and 5604-35, most of this latter series had their 1st Class accommodation removed in 1974 when they were reclassified 2SAP (Class 418), reverting later to their 2HAP condition. Then in 1982 a further reclassification took place when 46 of the 6001 series were merged into 23 four-car 4CAP units (Class 413) and renumbered in the 3200 and 3300 series, in which form they were still at work at the end of 1994.

Of the earlier two-car sets, the 2NOLs were withdrawn by August 1959, the ever-economical Southern Region utilising the frames for their successors, while both the 2BIL and 2HAL units survived until the end of 1971.

Passing mention should be made of the 194 'High Density' 4VEP (Class 423) 90 mph main-line units introduced in 1967, originally in blue livery and numbered from 7701 upwards. They have since been renumbered in the 3000 series, with a 'face-lifted' version in the 3400s from 1988 onwards. Widely used, their duties bring them in to our orbit by their calls at suburban stations such as Bromley South, East Croydon and Surbiton.

THE 1970S AND '80S

The next generation of EMUs was heralded by the appearance in 1972 of the aluminium-bodied 4PEP units, Nos 4001-2, with a solitary 2PEP companion, No 2001. As first built No 4001 had one car in silver-grey livery and the remaining three in blue, and the original classification was 4PER - Prototype Electro Rheostatic! With passenger-operated sliding doors, two powered bogies on each coach and

generous 'standee' accommodation, the wits soon interpreted 'PEP' as 'Pack 'em in perpendicular'!

After extended trials throughout the 1970s they were transferred to the Derby Research Centre, having paved the way for the 43 four-car units of Class 508, built at York and allocated to the South Western Division. The seating was increased to 320 as compared to 280 in a 4PEP, but after a stay of just five years they were sent north to Merseyrail, each leaving behind a trailer car to be incorporated in their successors of Class 455. These were introduced in 1982 and comprised 145 four-car units in three batches, like their predecessors gangwayed throughout. They are equipped with pressure heating and ventilation systems, and with driver-guard communication and public address facilities. The second batch, series 5700, incorporate the Class 508 trailers, distinguishable by their lower roof profile, while the first batch, series 5800, have a rather ugly square cab frontage.

Based at Selhurst and Wimbledon depots, they operate on the South Central and South Western Divisions and, while their performance is beyond reproach, some quirk - presumably in their suspension - often produces a continuous squawk akin to that of a demented parrot! Nevertheless, with their superior acceleration they represent a major advance from the days of the 4SUBs.

Next in succession come the 'Thameslink' Class 319s of 1987, which, while covering outer-suburban services on South Eastern and South Central routes, are of course the prime movers on Midland metals out to Luton and Bedford. All 86 units are allocated to Selhurst depot, the final 26 of sub-class 319/1 being distinguished by the provision of 1st Class accommodation, variations in the designs of the panels alongside the couplers, and in the NSE livery. Such is progress that the 100 mph capability of the 319s is virtually dou-

The experimental 4PEP units of 1972 ushered in a new era of 'High Density' stock on the Southern Region, though only two were built to this particular design. During several years of intensive trials they are seen at Clapham Junction on 11 March 1975. Note the silver car in an otherwise 'Rail Blue' unit No 4001. *F. Hornby*

Left Developed directly from the 4PEPs came Class 508 in 1979, destined for five years' service on the South Western section before removal to pastures new on Merseyside. No 508014 leads a Hampton Court train past East Wimbledon depot on 29 July 1981. *F. Hornby*

Below left The ungainly front-end design of the first batch of Class 455 units is clearly seen in this shot of a 5800 series approaching Claygate on 25 August 1993. South Western section suburban services have been monopolised by this class for some years. *F. Hornby*

ble that of the pioneer pre-Grouping trains. They have the added refinement of thyristor chopper control, which was tried out in the last five units of Class 455.

THE 1990S

The present decade has seen the appearance of the 24 Class 456 two-car units from BREL York, their entry into service being delayed until 30 September 1991 while the driving seat position was altered to suit the requirements of 'driver only' operation. They are currently confined to 'Network South Central' - the former Central Division - where off-peak a single unit covers duties previously rostered for a four-car set. They can, however, run in multiple with each other and with Class 455, though their couplings and controls are not compatible with those of Class 319. Remarkably they are powered by the same EE507 traction motors as employed on the 4EPBs of 1951,

but, with disc brakes, fluorescent lighting and toilets, they bring unheard-of refinements to such backwaters as the Wimbledon-West Croydon line!

On the South Eastern Division the scene has been transformed by the advent of the Class 465 four-car and 466 two-car 'Networkers', albeit delayed while various problems have been sorted out. Built from 1991 onwards by BREL York/ABB and by GEC/Metro-Cammell with 20-metre aluminium bodies and 'collision-proof' ends, they incorporate three-phase traction technology, thyristor controls and regenerative braking. There are surprising variations in the batches from the two manufacturers, as even the cab layouts and bogies differ, and while the units from York are 'home-made', the bodies for those completed by GEC/Metro-Cammell are imported from Italy. In service they are confined to routes on which the signalling has been modified, as proved necessary due to interference from the 'high-tech' electronics in the traction motors. There are four of these per bogie, producing a maximum output of 1,875kW and a 75 mph top speed. Seating is 348 (all Standard Class) per four-car unit in the '2 + 3' 'High Density' mode, and platform and track alterations permit three such units to work in multiple. The total fleet comprises 147 Class 465 and 43 Class 466 units.

In conclusion it is worth mentioning that numerous superannuated passenger vehicles, mostly of 4EPB and 2EPB origin, still serve for inter-depot stores duties. Also, Bulleid 4SUB No 4732 and 4EPB No 5001 have been restored to green livery and have been much in demand for enthusiasts' specials.

Rarely seen above ground are the 12 'tube'-sized motor coaches of the Waterloo & City line, operating at 630V DC on the 1 m 46 ch 'non-stop' run between Waterloo and Bank. The Class 482 vehicles now in service are based on London Underground's Central Line 1990 stock, replacing the Class 487s of 1940 vintage. The operation of this line, opened by the LSWR in August 1898, is now the responsibility of London Underground Ltd.

HEADCODES

In 1948 most of Southern Region's suburban traffic was still worked by pre-war stock, on which services were identified by lettered headcodes, displayed on centrally mounted stencilled plates. The letters used included 'H.O.V.I.S.', as per the famous advertisement, together with J, L, P and D, with permutations by the addition of bars and single or double dots above the letters. Even so, thanks to the proliferation of routes, the same headcodes were perforce used on more than one Section.

Until the advent of the Bulleid units the only exceptions, other than main-line stock, were on the South London and Wimbledon-West Croydon lines, both identified by route No 2.

From the Bulleid 4SUBs onwards, route numbers came into universal use, displayed at first on two-character stencilled panels and later on roller blinds. Nos 1-99 were all taken up, the majority with two or more uses. On the Eastern Section even numbers distinguished services using Charing Cross, and odd numbers those for Cannon Street, while on the Central Section Victoria services were allocated the even and London Bridge the odd numbers.

Perhaps it was fortunate therefore that when Class 508 units entered service in 1979 they were confined to the South Western Division and thus only to one terminus, as no provision was made for route numbers. They had separate blinds above the near and off-side cab windows, one showing the destination and the other either the starting place or 'via. . .' as applicable. Initially the same applied to their Class 455 successors, but small two-digit route numbers were incorporated later. The Class 319 Thameslink units display headcodes consisting of two digits - or a letter and one digit - over the nearside, and the destination over the offside cab windows. In the most recent Classes 456, 465 and 466, destination and route numbers are combined in 'dot matrix' displays at the top of the drivers' windows. From May 1991 the appropriate headcodes have been shown at the head of each column in the timetables, at the suggestion of passenger pressure groups.

LIVERIES

At nationalisation the Southern Electric fleet remained in the traditional green livery with, for a time, an 'S' prefixing the unit numbers. The words 'British Railways' were later replaced by the 'Lion and Wheel' emblem. In common with multiple unit stock on other Regions, 'Rail Blue' was adopted in 1966, enlivened by yellow end-panels from 1969. Blue-grey became standard from the early 1980s and - as the 'Jaffa Cake' livery adopted by the Southern Eastern sector a few years later was confined to main-line stock - remained so until the introduction of Network SouthEast's 'patriotic' red-white-blue (and grey) colour scheme from May 1986.

Only we 'oldies' remember the joys of riding in units like these with advertisements in each compartment showing five motor coaches with headcodes spelling the name of a popular brand of brown bread! No 4251, seen at Clapham Junction in March 1955 on a Kingston roundabout service, consists of converted LB&SCR stock, with a Bulleid 4SUB in tow. *F. Hornby*

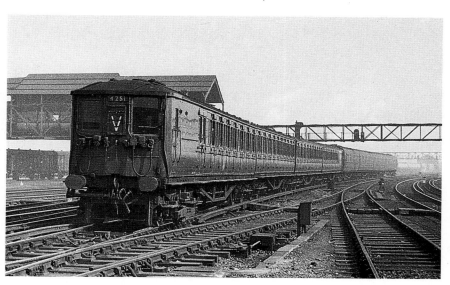

10

SOUTHERN REGION SOUTH EASTERN DIVISION

Old traditions die hard, and over 90 years after the fusion of the former rival South Eastern and London, Chatham & Dover companies in 1899, it is still convenient to deal with the South Eastern Division in two parts, which coincide broadly with the 19th-century ownerships.

This first part of this chapter covers the lines of SER origin with their termini at Charing Cross and Cannon Street, and the second part the former LCDR lines from Victoria, Holborn Viaduct and Blackfriars. It will be noted, however, that there has been some overlapping since the Grouping, perpetuated after nationalisation, with services between the former LCDR termini and Dartford. The two sets of lines are identified on the map overleaf.

None of the route mileage of the combined

SE&CR was electrified prior to the Grouping of 1923. Although the matter had been considered during the Edwardian era, the project was postponed due to the outbreak of the First World War and subsequently shelved. Thus the heavy suburban traffic on both sections continued to be worked by an army of 0-4-4Ts until the mid-1920s by which time, under Southern Railway auspices, the third rail was being laid with commendable speed. By the end of the decade all suburban routes were energised, though stopping short at Orpington on the former SER main line until extended to Sevenoaks in 1935.

The heading 'Kent Link', under which services on all these lines have appeared in recent timetables, has been abandoned in favour of 'South Eastern'.

FORMER SER LINES FROM CHARING CROSS AND CANNON STREET

To Dartford via the North Kent, Bexleyheath and Loop lines
Mid-Kent line to Hayes, Addiscombe and Selsdon
Main line to Sevenoaks and branches (Grove Park-Bromley North and
Dunton Green-Westerham)

As mentioned in our introduction, the London & Greenwich Railway was a pioneer 'commuter line', which eventually formed part of the first of the three routes that reached Dartford in 1849, 1864 and 1885 respectively. During these years Addiscombe, Bromley North, Hayes and Selsdon were all rail-connected, while the main line reached Tonbridge via Orpington and Sevenoaks in 1868, giving a more direct route

than the original one via Redhill! The Westerham branch was added to the network in 1881.

Even by the turn of the century Charing Cross and Cannon Street were handling between them 23¾ million passengers annually, many of whom continued to endure the discomfort of six-wheeled carriages into the early Grouping years. The advent of the fast and frequent electrics in the 1920s must have been hailed

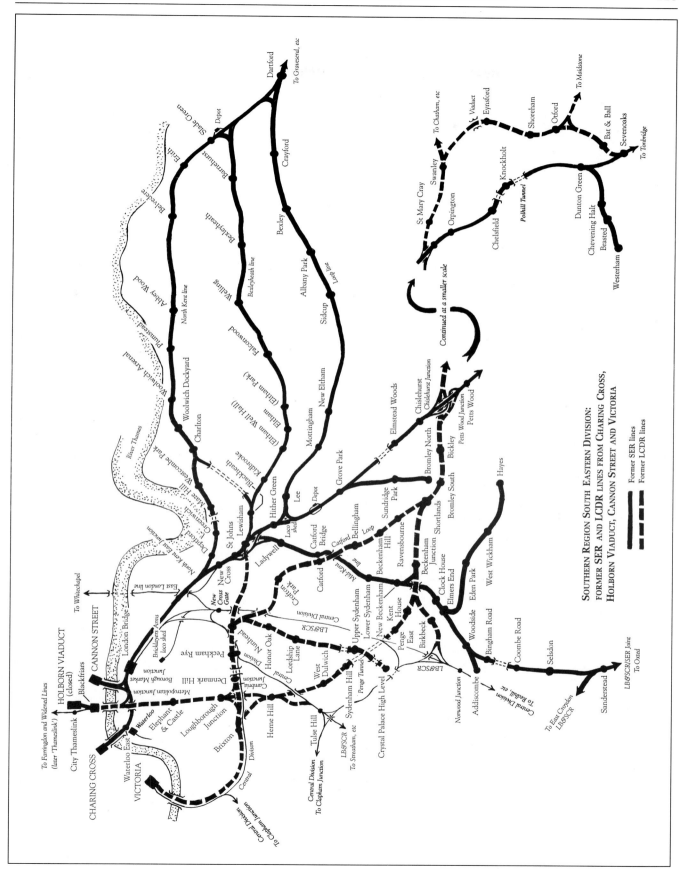

SOUTHERN REGION SOUTH EASTERN DIVISION: FORMER SER AND LCDR LINES FROM CHARING CROSS, HOLBORN VIADUCT, CANNON STREET AND VICTORIA

Former SER lines
Former LCDR lines

Former SER suburban lines from Charing Cross and Cannon Street to Dartford, Sevenoaks and branches

Miles	Name	Opened	Closed	Notes
From Charing Cross				
	Charing Cross	1/1864		
¾	Waterloo East	1/1867		'Waterloo' to 5/1977
	Cannon Street	9/1866		
1¾	London Bridge	12/1836		
North Kent line				
5	Deptford	2/1836		Closed 3/1915-6/1926
5½	Greenwich	12/1838		Present station from 1/1877
6¼	Maze Hill	2/1878		Originally 'Greenwich Maze Hill'
7	Westcombe Park	5/1879		Originally 'Coombe Farm Lane'
7½	Charlton	7/1849		
8¾	Woolwich Dockyard	7/1849		
9¼	Woolwich Arsenal	11/1849		
10	Plumstead	7/1859		
11½	Abbey Wood	1850		Rebuilt 5/1987
13	Belvedere	3/1859		
14¼	Erith	7/1849		
15¼	Slade Green	1900		'Slades Green' to 9/1953
Bexleyheath line				
6	Lewisham	7/1849		'Lewisham Junction' to 7/1929
7	Blackheath	7/1849		Restored 1982-5
	Blackheath-Charlton spur - no intermediate stations			
8	Kidbrooke	5/1895		
9	Eltham (Well Hall)	5/1895	3/1985	'Well Hall & North Eltham' to 9/1927
9¼	Eltham	3/1985		
9½	Eltham Park	7/1908	3/1985	'Shooters Hill & Eltham Park' to 10/1927
10½	Falconwood	1/1936		
11½	Welling	5/1895		Closed 1/1917 to 9/1935
12¾	Bexleyheath	5/1895		
14	Barnehurst	5/1895		
Loop line				
7	Hither Green	6/1895		
7¾	Lee	9/1866		
9½	Mottingham	9/1866		'Eltham & Mottingham' to 10/1927
10¼	New Eltham	4/1878		'New Eltham & Pope Street' to 10/1927
12	Sidcup	9/1866		
12¾	Albany Park	7/1935		
13¾	Bexley	9/1866		
15¼	Crayford	9/1866		
Dartford				
17 via Bexleyheath		7/1849		
17¼ via Greenwich				
17¼ via Sidcup				
18¾ via Blackheath & Woolwich				

Miles	Name	Opened	Closed	Notes
Main line to Sevenoaks				
5	New Cross	10/1850		'New Cross (SER)' to 1923
5½	St Johns	6/1873		
9	Grove Park	11/1871		
10¼	Elmstead Woods	7/1904		'Elmstead' to 10/1908
11¼	Chislehurst	7/1865		
	Loops to St Mary Cray opened 6/1904			
12½	Petts Wood	7/1928		
13¾	Orpington	3/1868		
15¼	Chelsfield	3/1868		
16	Knockholt	5/1876		'Halstead for Knockholt' to 10/1900; closed 1981-5/1984 after fire
20½	Dunton Green	3/1868		
22	Sevenoaks	3/1868		'Sevenoaks (Tubs Hill)' to 6/1950
From Charing Cross to Elmers End via Ladywell spur				
6¾	Ladywell	1/1857		
7½	Catford Bridge	1/1857		
9	Lower Sydenham	1/1857		New station 1906
9½	New Beckenham	4/1864		
10¼	Clock House	6/1890		
11	Elmers End	4/1864		
Hayes branch				
11	Elmers End			
12½	Eden Park	5/1882		
13¼	West Wickham	5/1882		
14½	Hayes	5/1882		
Addiscombe and Sanderstead lines				
11	Elmers End			
12	Woodside	1871	9/1963	
13	Addiscombe	4/1864		'Addiscombe (Croydon)' to 6/1955
12¾	Bingham Road	9/1935	5/1983	Date reopened; 'Bingham Rd Halt' 8/1885-1/1917
13¾	Coombe Road	9/1935	5/1983	Date reopened; 'Coombe Lane' 8/1885-1/1917)
14¼	Selsdon	9/1935	5/1983	Date reopened; 'Selsdon Road' 8/1885-1/1917
15	Sanderstead	3/1884		
Bromley North branch				
9	Grove Park			
10¼	Sundridge Park	1/1878		Originally 'Plaistow' to 1894
10½	Bromley North	1/1878		Originally 'Bromley' to 1899
Westerham branch				
20½	Dunton Green			
21¾	Chevening Halt	4/1906	10/1961	
23¾	Brasted Halt	7/1881	10/1961	'Brasted' to 9/1955
25¼	Westerham	9/1881	10/1961	

with relief, and it sparked off a building boom that pushed the boundaries of London's built-up areas ever further to the south-east. Only the Westerham branch remained steam operated after 1935, until its demise in October 1961.

Mention must also be made of the ex-SECR branches from Purley to Caterham and Tattenham Corner, served traditionally by trains from either Charing Cross or London Bridge along the former LB&SCR main line through Norwood Junction. They appear in the BR timetable for the Central (now South Central) Division and will therefore be dealt with in the later relevant chapter.

ROUTES AND INFRASTRUCTURE

BR has a monopoly of rail transport in the south-eastern suburbs, save for the Metropolitan's East London Line to New Cross and New Cross Gate. Thanks to a

profusion of routes and connecting spurs, numerous permutations are possible both for normal traffic and in emergencies, the classic example being Dartford, which has, at one time or another, been served by trains from six London termini. This number is now reduced to three, of which Victoria's contribution is confined to the Bexleyheath line.

The other two are Charing Cross and Cannon Street, of South Eastern Railway origin and both on the north bank of the Thames, convenient for the West End and City respectively and fully justifying the great expense incurred in their construction in the 1860s. Neither rank in size among the major stations, Charing Cross having a modest six platforms and Cannon Street seven (recently reduced from eight), but thanks to the quick turn-round of multiple unit trains their capacity is still formidable. Much of their original character has disappeared in the process of modernisation, though amenities around the concourses have certainly been improved. Both are directly served by London Underground, Charing Cross by the Bakerloo, Jubilee and Northern Lines and Cannon Street by the District and Circle Lines.

Despite modernisation, viewed from across the river Charing Cross does still offer the illusion of a traditional high-arched terminus and - nice touch - the old 'SR' coat of arms is still prominently displayed. Suburban trains monopolise platforms 1-3, lengthened to take 10 coaches in 1954 and, more recently, for the 12-car

Above left The suburban platforms at Charing Cross in this 1957 view are occupied by 4EPB units, two of which bear their original numbering with an 'S' prefix. Note the even-numbered headcode as assigned to Charing Cross trains, also the station roof as rebuilt after its disastrous collapse in December 1905. *N. L. Browne*

Left Cannon Street station as seen on 23 June 1982 is in an interim state of rebuilding, having lost its fine arched roof but not yet acquired the flat 'raft' that covers the platforms today. The 15-storey office block dominates the view and a section of the old wall can be glimpsed on the right. The trains are 4EPBs in blue-grey livery, all belonging to sub-class 415/2 with BR-designed bodywork. *F. Hornby*

'Networkers' of the 1990s. The two local tracks cross the river on the original Hungerford Bridge of 1866, with the later structure dating from 1877 alongside. When repairs were carried out in 1979 it was stated that 400 trains were using the local tracks daily. Once across the Thames the lines are carried on brick arches through Waterloo East, where the four platforms are lettered A-D to avoid confusion with the adjacent terminus - most local services use A and B.

Cannon Street station is closed at weekends and bustles with activity only at weekday peak hours, outside which only platform 1 is in use for the 'skeleton service' of four trains in and out hourly. The road frontage is hidden behind a 15-storey block erected in 1965, but at the outer end the two 135-foot towers and sections of the old wall have survived the rebuilding. In place of the arched roof, removed in 1959, is a raft supporting a three-tiered edifice. Four platforms, suitably lengthened, are adequate for the peak-hour suburban traffic.

The tracks across the river bridge diverge at the south end to form a triangle junction with the line from Charing Cross. Originally there were three tracks curving towards Charing Cross and four eastwards towards London Bridge, but these have been slimmed down to one and three respectively, in the latter case to make allowance for the more generous dimensions of the 'Networker' vehicles. There are only two tracks across the base of the triangle between Metropolitan and Borough Market junctions, the latter, at the eastern end, being notorious as one of the busiest intersections in the country. In the 1960s on average one train tra-

versed it every 36 seconds during the busiest evening rush hour, and 1,200 in a day.

Between Waterloo East and Metropolitan Junction the line southwards from Blackfriars crosses overhead at right-angles with a steeply graded spur, currently used by 'Thameslink' services via London Bridge, connecting the two routes. The South Eastern Division through station at London Bridge consists of three island platforms with faces numbered 1-6 from north to south, of which Cannon Street local services use Nos 1 and 2. Since track replanning in the mid-1970s there have been seven running lines - one of them reversible - for SE Division trains eastwards for 2 miles to North Kent East Junction, where the northernmost of the three routes to Dartford diverges.

Never far from the river, the North Kent line follows the course of the London & Greenwich Railway,

Above right The notorious Borough Market Junction is seen during track relaying in June 1982, from a train on the curve into Cannon Street. The 4EPB on the left is traversing the two-track bottleneck between the two junctions on the line to Charing Cross. *F. Hornby*

Right All three island platforms at London Bridge's South Eastern Section station can be seen in this view from a train arriving at platform 6 on 20 August 1976. The footbridge may not be elegant but there can be no disputing the ability of this station to handle large numbers of trains and passengers expeditiously. *F. Hornby*

crossing Deptford Creek by a swing bridge, continuing eastwards to Belvedere then south-east through Slade Green, with 12 stations in as many miles. The line is easily graded but there are numerous tunnels between Greenwich and Plumstead, in which the tracks had to be lowered or realigned to accommodate the 'Networkers'.

The present Greenwich station, dating from 1877, is the third to be built there and has withstood the ravages of time particularly well. By contrast Maze Hill, next along the line, was rebuilt in 1972 with a glass-fronted booking hall intended as a prototype for other stations. To avoid interference with the nearby Greenwich Observatory a centrally placed fourth rail was laid hereabouts, bonded to the running lines to increase their capacity for the return current. Woolwich Arsenal station has also been the subject of renovation, completed in 1993 with a 'lighthouse' structure over the entrance. The industrial decline of this area - notably of the Arsenal itself - has been off-set by the growth of the Thamesmead housing development north of the line and east of Plumstead, where there are sidings for stabling EMUs outside peak hours.

The next two stations, Abbey Wood and Belvedere, have been modernised out of recognition, but Erith survives in typical 'South Eastern Railway' condition even to the staggered platforms. The building has been nicely renovated and the general effect is spoiled only by a rather angular footbridge. Just beyond Slade Green is the main EMU depot, which, though updated to deal with 'Networkers', retains a building opened in 1901 as a steam locomotive shed.

The Bexleyheath route to Dartford parts company with the main line at St Johns, scene of a derailment involving steam and local electric trains in dense fog on 4 December 1957. The station there has since been reduced to a single island platform for the slow lines at which, save at peak times, only Mid-Kent line trains call. The map highlights the complexity of the flying, burrowing and flat junctions in this area, cen-tred on Lewisham, where a line from Nunhead comes in from the west, while the Bexleyheath and Mid-Kent lines, and a spur back to the main line, branch off at the east end. The station building serving this busy shopping centre is in the angle between the two diverging pairs of platforms.

The Bexleyheath line proceeds east for 9 miles through seven stations before joining the North Kent line near Slade Green by means of a triangle junction 1½ miles short of Dartford. Blackheath, the first sta-tion beyond Lewisham, retains much of its pre-Grouping appearance save for the loss of the adjacent sidings. It is the junction for a line through a mile-long tunnel north-east to Charlton, which formed part of the original North Kent line before the gap between Greenwich and Charlton was bridged, and which pro-vides yet another alternative route to Dartford.

Kidbrooke station, a mile east of Blackheath, is an example of modern 'CLASP' prefabricated construc-tion. It was rebuilt in 1972 in anticipation of increased traffic from a nearby housing development, having hitherto been the least used sta-

Above left The motor cars help to date this picture of Greenwich station - taken on 16 June 1960 when Morris Minors were still rolling off the production line. The 1877 building is 'listed' as of archi-tectural merit and could scarcely be of greater contrast with the modern-age 'bus stops'. *F. Hornby*

Left Woolwich Arsenal station on the North Kent line was rebuilt during 1992/3, and the 'lighthouse' over the entrance is visible right of centre. Not much has changed at platform level, however, for which passengers, well sheltered from the elements, can be thankful! *F. Hornby*

Blackheath station on 11 May 1993, looking east and showing the now disused bay platform on the right-hand side. Beyond the station is the junction where the connecting line to Charlton leaves the Bexleyheath route to Dartford. *F. Hornby*

tion on the line. In March 1985 the next two stations, Eltham (Well Hall) and Eltham Park, were closed in consequence of the construction of the Rochester Way relief road alongside the line. A new Eltham station was opened midway between the two with a spacious forecourt incorporating a bus interchange, under which the new road tunnels at this point. The summit of the line is between Eltham and Welling near the 200-foot contour, approached by grades of 1 in 75 from the west and 1 in 80 from the east. Bexleyheath, the last station but one before Dartford, acquired its present buildings in 1931 and is centrally sited in a residential area that grew apace after electrification.

Hither Green is the junction for the Loop line - the southernmost of the three routes to Dartford - with platforms curving sharply away from those on the main line. A 'freight only' spur completes a triangle inside which the 1930s steam shed still survives as a diesel stabling point. The Loop line, double-tracked throughout like the other two, is easily graded save for two short lengths of 1 in 100, and there is still a good deal of open countryside along the way, with the River Cray close by at the eastern end. Of the seven stations, New Eltham and Sidcup are the most important, both having been rebuilt in recent years, while Bexley by contrast remains a well-preserved example of SECR timber construction. The junction at the Dartford end of the Loop line is another triangle; the connecting spur was laid for wartime traffic and, though not used by regular passenger services, is useful for empty stock movements.

Dartford station, at the convergence of the three routes, was rebuilt in 1973 with four through platform faces in place of three, all tracks being signalled for reversible running. About 350 passenger trains are dealt with daily including those to and from Gravesend and Gillingham, while a fair sprinkling of freight traffic passes through.

The Mid-Kent line (certainly not in *Mid* Kent and partly in Surrey!) has two alternative exits from the main line. One is via Lewisham station, while some peak-hour trains avoid Lewisham by using the spur from the main line at Parks Bridge Junction, the two routes coming together at Ladywell. The direction is then south through five stations to Elmers End, passing under the Catford Loop and the Chatham and Dover main line from Victoria en route. New Beckenham is no great distance from Beckenham Junction on the latter main line, and a spur - now singled - connects the two. This proves useful as Clock House, between New Beckenham and Elmers End, is in a dip and prone to flooding, at which times trains are diverted via the spur into the junction.

Elmers End has a bay platform for the shuttle service on the Addiscombe branch, which is 2 miles long with one intermediate station at Woodside. Until 1983 the latter was also a junction, for the Woodside & South Croydon Railway, built jointly by the SECR and LB&SCR to link up with the Oxted line at Selsdon. The two intermediate stations were separated by a 600-yard tunnel. The line was closed during the First World War, reopened and electrified in 1935, and closed again on 13 May 1983, since when part of trackbed has been built over. Selsdon was also served by a few Oxted line trains until June 1959.

Addiscombe station consists of an island platform, a third platform road having been removed in 1957. There is a four-track EMU shed, now disused but still intact, alongside the station. Initially this branch was considered more important than the other from Elmers End to Hayes, but the latter now enjoys the through services to and from London. It is 3½ miles long with two stations en route, and the terminus was rebuilt in 1935 in the 'Southern Electric' style of the period. Nowadays it has an island platform and no sidings. Both branches involve steady climbs from Elmers End, as steep as 1 in 89 on the line to Hayes, which is 200 feet above sea level.

Sevenoaks (pop 25,000), 22 miles from Charing

Cross on the main line, has long been the outer limit for stopping trains, as it was for the third rail until 1961. The route there is via New Cross and Hither Green, then south-east through a further eight stations. A steady 10-mile climb to Knockholt, partly at 1 in 120, is followed by a 4-mile descent to Dunton Green, of which 1½ miles are in Polhill Tunnel through the 500-foot hills.

At New Cross, the first station east of London Bridge, there are three through platforms plus a bay for the East London line. There are separate slow roads out to Orpington and the intermediate stations from Hither Green have platforms on all four lines. Grove Park, 2 miles beyond Hither Green, also has a bay platform for the Bromley North branch - 1½ miles long with an intermediate station just a third of a mile short of the terminus. The latter consists of the customary island platform and has an elegant station building of 1925 vintage.

The Victoria to Dover main line is crossed between Chislehurst and Petts Wood, with flying and burrowing connecting spurs that were remodelled in 1959 and again in 1993 with the 'Eurostar' trains in mind. Then follows Orpington (13¾ miles from Charing Cross) where, in the course of alterations in 1992, two additional terminal platforms were provided at the London end. At the same time the EMU shed was dismantled, although the four stabling sidings remain.

Dunton Green (20½ miles) was the junction for the 4¾-mile branch to Westerham until the latter closed in October 1961. Beyond the fringes of suburbia, the branch was single-track with two intermediate halts, and remained very much the 'country branch line' to the end. Preservation was considered, but was frustrated by road-building schemes.

Sevenoaks station, also served by trains via Swanley, was extensively rebuilt in 1976. The two island platforms remain, but those formerly flanking the outside tracks have been removed.

SIGNALLING

Thanks to a preponderance of flat junctions the South Eastern Division has always presented difficulties in train regulation, eased somewhat when colour-light signalling appeared at the London termini concurrently with electrification. Four-aspect signals were installed out to Borough Market Junction in June 1926 and were extended by the end of 1929 to Greenwich, Blackheath, Hither Green and Ladywell. Automatic colour-lights were also in place before the war on a short stretch of the Bexleyheath line, but no further progress was made for many

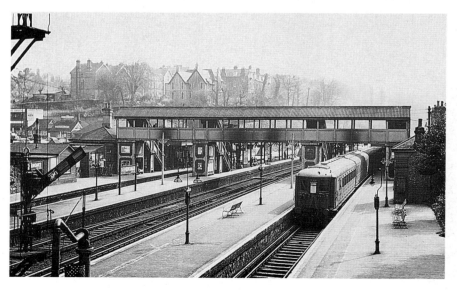

Above left The pleasing design of Bromley North station, as seen from the road, is evident in this view in February 1990. It now deals exclusively with the shuttle service to and from Grove Park on which the customary 2EPB has given way to a 'Networker'. *F. Hornby*

Left Sevenoaks station, looking east in March 1957, presented a very different appearance from today, thanks to the rebuilding in 1976. Note that the outer tracks are flanked by platforms on both sides, hemming in this pre-war 4SUB, strengthened by a Bulleid trailer. *F. Hornby*

years thereafter, save for a small installation in the Eltham area in 1954. Cannon Street box was destroyed by fire in April 1957, causing prolonged dislocation until December when a new box was prepared south of the river, incorporating a redundant 167-lever frame from the London Midland Region.

Colour-lights were installed between New Beckenham and Elmers End in August 1966, but it was 1971 before further attention was given to the Mid-Kent line. In the meantime all three routes to Dartford were tackled in 1970, and at the end of that year Dartford panel box took control of 257 colour-lights, eliminating 31 other boxes. There is, however, still a reminder of the past on the North Kent line, just east of Charlton, where a small mechanical box controls a level crossing. The Hayes branch lost its upper quadrants in September 1975, leaving Addiscombe as the last outpost of semaphore signalling, still operated from the platform-end box in 1994.

The London end was comprehensively dealt with in the 1970s; Cannon Street was closed for five weeks in August/September 1974 for track remodelling and resignalling, and London Bridge panel took over a wide area during 1975/76, including the Bromley North branch where the 1962 electro-mechanical box was duly closed. Charing Cross box, spanning the tracks near the platform ends, was removed with many others including the famous one at Borough Market Junction. To expedite this work, the two termini and Waterloo East were closed during the 1976 Easter weekend. The whole project cost £18 million - a sum that, at today's values, would seem a bargain!

Out on the main line also, the process of eliminating semaphore signalling and of reducing the number of boxes continued during the 1960s and 1970s. More recently the control of the former SER line at Chislehurst Junction complex and of the junction at Sevenoaks passed to the Ashford Integrated Electronic Centre, in April and June 1993 respectively.

SERVICES

Mention has already been made of the diversity of routes between London and Dartford, and full use was made of these in the early years following nationalisation. In the Summer 1948 timetable 189 stopping trains reached Dartford from the London termini on weekdays - 63 via the North Kent line, 55 via Bexleyheath and 71 along the Loop line. The great majority of these were from Charing Cross and Cannon Street, but there were eight from Holborn Viaduct and two from Blackfriars via the Nunhead-Lewisham Junction spur, all at peak hours. Some additional trains terminated short of Dartford, while others, including two starting from London Bridge, made a circuit of the North Kent and Bexleyheath lines via the spur between Slade Green and Barnehurst. A fast service between Charing Cross and Gillingham via Woolwich brought the daily total of down trains serving Dartford to over 200. A friend recalls that on Saturdays, when Charlton FC was playing at home, one or two of these made an extra stop for the benefit of fans.

An analysis from the same timetable in the accompanying table illustrates the variety of destinations of Dartford line trains leaving London on weekdays between 16.30 and 18.30. (A similar result would be obtained on Saturdays for departures between 12.30 and 14.30.) There are 51 trains, all 'Third Class Only'. Off-peak and on Sundays there were three trains per hour to and from Dartford on each of the three routes.

On the Mid-Kent line there were 111 weekday down trains, with an additional four shuttling from Elmers End to Hayes. In the peak hours trains from Cannon Street and Charing Cross served the three destinations - Addiscombe, Hayes and Sanderstead - using both routes, via Lewisham and via the St Johns-Ladywell spur. Many in the peak hours missed out St Johns and Lady Well (then spelt as two words). Typical times were as shown in the upper table overleaf.

To complete the 1948 picture, 79 weekday trains made their way down the main line from Cannon Street and Charing Cross, 28 of them diverging on to the Bromley North branch, supplemented by 25 from Grove Park. Just eight terminated at Orpington (also served from Victoria) and two at Chelsfield, while Sevenoaks (Tubs Hill) was journey's end for 41. This station, of course, also enjoyed calls by other, faster steam trains proceeding to Tonbridge and beyond, as well as by those on the old LCDR route via Swanley. The Westerham branch had 22 trains each way daily (15 on Sundays), steam-worked by class 'H' 0-4-4Ts with a two-coach push-pull set formerly used on the Sheppey Light Railway.

Space limitations preclude detailed reference to the many timetable changes implemented over the years, commencing in 1951 with cuts due to fuel shortages, reversed in the following year. The general trend has been for a reduction in off-peak services down to two per hour, and to one or two per hour on Sundays, but there have been exceptions. In the Summer 1967 timetable, for instance, the Bexleyheath and Loop line frequencies were increased to four per hour, while extra peak-time trains were run, some turning back at Sidcup where a siding was installed for this purpose. Three years later both lines reverted to three per hour on a par with the North Kent line. Further cuts were made from June 1981, reducing the off-peak service to half-hourly.

Perhaps inevitably the most noticeable changes have taken place on the branches, in particular on the Woodside-Selsdon line, which was the first to lose its Sunday trains, in 1951. Those on Saturday followed suit in 1967, by which time weekday trains were restricted to peak hours until complete closure in 1983.

Both the Bromley North and Addiscombe branches have also lost their Sunday services and their through trains, of which Addiscombe still had three up to October 1993. Shuttle services, currently at half-hourly intervals, operate on these branches from Monday to Saturday. One interesting working that has disappeared was a train in the small hours from Blackfriars to Bromley North, which then returned to Grove Park where it reversed, to continue down the main line to Orpington. On the Westerham branch, off-peak services were pruned from September 1955. The changing trends in off-peak frequencies over the years are summarised in the table below.

TYPICAL JOURNEY TIMES ON THE MID-KENT LINE, 1948

	Miles	Stops	Time (mins)	Average (mph)
Charing Cross-Hayes	14½	10	37	23.5
Charing Cross-Addiscombe	13	10	36	21.6
Charing Cross-Sanderstead	15	14	41	21.9

DESTINATIONS OF DARTFORD LINE TRAINS LEAVING LONDON ON WEEKDAYS BETWEEN 16.30 AND 18.30, 1948

From	To	Via	No
Charing Cross	Gillingham	Woolwich	2
	Gillingham	Sidcup	1
	Gillingham	Bexleyheath	1
	Gravesend	Sidcup	2
	Dartford	Greenwich/Woolwich	3
	Dartford	Blackheath/Woolwich	1
	Dartford	Bexleyheath	3
	Dartford	Sidcup	3
	Slade Green	Bexleyheath	4
	Barnehurst	Bexleyheath	1
	Crayford	Sidcup	1
	Plumstead	Greenwich/Woolwich	1
Cannon Street	Gravesend	Blackheath/Woolwich	2
	Gravesend	Sidcup	2
	Dartford	Greenwich/Woolwich	2
	Dartford	Blackheath/Woolwich	1
	Dartford	Sidcup	2
	Dartford	Bexleyheath	3
	Plumstead	Blackheath/Woolwich	1
	Slade Green	Greenwich/Woolwich	2
	Slade Green	Blackheath/Woolwich	2
	Crayford	Sidcup	1
	Bexley	Sidcup	1
Holborn Viaduct	Dartford	Sidcup	4
	Dartford	Bexleyheath	1
	Barnehurst	Bexleyheath	1
	Dartford	Bexleyheath	1
	Slade Green	Bexleyheath	1
	Barnehurst	Bexleyheath	1
		Total	51

An up Loop line train awaits departure from Lewisham Junction in June 1958 with unit No 4501 - a conversion from ex-LB&SCR steam stock - sporting head-code 'L'. These veterans soon succumbed to the growing numbers of steel-bodied 4EPBs and this example was withdrawn in January 1960. *N. L. Browne*

The total number of daily trains on the Dartford routes has dropped slightly, but those serving the Mid-Kent line have halved, thanks to the closure of the Woodside to Selsdon line and the elimination of through trains from the Addiscombe branch. On the main line fewer trains terminate at Sevenoaks, compensated by more

---

SR South Eastern Division: changing trends in off-peak frequencies, 1948, 1966 and 1993

From Charing Cross and Cannon Street to	Per hour, Summer 1948			Per hour, Summer 1966			Per hour, Summer 1993		
	Week	Sat	Sun	Week	Sat	Sun	Week	Sat	Sun
Dartford (via Greenwich or Blackheath)	3	3	3	3	3	3	2[1]	2[1]	1[1]
via Bexleyheath	3	3	3	3	3	2	2	2	1
via Loop line	3	3	3	3	3	2	2	2	1
Plumstead via Greenwich	-	-	-	-	-	-	2	-	-
Mid-Kent to Hayes	2	2	4[2]	2	2	2	2	2	1
to Addiscombe	1	2	-	-	-	-	-	-	-
to Selsdon or Sanderstead	1	2[3]	-	-	-	-	-	-	-
Elmers End to Addiscombe	-	-	2	2	2	2	2	2	-
Main line to									
Bromley North	-	-	-	2	2	-	-	-	-
Orpington	-	-	-	-	-	-	1[4,5]	1[4,5]	1
Sevenoaks	2	2	2	2	2	2	1[5]	1[5]	-[5]
Grove Park to Bromley North	2	2	2	-	-	2	2	2	-
Dunton Green to Westerham	1	1	1	-	-	-	-	-	-

[1] Plus two semi-fasts per hour to Gillingham
[2] Includes two per hour from London Bridge
[3] Last train at 15.22.
[4] Increased to two per hour in late evening.
[5] Also served by semi-fasts to Hastings/Ashford/Dover

Note From May 1994 the Bexleyheath line service has been supplemented by half-hourly off-peak trains to and from Victoria (via Nunhead).

On 3 June 1961 Class 'H' 0-4-4T No 31177 arrives at Westerham, evidently with enthusiasts among its passengers! Within four months this branch, a delightful survivor of a bygone age, would see its last train, leaving the 3,300 residents dependent on buses and their private cars. *F. Hornby*

semi-fasts calling there, while some 27 now terminate at Orpington as compared with only eight in 1948. There has been a net reduction of around 70 weekday stopping trains out of the London termini; departures to Dartford during the afternoon peak hours 16.30-18.30 are down by two to 49, as compared with 51 in 1948, the reduction being on the Loop line. Strood and Sidcup have joined the list of destinations in place of Crayford and Bexley, while Victoria takes the place of Holborn Viaduct and Blackfriars among the termini. (The peak-hour services between those two stations and the Dartford lines disappeared with the introduction of the 'Thameslinks' in 1988, with the latter making connections at London Bridge.)

Cannon Street's off-peak role has fluctuated somewhat over the years as the following 'trains per hour' figures show:

> 1948: 1 Dartford via North Kent; 1 Dartford via Sidcup; 1 Dartford via Bexleyheath
> 1972: 1 Dartford via North Kent; 2 Bromley North
> 1978: 2 Dartford via North Kent; 1 Dartford via Sidcup (plus 1 semi-fast to Gillingham); 1 Orpington; 1 Hayes
> 1984: 4 London Bridge
> 1993: 2 London Bridge; 2 Plumstead

TRACTION AND TRAINS

Save for the Westerham branch, which was customarily worked by Class 'H' 0-4-4Ts, and for isolated emergencies such as exceptionally severe weather conditions, all suburban traffic during the period under review has been worked by electric multiple unit trains. They have advanced from the SR-built 3SUBs, still in traffic well after nationalisation albeit strengthened by an additional trailer,

through the Bulleid 4SUBs and EPBs to the 'Networkers' of the 1990s. The 4SUBs disappeared from the Dartford lines in July 1960, but the unique pair of double-decker sets, introduced in November 1949, continued to ply to and from Dartford until October 1971. Less common were 2NOLs, which were reported on Holborn Viaduct-Dartford services in the late 1950s, while one paid a visit to the Selsdon line in July 1956, coupled to a four-car unit.

On the longer runs, via Dartford to Gravesend and Gillingham, the pre-war 2HALs yielded to new 2HAPs after 1957, and the latter were also seen on Bexleyheath and Hayes services in the 1960s.

By 1986 Slade Green's allocation consisted entirely of Classes 415 (4EPB) and 416 (2EPB) to the tune of 860 vehicles, but by this time the Gillingham-based 4CAPs, comprised of two pairs of 2HAPs, were participating in semi-fast rosters. Since none of the next generation of Class 508 or 455 units was allocated to the South Eastern Division, the slam-door EPBs have seen well over 30 years in service, although the survivors' days are numbered, thanks to the influx of 'Networkers'.

Until platform lengthening in the 1950s peak-hour trains were limited to eight vehicles, seating 690 in pre-war stock or 772 in post-war one-class centre-gangway coaches. Overcrowding was an occupational hazard until trains were strengthened to 10 coaches by the addition of 2EPBs from 1954 onwards, providing 958 seats per train. The Bexleyheath and Loop lines saw 10-car trains to and from Charing Cross in June 1954 and June 1955 respectively, and the North Kent line a year later. The first trial run to Sevenoaks by a 10-car train was in June 1954, while the Mid-Kent stations were adapted between 1955 and 1957, by which time Cannon Street's platforms were also lengthened. (It was just as well, as the number of passengers leaving there in the evening peak time had increased from 16,500 in 1939 to 23,500 in 1959, rising to 26,300 in 1967!)

In 1993, in preparation for the coming of the 'Networkers', 63 stations had their platforms lengthened once more to accommodate 12-car formations.

A thoroughly modern scene at Lower Sydenham on the Mid-Kent line on 22 June 1993 with 'Networker' units about to leave for Hayes. The station had been recently rebuilt in the 'chalet' style, replacing a typical SECR structure. *F. Hornby*

In spite of advances in technology, both as regards rolling-stock and signalling installations, there has been little scope for significant reductions in journey times, which remain virtually constant on the Dartford routes, varying from 44 to 48 minutes. There is nothing in today's timetable to compare with the 5.10 pm Cannon Street-Gillingham in 1948, which reached Dartford in 29 minutes with one stop only, at London Bridge! There has been a marginal speed-up of 2 minutes on the Charing Cross-Hayes run, and no material change as regards stopping trains to Sevenoaks. On the faster runs a 'Networker' appears to have the legs of a 'Schools' 4-4-0 by 2 minutes, inclusive of an extra stop en route.

DEPOTS

The only depot to which South Eastern Division suburban EMUs are allocated is Slade Green, strategically situated less than 2 miles from Dartford and home to the 'Networker' fleet and to the surviving EPBs. It consists of an eight-road shed - the old steam MPD - for berthing and routine maintenance, an eight-road building with pits, cranes and all the equipment for repairs, and additional berthing sidings on the opposite side of the running lines. Depot facilities have been recently upgraded at a cost of £23 million.

Extensive berthing facilities are also provided on both sides of the main line between Hither Green and Grove Park, with a total capacity of 27 12-car trains. Other stabling sidings are at Dartford, New Beckenham, Plumstead, Orpington, Sevenoaks and, until recently, Addiscombe. Those platforms at Cannon Street that are unused save at peak hours are also utilised for this purpose.

By comparison with the complex lines of SER origin,

FORMER LCDR LINES FROM VICTORIA (EAST), HOLBORN VIADUCT AND BLACKFRIARS

VICTORIA (EAST)-SEVENOAKS VIA HERNE HILL AND SWANLEY
HOLBORN VIADUCT/BLACKFRIARS-HERNE HILL
CATFORD LOOP (BRIXTON-SHORTLANDS VIA NUNHEAD)
NUNHEAD-CRYSTAL PALACE (HIGH LEVEL)
NUNHEAD-LEWISHAM JUNCTION

the former LCDR routes in the London suburban area are relatively straightforward. Their story begins in the late 1850s when the East Kent Railway obtained running powers westwards from Beckenham over the West End of London & Crystal Palace Railway, with temporary accommodation in the new

FORMER LCDR SUBURBAN LINES FROM HOLBORN VIADUCT, BLACKFRIARS AND VICTORIA (EAST) TO SEVENOAKS VIA SWANLEY, THE CATFORD LOOP AND BRANCHES TO CRYSTAL PALACE (HIGH LEVEL) AND LEWISHAM

Miles	Name	Opened	Closed	Notes
	From Holborn Viaduct			
	Holborn Viaduct	3/1874	1/1990	
	City Thameslink	5/1990		
¼	Blackfriars	6/1864		'St Pauls' to 1/1937
	Blackfriars-Metropolitan Junction spur opened 6/1878			
1½	Elephant & Castle	10/1862		
3½	Loughborough Junction	1872		Originally 'Loughborough Road' (Brixton Spur platforms from 1864)
	Loughborough Junction-Brixton spur opened 5/1863			
	Loughborough Junction-Cambria Junction spur opened 1/1872			
	From Victoria (East)			
	Victoria	8/1862		
3¼	Brixton	8/1862		
4	Herne Hill	8/1862		
	Herne Hill-Tulse Hill spur opened 1/1869			
5	West Dulwich	7/1863		
5¾	Sydenham Hill	1864		
7¼	Penge East	7/1863		
7¾	Kent House	1884		
8¾	Beckenham Junction	5/1858		
10	Shortlands	5/1858		Originally 'Bromley'
10¾	Bromley South	11/1858		'Bromley' to 1899
12	Bickley	7/1858		Formerly 'Southbourne Road'
	Bickley-Petts Wood loops opened 9/1902			
14¾	St Mary Cray	12/1860		
17½	Swanley	1862		'Sevenoaks Junction' to 1871; new station from 4/1939
	Lullingstone built 1939 - never used			
20¼	Eynsford	7/1862		
22¼	Shoreham	6/1862		
24	Otford	8/1882		'Junction' 1904-1929
25½	Bat & Ball	6/1862		'Sevenoaks (Bat & Ball)' to 6/1950
	Sevenoaks (Bat & Ball) to Sevenoaks (Tubs Hill) opened 1869			
26¾	Sevenoaks	3/1868		'Sevenoaks (Tubs Hill)' to 6/1950

Victoria station provided by the LB&SCR from October 1860. By August 1862 the company, now styled the London, Chatham & Dover Railway, had its own platforms alongside those of the LB&SCR, and by July 1863 an independent route in from Beckenham Junction via Herne Hill was open to traffic.

A branch from Nunhead to a high-level terminus at Crystal Palace opened in August 1865 and another from Swanley gained access to the SECR's Tubs Hill station at Sevenoaks in 1869. Holborn Viaduct - the 'City' terminus - opened in March 1874, the Thames having been bridged previously to a temporary station in December 1864. Blackfriars ('St Pauls' until 1937), with through and terminal platforms, followed in May 1886. For many years the longer-distance trains conveyed 'City' and 'West End' portions, which joined or divided at Herne Hill.

The Catford loop from Brixton to Shortlands, much used by boat trains as well as by local traffic, was completed in July 1892, with spurs northwards from both directions on to the Herne Hill-Holborn Viaduct line at Loughborough Junction.

The Nunhead-Greenwich Park branch, some 2

Miles	Name	Opened	Closed	Notes
Catford Loop				
	Holborn Viaduct			
4¼	Denmark Hill	12/1865		Destroyed by fire 3/1980 and restored
5	Peckham Rye	12/1865		
6	Nunhead	9/1871		New station 5/1925
	Nunhead-Lewisham Junction spur opened 7/1929 (freight), 9/1935 (passenger)			
7	Crofton Park	7/1892		
8	Catford	7/1892		
8¾	Bellingham	7/1892		
9½	Beckenham Hill	7/1892		
10¼	Ravensbourne	7/1892		
Crystal Palace branch				
	Nunhead	9/1871		
1½	Honor Oak	12/1865		
2¼	Lordship Lane	9/1865	9/1954	
3	Upper Sydenham	8/1884		
3¾	Crystal Palace & Upper Norwood	8/1865		'High Level' station

miles long with three intermediate stations, opened throughout in October 1888. Worked mainly by a shuttle service, it closed in January 1917 but was later partly utilised to form a goods loop from Nunhead to Lewisham Junction, completed by the SR in 1929. It was electrified and used for passenger services from September 1935.

ROUTES AND INFRASTRUCTURE

Victoria (Eastern Section) station, separated only by a wall from its Central Section neighbour, comprises eight platforms, with those for suburban traffic - mainly Nos 3 and 4 - flanked by the main-line ones. A carriage shed for both suburban and main-line stock is situated between the platform ends and Grosvenor Bridge over the Thames. There are four tracks as far as the divergence of the Catford loop at Brixton, where only the two main-line platforms remain, enlivened by life-sized bronze 'passengers'. Herne Hill, just three-quarters of a mile on, is the junction for the 'City' line from Blackfriars, and has up and down island platforms giving cross-platform connections. At the country end a spur curves away to the Central Division station at Tulse Hill.

Holborn Viaduct terminus consisted originally of six platforms, later reduced to five, in front of which a 10-storey office block was erected in 1963. Greatly dependent on business traffic, it is not surprising that there were no Sunday trains and that, from 1964, it closed at 3 pm on Saturdays. The non-electrified tracks 2 and 3 were lifted and the platforms removed early in 1973 and complete closure came in January 1990. Four months later the new through station, St Pauls Thameslink (shortly afterwards re-christened 'City Thameslink') was opened, with two 900-foot platforms, after the tracks had been slewed. It is reached from Blackfriars down a 1 in 29 gradient and through an 1,890-foot tunnel.

Blackfriars station, less than half a mile distant, comprises two through and three terminal platforms. Two of the latter were lengthened in the 1950s to accommodate 10-car trains and are utilised off-peak, together with two nearby sidings, for stabling empty stock. When rebuilding took place - completed in November 1977 - stones from the old structure on which were engraved the names of 54 destinations at home and abroad, were incorporated into the wall of the new concourse, as a reminder of bygone glories! Nowadays the terminal platforms see nothing more exotic than a handful of peak-time semi-fasts to and from Rochester and Ashford. Blackfriars has access to the Circle and District Lines, an amenity not shared by Holborn Viaduct, which was some distance from the nearest Underground station.

It is worth mentioning that, in the short distance between these two main-line stations, there was once a third - Ludgate Hill - opened in 1865 and closed with the advent of electrification in March 1929.

The line southwards from Blackfriars, once across the river, is carried largely on brick arches along the

Left The 'passengers' in this Brixton station scene are in fact life-sized (and lifelike) replicas. The Catford Loop diverges behind the buildings on the left and the South London line crosses at an angle over the girder bridge. *F. Hornby*

Below left Connecting trains wait on either side of the up island platform at Herne Hill on 16 January 1986. A West Croydon-Holborn Viaduct train, led by a 2HAP, is on the right, while that on the left is bound for Victoria. *F. Hornby*

Victoria via Crystal Palace.

The Catford loop rejoins the main line at Shortlands, 10 miles from Victoria, having formed an 8-mile alternative route from Brixton. There are eight stations on the loop, of which the first two, Denmark Hill and Peckham Rye, are shared with the South London line from Victoria to London Bridge. The third station, Nunhead, was a three-way junction until closure of the branch to Crystal Palace (High Level), but still sees passenger and freight trains routed along the spur to Lewisham Junction. The station consists of a 520-foot island platform of 1925 vintage, elevated sufficiently to give a fine northerly panorama.

The Crystal Palace branch, 3¾ miles long, was never as successful

four-track section through Elephant & Castle to Loughborough Junction. The former, close to the busy traffic intersection, has access to the Northern Line and to the southern terminus of the Bakerloo Line. At Loughborough Junction only the island platform on the line south to Herne Hill remains, though there are still traces of those on the connecting spur eastwards on to the Catford loop.

Two tracks continue to the junction at Herne Hill, beyond which the main line skirts the playing fields of Dulwich College, then, at the summit of a 1 in 101 climb, plunges into the 1¼-mile Penge Tunnel between Sydenham Hill and Penge East. There is a short four-track section through Kent House, where the two island platforms are reached by a subway from the original two-storey station building on the up side. Beckenham Junction, where a spur comes in from the Mid-Kent line, has bay platforms facing London on both up and down sides, the former for Central Division trains to and from

as expected. It had the disadvantages of two tunnels and of 1 in 68 grades, which must have been a trial in steam days with three stations averaging only three-quarters of a mile apart. However, the terminus was imposing beneath its high glass roof, with four tracks flanking three island platforms, and with a vaulted subway leading to the Palace grounds.

The Nunhead-Lewisham spur is mostly in cuttings, with no intermediate stations, and diverges from the course of the old Greenwich Park branch to curve round into Lewisham.

Crofton Park, the next station along the Catford Loop, has a small and inconspicuous building on a road bridge, and is followed by Catford, where the prefabricated 'CLASP' platform structures contrast unfavourably with those of its near neighbour at Catford Bridge on the Mid-Kent line. The remaining 2 miles or so to Shortlands are bordered by several open spaces, a pleasant change from the 'inner city' surroundings at the Brixton end of the loop.

Right In March 1957 Holborn Viaduct still had the appearance of a conventional old-style terminus, albeit somewhat cramped. Note the parcels vans on non-electrified track; this traffic continued to be dealt with there until the 1959 Kent Coast electrification. The overall roof was removed in 1967. *F. Hornby*

Middle right Blackfriars terminal platforms are depicted in this photograph taken in March 1971 with 4EPB units occupying all three tracks. The wooden platform extensions (to reduce weight on the river bridge) responded noisily to the pounding of rush-hour feet! The girder bridge on the left has since been removed. *F. Hornby*

Bottom right Were it not for the BR logo above the upstairs window the solid brick-built station building at Kent House could easily pass for a Victorian private residence. The four tracks through the station are on a level with the first floor. *F. Hornby*

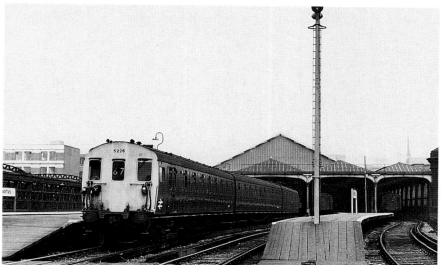

Like the main line, the loop has its saw-tooth ups and downs, but is free from tunnels save for a short one at Denmark Hill.

Beyond the junction at Shortlands the main line was quadrupled to Bickley in the 1890s, extended to Swanley in May 1959. Bromley South, the first station east of Shortlands, is the most important in the area, with two island platforms linked by bridges at either end. It has been twice modernised, in 1959 and 1987, and, with the nearby branch terminus at Bromley North, serves a catchment area with 200,000 residents.

Continuing eastwards, between Bickley and St Mary Cray is the complex of junctions where the former LCDR and SER main lines cross at an angle. There are flying and burrowing junctions between the two, remodelled in 1993, which enable stopping trains from Victoria (East) to terminate at Orpington. At St Mary Cray the SR station buildings of 1936 construction survived the alterations that accompanied the quadrupling of 1958-59 when the erstwhile

Bat & Ball station on the Otford-Sevenoaks section retains its traditional architecture in this 1962 scene looking towards Swanley. The distant sidings, well filled with open wagons at that time, have long since disappeared, made redundant by the dwindling demand for household coal. *B. W. Brooksbank*

staggered platforms were replaced by two parallel 'islands'. The Chatham and Dover main line continues on its eastward course through Swanley, but we, in our suburban survey, part company from it at the junction, a few hundred yards past the 1939-built station.

The double-track branch to Sevenoaks and Maidstone, electrified in 1935, veers south, following the winding course of the River Darenth and passing close to Lullingstone Castle. This is truly 'outer suburban' territory, serving small and select communities in attractive rural surroundings. The Maidstone line parts company at Otford, followed by Bat & Ball, the last of the four intermediate stations, on the northern outskirts of Sevenoaks. The line then makes its curving approach to the main-line station - the erstwhile Tubs Hill. This route to Sevenoaks is over 4 miles longer than that from Charing Cross, and appreciably slower, but has much to recommend it if time is not of paramount importance.

worked three-position semaphores were installed in 1920, only to be replaced by conventional colour-lights in the late 1930s. At Holborn Viaduct, coincidental with electrification in March 1926, the first four-aspect colour-lights in the world, complete with route indicators, controlled the line out to Elephant & Castle. Seven manual boxes were then replaced by new ones at Holborn Viaduct and Blackfriars, but the latter was a wartime casualty, and its successor was completed in January 1946.

The Nunhead to Lewisham Junction spur also had the benefit of four-aspect colour-lights when opened for freight traffic in 1929, but the Catford Loop continued to be semaphore signalled for another 30 years. New boxes were opened at both ends of the loop in 1959, while on the main line a brick-built manual box had been commissioned at Herne Hill in 1956. The remaining semaphore signalling out to Swanley, including automatic upper quadrants installed beyond St Mary Cray in 1934, were replaced by colour-lights in June 1959. Swanley box survived until June 1983, when its functions were absorbed by Clapham Junction panel. Colour-lights appeared between Swanley and Otford in 1971.

Victoria (Eastern) box closed in May 1979 and control was transferred to the Central Division box,

SIGNALLING

Long before nationalisation, in different ways and at different times, the most up-to-date signalling techniques had been applied at the former LCDR termini. At Victoria (East), American-style electrically

A Victoria-Gillingham train of four 2HALs speeds through Beckenham Junction on 30 August 1958 with a splendid array of semaphore signals as a background. The extreme left-hand signal arm controls the bay platform for trains to Victoria via Crystal Palace. *N. L. Browne*

itself made redundant by a panel in Clapham Junction signalling centre from May 1980, overseeing movements from Victoria and Holborn Viaduct. During the next two years this centre extended its sphere of operations as far out as Otford.

SERVICES

In BR's first year the termini at Blackfriars, Holborn Viaduct and Victoria (Eastern Section) dispatched 153 weekday suburban trains to destinations on former LCDR routes - less than half the number operating on the lines of SER origin. Additionally there were 15 departures from the City termini to the Dartford lines via the Nunhead spur, plus 48 from Blackfriars and one from Holborn Viaduct to Wimbledon or West Croydon. These gained Central Section metals via the Herne Hill-Tulse Hill spur and some continued to London Bridge via Norwood Junction.

Although fewer permutations were possible than on the ex-SER network, there was no lack of variety as the accompanying table shows.

Afternoon peak services were also far fewer than those from Charing Cross and Cannon Street - just 29 in the two hours as compared with 77.

Short workings comprised 13 shuttling between Nunhead and Crystal Palace and one each - in the 'unsocial' hours - from Herne Hill to Beckenham Junction and Bromley South to Orpington.

On Sundays there were 103 departures from London, of which Victoria's contribution was 34, all to Orpington. Surprisingly, in view of the deathly hush that descends on the City on the Sabbath, there were 69 departures from Holborn Viaduct, of which 33 traversed the Catford loop en route to Sevenoaks. The same number made their way to West Croydon via Wimbledon, while yet another 33 plied between Nunhead and Crystal Palace; all these services were at half-hourly intervals.

With the majority of trains calling at all or most stations high speeds were out of the question, most services being scheduled at between 21 and 27 mph, save for a Victoria-Bickley run with only two stops, timed at an indecent 36 mph!

During BR's 46 years of stewardship the principal changes resulted from the closure of the Crystal Palace branch in 1954, the population shift from the inner to outer suburbs, the spread of business travel hours and the reintroduction of north-south through services in 1988, with the closure of Holborn Viaduct. The role of the City termini was gradually eroded, as for example in 1963 when the four night trains to Orpington were discontinued, and in June 1964 whereafter Holborn Viaduct was closed between 14.00 on Saturday and midnight on Sunday. (Nevertheless in July 1967 the three arrival platforms there still dealt with 22 trains between 08.00 and 09.00, and 30,000 passengers still used the station daily.)

As of 1966 the weekday tally of down stopping trains on ex-LCDR lines had dropped to 107, inclusive of just three from Blackfriars (all in the afternoon peak), evidence of a thinning out of services besides the loss of those to Crystal Palace. Journey times were unchanged, give or take a minute, though minor improvements had resulted from the quadrupling of the line between Bickley and Swanley in 1959, when the Kent Coast electrification heralded more frequent trains over longer distances.

Much the same level was maintained into the 1970s, with half-hourly off-peak frequencies on the Victoria-Orpington and Holborn Viaduct-Sevenoaks via Catford

---

SUBURBAN TRAIN SERVICES ON FORMER LCDR LINES, 1948

From	To		Total weekday trains	Total trains 16.30-18.30
Victoria	Orpington		42	5
	Sevenoaks (Tubs Hill)		1	-
	Bickley		3	2
	Herne Hill		2	1
		Total	48	8
Blackfriars	Orpington*		3	-
	Sevenoaks (Tubs Hill)*		2	-
	Bickley		1	-
	Crystal Palace		22	6
		Total	28	6
Holborn Viaduct	Orpington*		19	4
	Sevenoaks (Tubs Hill)*		40	6
	Bickley		7	4
	Crystal Palace		3	-
	Swanley		1	1
	Bellingham*		7	-
		Total	77	15
		Grand total	153	29

* via Catford loop

Left A tug noses between the piers of the old bridge at Blackfriars in August 1994 while a Class '319' unit awaits departure on a southbound Thameslink service. The city skyline contrasts Wren's masterpiece with some less elegant modern creations. *F. Hornby*

Below left Bellingham station on the Catford Loop plays host to EMU No 319164 on a Thameslink service to Sevenoaks on 15 July 1992. This is one of the second series comprising 26 units built at York in 1990. *F. Hornby*

remainder through from the Midland Division. The Thameslink service does not operate on Sundays, when Blackfriars is closed.

In the same timetable the Victoria-Orpington service, half hourly off-peak and on Saturdays, aggregated 40 weekday trains; on Sundays an hourly services sufficed, reinforced by the half-hourly semi-fast to Ashford. On this day there were no trains between Otford and Sevenoaks.

During the afternoon peak hours six trains still depart from the terminal platforms at Blackfriars to destinations ranging from Beckenham Junction to Ashford. Prior to the introduction of Thameslink, the Wimbledon-Holborn Viaduct service had been diverted to London Bridge, thus freeing the paths required between Blackfriars and Loughborough Junction for the new through trains.

services. Some economies were made on all sections in 1976 in an attempt to reduce the suburban fleet, and again in 1984/85.

A more drastic reshaping came with the advent of 'Thameslink' in April 1988, with an enhanced flow of trains across Blackfriars Bridge, linking the Midland with the Central and South Eastern Divisions. On former LCDR territory Sevenoaks, Orpington and Bromley South were the beneficiaries at first. Then in 1992 the service was concentrated on Sevenoaks (via Catford and Swanley) at half-hourly intervals, alternate trains taking 51 and 61 minutes to and from Blackfriars, the faster ones omitting nine stops and averaging 32.9 mph. This does in fact entail smart running, as for example between Bromley South and Sevenoaks, 16 miles in 18 minutes with three stops. The 1993/94 timetable listed 36 weekday southbound trains, with seven starting from Blackfriars and the

TRACTION AND TRAINS

Electrification of suburban routes of LCDR origin having been completed by 1935, all services thereafter have been in the capable hands of electric multiple units, though faster steam trains continued to call at Bromley South and Sevenoaks until the third rail was extended to the Kent Coast in 1959. As these were worked by anything from pre-Grouping 4-4-0s to BR Standard 4-6-0s, they brought welcome variety to the otherwise monotonous procession of EMUs. As on the former SER lines these included pre-war SR-built units throughout the 1950s, as well as post-war 4SUBs and 4EPBs, with 2HAPs replacing 2HALs on outer-suburban duties.

Right Class 413/2 4CAP EMU No 3207 wends its way through Loughborough Junction on 22 July 1992 on a peak-hour service bound for Blackfriars. The 4CAPs consist of pairs of erstwhile 2HAPs joined in holy wedlock! Note the TV screens for 'OPO' operation and the bridge carrying the Catford Loop and South London tracks. *F. Hornby*

Below right A 'face-lifted' Class 415/2 4EPB No 5624 pauses at the down Catford Loop platform at Peckham Rye en route to Sevenoaks on 10 February 1988. Though still in blue-grey livery, the cab-front bears a small 'NSE' insignia. *F. Hornby*

The slam-door stock remained predominant until the advent of the Selhurst-based Class 319s on Thameslink services. More recently still, once sufficient units were available, Class 465 and 466 'Networkers' from Slade Green have supplanted the older stock. There is no major depot dedicated exclusively to the ex-'Chatham' suburban routes, but there are stabling facilities at Victoria, Blackfriars, Bellingham and Beckenham Junction; until its closure, units also berthed overnight at Crystal Palace (High Level).

11

SOUTHERN REGION CENTRAL DIVISION

Main lines:
Victoria-Redhill and London Bridge-Windmill Bridge Junction
Secondary lines:
London Bridge-Battersea Park via Peckham Rye;
Balham-Beckenham Junction and Sydenham;
Peckham Rye-Sutton via Streatham; West Croydon-Sutton;
Sutton-Streatham via Wimbledon; West Croydon-Wimbledon;
Sutton-Dorking
Branches:
Sutton-Epsom Downs and Purley-Caterham & Tattenham Corner
Oxted line:
South Croydon-Oxted

The Central Division yields nothing to its South Western and South Eastern neighbours in complexity. It is particularly noteworthy for the profusion of loop lines and spurs over which a variety of 'roundabout' services are operated, out of London and back again after making a circuit through the suburbs.

The way was paved by the opening of the London & Croydon railway, 10¾ miles long from London Bridge to West Croydon, in June 1839, extended southwards from Norwood two years later, while access was gained to a West End terminus at Victoria in 1860. By this time the London Brighton & South Coast Railway had been in existence for 14 years, and within the next decade almost the whole of the suburban network was in place. By the turn of the century the LB&SCR had long been operating intensive local services, for which purpose a fleet of tank engines was stationed at Battersea Park, New Cross Gate and smaller outlying sheds. Growing tramway competition then resulted in a decline in traffic, which was reversed by the AC overhead electrification from 1909 onwards. In all 40 route miles were so equipped, the last section being completed by the Southern Railway in 1925. In addition to multiple units, the stock included 60 motor luggage vans, which ended their days converted by the SR into brake vans for fast freights.

By May 1930 all ex-LB&SCR suburban routes including those previously 'under the catenary' were electrified on the SR third-rail 600V DC system. This was extended from Coulsdon North down the main line to Brighton, completed in 1932. Thus, by nationalisation in 1948, the only steam-operated route was that leaving the main line at South Croydon, via Oxted to Tunbridge Wells, East Grinstead and beyond. With this exception, multiple units reigned supreme in the suburban area, relegating steam traction to local freight traffic.

ROUTES AND INFRASTRUCTURE:
MAIN LINES

The two main lines from London Bridge and Victoria merge at Windmill Bridge Junction, continuing southwards thence through East Croydon and Redhill.

At Victoria local trains use platforms 9 to 12, nearest to the adjacent South Eastern station; Nos 13 and 14 are reserved for the 'Gatwick Expresses', while semi-fasts share Nos 15-19 with the main-line services. In the early 1900s the platforms had been lengthened sufficiently to take two trains each, with centre release roads between the extensions. Eighty

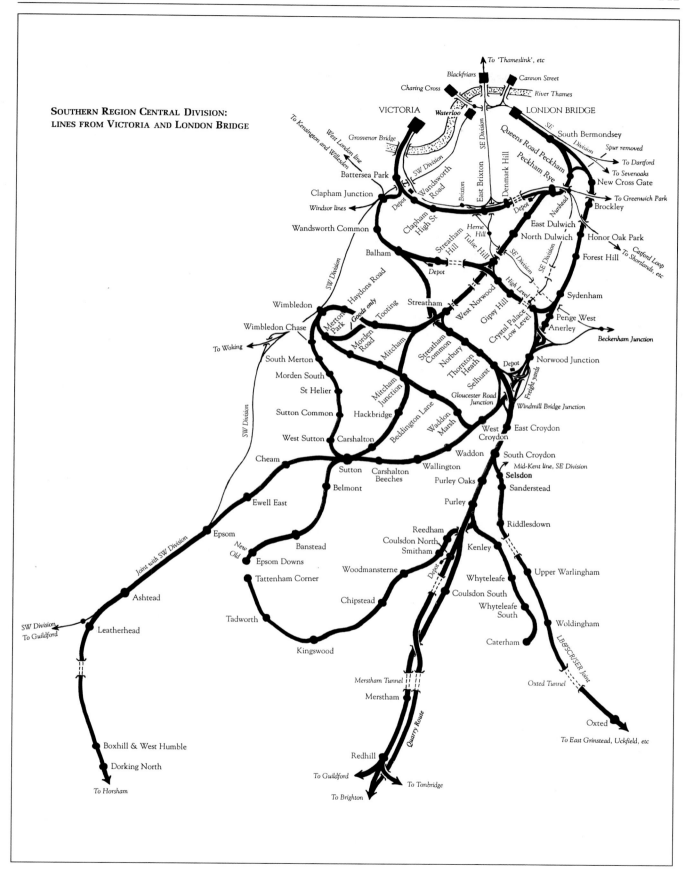

SOUTHERN REGION CENTRAL DIVISION:
LINES FROM VICTORIA AND LONDON BRIDGE

Central Division suburban lines from Victoria and London Bridge

Miles	Name	Opened	Closed	Notes
From Victoria				
	Victoria	10/1860		
1¼	Battersea Park	5/1867		'York Road' to 11/1877
2¾	Clapham Junction	3/1863		
4	Wandsworth Common	12/1856		Terminus to 3/1858; new station opened 11/1869
4¾	Balham	12/1856		'& Upper Tooting' to 10/1969
6½	Streatham Common	12/1862		'Greyhound Lane' to 1870
7½	Norbury	1878		
8¾	Thornton Heath	12/1862		
9½	Selhurst	1865		
10½	East Croydon	7/1841		Rebuilt 1898 and 1992
11¼	South Croydon	1865		
12½	Purley Oaks	11/1899		
13½	Purley	7/1841		'Godstone Road' to 10/1847; closed 1847-56; 'Caterham Junction' 8/1856-10/1888
15	Coulsdon North	12/1899	10/1983	'Stoats Nest' to 1911; 'Coulsdon' to 7/1923
15½	Coulsdon South	1889		
19¼	Merstham	12/1841		
21	Redhill	7/1841		Originally 'Reigate Junction'; on present site from 1844
Balham to Beckenham Junction				
4¾	Balham			
5¾	Streatham Hill	12/1856		'Streatham' to 1868
7	West Norwood	12/1856		'Lower Norwood' to 1/1886
8	Gipsy Hill	12/1856		
8¾	Crystal Palace	6/1854		'Low Level' to 6/1955
	Crystal Palace-Sydenham spur opened 10/1854			
	Crystal Palace-Norwood Junction spur opened 1/1857			
10¼	Birkbeck	3/1930		
11¾	Beckenham Junction	5/1858		LCDR station opened 1/1857
Balham to Dorking				
4¾	Balham			
8¾	Mitcham Junction	10/1868		
10	Hackbridge	10/1868		
10¾	Carshalton	10/1868		
12	Sutton	5/1847		
13	Cheam	5/1847		
14½	Ewell East	5/1847		'Ewell' to 7/1923
16	Epsom	5/1847		New station opened 1929
18	Ashtead	8/1859		
19¾	Leatherhead	2/1859		New station from 1867
23	Boxhill & West Humble	3/1867		'& Burford Bridge' to 1969
23¾	Dorking	3/1867		'Dorking North' to 9/1967
Norwood Junction/Selhurst to Sutton				
	Norwood Junction-Selhurst spur opened 1/1862			
10¼	West Croydon	6/1839		'Croydon Town' to 4/1851; rebuilt 1933/34
11½	Waddon	2/1863		
13	Wallington	5/1847		'Carshalton' to 9/1868; new station opened 9/1883
13¾	Carshalton Beeches	10/1906		'Beeches Halt' to 4/1925
Epsom Downs branch				
12	Sutton			
13¼	Belmont	5/1865		'California' to 1875
14¾	Banstead	5/1865		'& Burgh Heath' 1898-1928
16¼	Epsom Downs	5/1865	2/1989	
16	Epsom Downs	2/1989		New station
From London Bridge				
	London Bridge terminus	1850-54		
2¾	New Cross Gate	6/1839		New Cross to 1/8/1923
3¾	Brockley	1871		
4¾	Honor Oak Park	1886		
5½	Forest Hill	6/1839		Originally 'For Lordship Lane'
6½	Sydenham	6/1839		
7	Penge West	1863		'Penge Bridges' to 1879

Miles	Name	Opened	Closed	Notes
7½	Anerley	6/1839		
8½	Norwood Junction	6/1839		'& South Norwood' to 6/1955
From Holborn Viaduct				
8½	Tooting	10/1868		'Tooting Junction' until new station opened in 1894; line was LBSCR/LSWR Joint
10	Haydons Road	10/1868		
From London Bridge				
1¼	South Bermondsey	8/1866		Present station opened 6/1928; bombed 1940
2¾	Queens Road Peckham	8/1866		Rebuilt 1977
3½	Peckham Rye	8/1866		Rebuilt 1961
4¼	East Dulwich	10/1868		'Champion Hill' to 1888
4¾	North Dulwich	10/1868		
6¼	Tulse Hill	10/1868		
	Tulse Hill-Streatham Hill spur opened 1/1871			
	Tulse Hill-West Norwood spur opened 1/1870			
7¾	Streatham	10/1868		
	Streatham-Streatham Common spur opened	1/1886		
4¼	Denmark Hill	8/1866		Destroyed by fire 3/1980 and restored
5	East Brixton	8/1866	1/1976	'Loughborough Park' then 'Loughborough Park & Brixton' to 1894
6¼	Clapham High St	5/1867		'Clapham' to 5/1989
6¾	Wandsworth Road	5/1867		LCDR platforms closed 4/1916
West Croydon to Wimbledon				
10¼	West Croydon			
1¼	Waddon Marsh	7/1930		'Halt' when opened
2½	Beddington lane	10/1855		'Beddington' to 1887
3	(Mitcham Junction)	10/1868		
3¾	Mitcham	10/1855		
5	Morden Road Halt	1857		'Morden Halt' to 7/1951
5½	Merton Park	1870		'Lower Merton' to 9/1887
6¼	(Wimbledon)			
Sutton to Wimbledon				
	Sutton			
1	West Sutton	1/1930		
1¾	Sutton Common	1/1930		
2¾	St Helier	1/1930		
3	Morden South	1/1930		
3¾	South Merton	7/1929		
4½	Wimbledon Chase	7/1929		
5½	(Wimbledon)			
Caterham branch				
13½	Purley			
14½	Kenley	8/1856		'Coulsdon' to 12/1856
15¾	Whyteleafe	1/1900		
16¼	Whyteleafe South	8/1856		'Warlingham' to 6/1956
18	Caterham	8/1856		
Tattenham Corner branch				
13½	Purley			
14	Reedham	3/1911		'Halt' to 7/1936; closed 1/1917-1/1919
14¾	Smitham	1/1904		Closed 1/1917-1/1919
15½	Woodmansterne	7/1932		
16½	Chipstead	11/1847		Originally '& Banstead Downs'
19	Kingswood	11/1897		Originally '& Burgh Heath'
20¼	Tadworth	7/1900		Originally '& Walton on the Hill'
21½	Tattenham Corner	6/1901		Closed 1914-28
Oxted line				
11¼	South Croydon			
11½	Selsdon	1885	5/1983	'Selsdon Rd' to 9/1935
12¼	Sanderstead	1884		
13½	Riddlesdown	1927		
15¼	Upper Warlingham	1884		
17	Woldingham	1885		Originally 'Marden Park' to 1894
20¼	Oxted	1884		'Oxted & Limpsfield' to 1969

years later they were slightly shortened again when the concourse was widened, and the release roads were removed. Victoria is reputed to be BR's most profitable station and, down below on two levels, the Circle, District and Victoria Lines provide connections to all the other main-line termini.

Once clear of Victoria the up and down local lines are on the east side of the fast pair, and remain so until the positions are reversed by a flyover where the 'Quarry Route' begins near Coulsdon. There is a steep gradient from the platform ends up to the Grosvenor Bridge across the Thames, followed by a steady climb for 17 miles, averaging around 1 in 200 with short interruptions, to a summit at Merstham Tunnel.

South of the river the South London line diverges at Battersea Park station, with its three-storey 'listed' building. Shortly afterwards the main line crosses diagonally over the South Western Division's tracks from Waterloo, descending to run parallel with them

through Clapham Junction. Although the only physical link between the two Divisions (a little-used shunt spur) was removed some years ago, there is a constant interchange of passengers at 'Britain's Busiest Station' with its 17 platforms.

The Central Division tracks bear away through Wandsworth Common and there are three more changes of direction, with as many junctions (near Balham, Streatham Common and Selhurst) in the next 6 miles to East Croydon. Most of the six stations along this stretch retain their solid LB&SCR brick-built structures, with platforms for all four tracks, although those for the fast lines see little use. However, the old station at Balham, dating from 1856, was rebuilt in the 1950s with two new island platforms.

At Windmill Bridge Junction the four tracks from Victoria meet those from London Bridge, while the route to Sutton, accessible from both main lines, branches off in a westerly direction. This junction is complicated thanks to the fact that the local lines from London Bridge, unlike those from Victoria, are outside the fast tracks. The layout was simplified somewhat in a remodelling in 1982/83 when a new local line flyover was constructed between Selhurst and Windmill Bridge. The Central Division's EMU repair and maintenance depot is at Selhurst, and was greatly extended in 1986 in order to care for the 'Thameslink' fleet. It is alongside the Norwood Junction to Selhurst spur, which in the past facilitated direct running between the two London termini but which in recent years has been utilised only for empty stock movements.

Above left The approach to Victoria as seen on 15 July 1992 with a Class 455 EMU on an outward-bound local service climbing the grade to Grosvenor Bridge. The South Eastern Division carriage sheds are behind the train and the empty shell of Battersea Power Station dominates the skyline. *F. Hornby*

Left Reconstruction is in full swing at East Croydon on 24 August 1991 as a 'Space Age' station arises from the remnants of the old. The new platform ramps and the suspension bridge supporting the booking office are taking shape. The Class 455 unit is bound for Charing Cross from Caterham. *F. Hornby*

A panorama of the Norwood Junction/Selhurst complex as seen looking east from a road bridge on 31 March 1957. Gloucester Road Junction signal box is on the left while the tracks at centre and right foreground are from Norwood Junction to East Croydon. The 4SUB with headcode '39' is passing under the main line from Victoria en route from London Bridge to Epsom.
N. L. Browne

East Croydon station has long been one of the most important on the Central Division, the more so since the 1960s boom in office buildings close by. It thus attracts significant traffic in its own right besides much exchange of passengers between local and main-line services. As a measure of its importance, the only trains not currently calling there are the quarter-hourly 'Gatwick Expresses'. It was transformed out of all recognition in 1991/92 apart from retaining its three island platforms, when the old entrance buildings were swept away and replaced by an airy glass structure on a suspension bridge at the south end.

There is a fifth (reversible) road southwards to the junction with the Oxted line at South Croydon, and four tracks thence through Purley. At this station there are two additional platforms on the down side, for the Caterham and Tattenham Corner branches.

Coulsdon North station closed in October 1983, two months after the nearby EMU depot fell into disuse. Beyond here stopping trains for Redhill and Horsham use the original main line which, prior to the 1923 Grouping, was, for historical reasons, owned by the South Eastern & Chatham Railway. Since April 1900 fast trains have used the 6⅞-mile 'Quarry Route', which bypasses the stations between Coulsdon and Earlswood. Both pairs of lines are in tunnels for over a mile, while from South Croydon all the way to Merstham the present railway closely follows the route of the horse-worked Croydon, Merstham & Godstone Railway of 1805.

Redhill, with a single down and an up island platform, is the junction for the ex-SECR lines eastwards to Tonbridge and westwards to Guildford. The former route was electrified during 1994, but on the latter the third rail extends only to Reigate where some outer-suburban services terminate.

Returning to central London, London Bridge terminus, in sharp contrast to Victoria, sees only local traffic outside peak hours, and is sometimes almost deserted at quiet periods. It is less well connected by Underground, being served (since 1900) only by the Northern Line.

Local trains use most of the 10 platforms as required, while others have units stabled off-peak. Nos 7 and 8 are hemmed in between the SE Division platforms and the covered station, in which platforms 9-13 are lengthy while 14-16 can comfortably accommodate eight coaches. Thameslink services for Central Division destinations, and off-peak and weekend Caterham trains starting and terminating at Charing Cross, use the 'South Eastern' through platforms. Prior to alterations in the 1970s there were 15 terminal platforms, but with decreasing traffic five were removed, concurrently with simplification of the approach tracks. These were reduced from six to four, including one signalled for reversible running.

The Peckham Rye line diverges 1½ miles out, then the main line parts company from the SE Division tracks and heads for Norwood Junction, following the route of the old Croydon Canal, with seven intermediate stations. The first of these is New Cross Gate, with a bay platform for London Underground's East London Line; the old locomotive sheds on the up side have long disappeared, as indeed have the stabling sidings that replaced them.

The following six stations have platforms for the local lines only, those at Sydenham being staggered, and few traces of their old buildings remain. There is a climb of 1 in 100 for the first 3 miles from New Cross Gate (where the old canal had ascended by a series of locks), followed by three virtually level miles to Norwood Junction. Connecting spurs from Crystal Palace join the slow lines at a flying junction south of Sydenham, as do others facing southwards near Norwood Junction, close to where the line to Beckenham Junction crosses overhead.

Norwood Junction station has survived relatively unscathed, with seven platforms for six running lines, Nos 6 and 7 being used only by a few early morning services. Southwards from Norwood trains for East Croydon climb up to Windmill Bridge with a good view of Selhurst depot, while those for Sutton burrow beneath the Victoria tracks, meeting a spur from Selhurst at Gloucester Road Junction.

ROUTES AND INFRASTRUCTURE: SECONDARY LINES

We now retrace our steps as far as South Bermondsey Junction, at the approaches to London Bridge, where two tracks curve away through South Bermondsey and Queens Road Peckham to Peckham Rye. The line is elevated on arches and embankments and the first two stations consist of somewhat windswept island platforms, South Bermondsey having been rebuilt in 1974. Peckham Rye is entered after passing beneath the SE Division main line from Victoria, the platforms for the two Divisions being connected by a long subway. The Central Division side was rebuilt in 1961 when the old wooden platforms were replaced by an island.

Thus far the tracks from London Bridge have been shared by several services, but two routes divide just west of the station, for Victoria via the South London loop line, and for Sutton via Tulse Hill. From 1909 to 1969 there were car sheds, built by the LB&SCR, in the angle between the two lines.

The South London line, the innermost of the loops, was opened throughout in May 1867. The distance between the two termini by this route is 8¾ miles with seven intermediate stations - originally eight until East Brixton closed in 1976, having lost traffic to the nearby London Underground Victoria Line. The South London was the pioneer line electrified by the LB&SCR in 1909 and was converted to the third-rail DC system by the SR in 1928. Between Peckham Rye and Wandsworth Road it is parallel to the former LCDR main line, and this section carries a considerable freight traffic, joining or leaving it at Factory Junction. Apart from Peckham Rye, the only interchange station between the two lines is at Denmark Hill, where the building on the overbridge has been restored after a fire in 1980. By contrast Clapham High Street and Wandsworth Road are unstaffed stations with platforms for the South London tracks only; the old building at Clapham High Street is 'listed' and survives in commercial use. The line overlooks Stewarts Lane depot on the final stretch into Battersea Park, where it has its own separate platforms before joining the main line

Above left The South London line platform at Denmark Hill is host to a Victoria-bound 2EPB unit No 5675 on 23 June 1982, while a Class 73 electro-diesel powers a freight on the SE Division down line. *F. Hornby*

Left The low-level station at Crystal Palace is but a pale shadow of its former self, roofless and with only peak-hour trains to break the silence. A 4EPB unit is seen on a London Bridge service on 2 April 1985, since when the bay platform tracks on either side have been removed. *F. Hornby*

into Victoria. As much of the route is on viaducts or embankments, the LB&SCR's title of 'Elevated Electric' was particularly apt.

The second of the loops is between 2 and 3 miles further out, leaving the main line from Victoria by a flat junction at Balham and joining the line into London Bridge at Sydenham. It is 5 miles between the two junctions and was opened throughout in December 1856. Between Balham Junction and Streatham Hill there are sheds and sidings for electric multiple units, and Streatham Hill has a bay platform, also now used for stabling empty stock. At the east end of the station is a 443-yard tunnel before the line from Peckham Rye to Sutton is crossed, with connecting spurs into Tulse Hill from both directions. Beyond Gipsy Hill another tunnel, 756 yards long, penetrates the high ground once crowned by Crystal Palace, the eponymous station being within yards of the tunnel's eastern mouth. Here the line divides, the right fork for Beckenham and Norwood Junctions passing between two through platforms while the left, for Sydenham, enters a once imposing but now dilapidated edifice. Built in 1854 to handle vast crowds visiting the Palace, it once boasted two terminal bays, two through platform roads and two sidings under a high roof. Its usefulness diminished overnight when the Palace was burned down in 1936, and the terminal roads and sidings have been lifted while the roof has long since been dismantled. A few London Bridge to London Bridge 'roundabout' trains call at peak hours, but at other times it is deserted. The old entrance building is no longer in BR ownership, but a small glass replica of part of the Palace was erected in 1980 to accommodate a new booking office.

The Beckenham Junction route bears south before crossing the main line from London Bridge, and was singled through Birkbeck in February 1983. There is a connection on to the South Eastern Division main line at Beckenham Junction, but all trains terminate there in a bay platform. It is possible that the Birkbeck-Beckenham Junction stretch may one day be shared with part of the proposed Croydon 'Tramlink'.

The line south-westwards from Peckham Rye to Sutton was completed in 1868, linking what were then isolated communities, and to

this day still crossing something of a 'no man's land' in the vicinity of Hackbridge. It is used between Peckham Rye and Streatham Junction by trains following the longest of the 'terminus to terminus' services, via Wimbledon, Sutton and Selhurst, and in peak hours by another, to and from London Bridge via Mitcham Junction instead of Selhurst. Three lines are crossed within 3 miles between North Dulwich and Mitcham Junction - needless to say with connecting spurs at all three crossings - while a short length through Mitcham Junction station is shared with the Wimbledon to West Croydon line. Tulse Hill, approached from the north through Knight's Hill Tunnel with its ornate portals, is a focal point for several services, including 'Thameslinks' via the connecting line from Herne Hill, and with three choices of route at the southern end. Thus its platforms are continuously busy, with many passengers changing trains through the subway or by the footbridge added in 1962.

After two more tunnels a flyover junction beyond Streatham station offers three more alternatives - right to Wimbledon, straight on for Sutton, or left to join the main line from Victoria at Streatham Common. As one can well imagine, in pre-colour-light days manual signal boxes were in close proximity hereabouts, operating impressive clusters of semaphores! A large area alongside the line between Streatham and Mitcham Junction was occupied by Eardley carriage yards, with hundreds of vehicles stabled in 26 sidings until they were removed in 1960. Then follow the reverse curves in and out of Mitcham Junction and re-entry into the built-up area around Carshalton, before joining the route from West Croydon close to Sutton station.

Sutton is an important centre where lines converge from five directions, and in recent years has come to

Birkbeck station, between Crystal Palace and Beckenham Junction, is now on a single-line section although the old up platform is still in place. The digital clock registers the 'on time' arrival of the 09.52 from Victoria. *F. Hornby*

resemble Croydon with its skyline punctuated by tower blocks. The station was rebuilt in 1928 in the neat 'Southern Electric' style typical of that period. There are four long platforms, two straight on and two for the Epsom Downs branch, curving away sharply to the south. The first line to reach Sutton was from West Croydon in 1847, originally with one intermediate station but with two more added in later years. West Croydon first opened in 1839 as the terminus of the London & Croydon Railway, but took its present form in 1933/34. Apart from the two through platforms there is a bay facing London and a short one at the opposite end for the shuttle service to Wimbledon. There were still several berthing sidings for EMUs on the site of the old loco shed well into BR years, but these have all been removed.

Wallington is the oldest of the three stations en route to Sutton, but has twice been rebuilt, most recently in 1983 when it was incorporated into a multi-storey office block. Semi-fast trains running non-stop over the 4½ miles between West Croydon and Sutton can attain speeds in excess of 60 mph.

Contrasting in age and in the style of its stations is the Sutton to Wimbledon line, completed by the SR in 1930 with the twofold objective of serving the new LCC St Helier estate while also discouraging threatened incursions into the area by the District or Northern Lines. It branches off the Epsom route a quarter of a mile west of Sutton, descending steeply into a cutting and describing a semi-circle around the outskirts of the town. It is 5½ miles long with six intermediate stations, all consisting of 520-foot island platforms, though the entrances and booking offices vary. West Sutton is convenient for Sutton United football ground and, before recent alterations, resembled a wartime concrete blockhouse! It was, however, kept spotlessly clean by its then custodian, Jim Iddenden, who won awards for helpfulness and courtesy prior to his retirement.

Morden South station overlooks the Northern Line car sheds, but the siding to the Express Dairy depot has disappeared, as indeed have virtually all the yards and sidings in the area, mostly in the 1960s. The line is double-track, with formidable switchback gradients, reverse curves, and 24 bridges along its course. There are still tracts of open ground bordering the line, which never fully fulfilled expectations, but it forms part of the outermost of the 'roundabout' routes, and traffic is brisk enough at peak times when it also sees the occasional Thameslink service. One scarcely imagines that its SR planners could have visualised through trains from Luton! The line approaches Wimbledon on separate tracks alongside the South Western Division main line and shares an island platform at that busy station with the West Croydon shuttle service.

The continuation to Streatham, 3½ miles long, is much older, having been opened jointly by the LB&SCR and LSWR in 1868 with two stations, at Haydons Road and Tooting. The latter lost its junction status when the line from Merton Park was severed, long after passenger services had ceased in 1929.

The West Croydon-Wimbledon line service is, and always has been, self-contained, worked since electrification by two-car units. It was opened in 1885, passing into LB&SCR ownership a year later, and is 6 miles long. It is now single-track save for short lengths at the Wimbledon end and close to Mitcham Junction, but even after nationalisation there were still many sidings, including those servicing a gas works and power station near Waddon Marsh. There was also a large permanent way depot near Mitcham Junction until 1966, hence an independent goods line from West Croydon was fully justified and remained in use until February 1976. Thus a journey along the line was enlivened by glimpses of 'private owner' locomotives as well as those working BR freights.

For most of the way from West Croydon to half a mile beyond Mitcham Junction the trackbed follows that of the Surrey Iron Railway (1803-46), horse-worked and laid to a gauge of 4 ft 2 in. Waddon Marsh, Beddington Lane and Morden are all halts, but Mitcham has a 'listed' station house of some antiquity, now used as offices, while Merton Park's building reflected its importance as the junction for the erstwhile line to Tooting. This remained open for freight until May 1975, although truncated to Merton Abbey since 1968. The crossing loops at Waddon Marsh and Merton Park having been removed, the line is now worked by a single unit.

We return to Sutton to follow, last but not least, the line to Dorking, which was opened as far as Epsom in 1847. Until the early 1950s there were four tracks from Sutton West Junction through Cheam, to allow Portsmouth and Bognor fast trains to overtake the locals, and the centre roads remained in place at Cheam station until 1978.

Epsom, at the junction with the line from Waterloo via Raynes Park, is a prosperous town, which, with its immediate surrounds, has a population close to 70,000. A new station was built in 1929 with two 650-foot island platforms, overlooked by a 60-lever signal box on a gantry. The four tracks are signalled for reversible working and there are stabling sidings for EMUs at the country end. Services beyond Epsom through Leatherhead and on to Dorking are shared with the SW Division trains, passing through tracts of still unspoiled countryside, following the Mole valley for the last few miles. One of the intermediate stations, Boxhill & West Humble, is in an attractive setting at the foot of the North Downs, contrasting in architectural style with Dorking's modern buildings. Although the line continues southwards through Horsham to the Sussex Coast, Dorking is the outer terminus for suburban trains and has three platform roads and berthing sidings.

ROUTES AND INFRASTRUCTURE: BRANCHES

All three branch lines in the Central Division's suburban area climb from relatively low ground on to the slopes of the Downs, and two of them have derived much traffic over the years from race meetings at Epsom. The shortest of the three, from Sutton to Epsom Downs, is 3¾ miles long, having opened in 1865 with two small intermediate stations. The steepest gradient is 1 in 50 and the original terminus was 355 feet above sea level with nine platform roads, six of which were later electrified. Time was when it handled a heavy race traffic, but the 'specials' ceased in 1950, followed by withdrawal of the modest freight traffic in 1969. Until 1972 EMUs stabled overnight at the terminus, but after that year only two platforms remained. The line was singled in October 1982 and Epsom Downs station closed completely in February 1989, replaced by a new one with a single platform and two-storey building, 300 yards closer to Sutton; by this time the other two stations were unstaffed.

Both the other branches leave the main line at Purley, sharing a common exit from the station for the first few yards, whereafter the Caterham branch climbs steadily, in close proximity for some 2 miles with the Oxted line on the other side of the valley. It is 4¼ miles long and opened in 1856, initially with two intermediate stations, joined in 1900 by a third at Whyteleafe. Kenley station building is in an attractive 'Alpine Chalet' style, as was the original one at Caterham until rebuilt in 1899. The terminus is 430 feet above sea level, so freights, which ceased to run in September 1964, and occasional troop specials were faced with a stiff climb on the outward journey. The centenary in 1956 was celebrated with a special train hauled by a Stroudley 'A1X' 'Terrier' 0-6-0T in yellow livery,

with an ex-SECR 'birdcage' set as a reminder that this - and indeed both branches from Purley - was owned by that company before the Grouping.

The Tattenham Corner branch, completed in 1901, had been opened in stages, and the last section beyond Tadworth was closed again from 1914 to 1928. After parting from the Caterham line it passes close to the old Purley engine shed - still intact although the last locomotive dropped its fire there in 1928 - then dives under the main line. It runs parallel with the latter for the first 1¼ miles so that, when Coulsdon North on the main line closed in 1983, passengers were able to use Smitham station on the branch with little inconvenience. From that point there is an almost continuous climb at 1 in 80 or 1 in 100 for 5 miles, and despite a descent thereafter, the terminus is still at an altitude of 490 feet.

The branch is 8 miles long and Tattenham Corner, by virtue of its proximity to the racecourse, resembled its LB&SCR neighbour in being lavishly provided with six platforms and numerous sidings. The layout was reduced to three platforms in 1970, where multiple units stable overnight. The SECR timber building was severely damaged on 1 December 1993 when an early morning arrival failed to stop and ploughed into it.

ROUTES AND INFRASTRUCTURE: OXTED LINE

Jointly owned until the Grouping by the LB&SCR and SECR, the Oxted line branches off the main line at South Croydon and climbs for 6 miles to Woldingham, before descending through a tunnel 1 mile 500 yards long to Oxted. Another engineering feature of note is the high viaduct near Riddlesdown. In earlier BR days, in addition to East Grinstead and Tunbridge Wells West services, there were others to

Most of the grass-grown platforms at Epsom Downs were trackless when recorded on 15 March 1985, with a 4EPB on a service from Victoria. There were few houses in the immediate vicinity of this station, which, in its prime, boasted nine platforms plus carriage sidings. *F. Hornby*

and from the South Coast, all calling at suburban stations, particularly East Croydon. Being steam-hauled until the advent of the diesel-electric multiple units, they enhanced the scene with a wide variety of motive power.

After closures from the late 1950s onward the only surviving routes are to East Grinstead and Uckfield, dividing at Hurst Green, the first station out of Oxted. There was a connection with the Woodside & South Croydon line at Selsdon and the third rail continued thence to Sanderstead. However, Oxted line trains ceased to call at Selsdon from June 1959, and the electric service from the Woodside line was withdrawn in May 1983. Some four years later the line from South Croydon through Oxted to East Grinstead was electrified, most of the stations being suitably renovated. Prior to this Selsdon and Upper Warlingham stations were of SECR and Sanderstead and Woldingham of LB&SCR design, emphasising the old joint ownership of the line.

SIGNALLING

The transition from semaphore to colour-light signalling in the Central Division's suburban area was spread over a period of no less than 60 years, commencing in the late 1920s. Prior to nationalisation the only major modernisation, other than at the two London termini and their approaches, had been southwards from Coulsdon North via the 'Quarry Route'. This was carried out before electrification to Brighton in 1932 and did not affect the older route via Redhill, used by stopping trains. However, a few semaphores were replaced between Streatham Common and Selhurst in 1936, and further out, in the Dorking area, in May 1938.

The first project undertaken by BR covered the main line out of London Bridge, from Bricklayers Arms Junction to Norwood North Junction in October 1950, when three power boxes replaced eight mechanical ones. The other main line, from Battersea Park to Selhurst, followed in 1952, and the junctions between there and East Croydon were dealt with in 1954. A year later the line southwards to Coulsdon North was converted, linking with the 1932 installations, but the old route via Redhill remained semaphore-controlled until 1983 (and the south end of Redhill station well into 1984). Similarly, although some of West Croydon's upper quadrants were replaced in 1954, it was 30 years more before that station was fully converted, when 'A' box on a gantry at the Norwood end was closed and dismantled.

Other landmarks swept away included the impressive gantry of pre-Grouping signals at the north end of East Croydon, the South box at Clapham Junction, perched high enough to overlook adjacent bridges, and, later on, the box spanning the platforms at Battersea Park.

The remaining lines, including the loops, were gradually tackled during the three decades commencing with the 1960s. The Epsom-Leatherhead section received attention in 1964 together with some intermediate signals near Carshalton and others on the Epsom Downs branch, a process continued on the latter in 1969. In that year the Balham to Beckenham Junction line (part of the old 'West End of London & Crystal Palace') and Mitcham Junction to Sutton stretches were dealt with, in addition to Epsom station and the junctions in the Tulse Hill area.

The pace was maintained in the 1970s, commencing with Purley to Tattenham Corner in November 1970, followed by Leatherhead-Dorking (December 1971), and between West Croydon and Sutton (November 1972). By this time the earlier post-war installations were themselves outdated and the 1928-built box at London Bridge gave way in 1974 to the Signalling Centre controlling both Central and South Eastern Division tracks. The first Central Division route incorporated was that through Peckham Rye, followed by the main line towards Norwood Junction in 1975.

Just prior to replacement by colour-lights in July 1950, upper quadrant semaphores stand guard at the south end of Balham station, then undergoing alterations. The line ahead is for Crystal Palace, while the main line curves to the right. Note the old signal box, soon to be made redundant. *A. J. Pike*

The London Bridge scheme was but the harbinger for two others, even more ambitious, designed to reduce the number of signal boxes - and signalmen - to a minimum. The first concentrated the control of both Central and South Eastern Division routes into a new centre at Clapham Junction (originally intended to be at Victoria and sometimes referred to as such), replacing 35 boxes in all. It opened in May 1980 and, when completed, regulated Central Division traffic on the lines to Thornton Heath, Beckenham Junction, Cheam and from Battersea Park to Peckham Rye. In conjunction with this project, the remaining semaphores were eliminated from the Tooting-Wimbledon-Sutton, Cheam-Sutton and Wimbledon-West Croydon sections. On the latter the level crossings were thereafter operated with the aid of closed-circuit television. The box at Epsom Downs was destroyed by fire in November 1981 and the service was restricted to a shuttle from and to Sutton until that branch was also linked to Clapham Junction centre a year later. In October 1982 Sutton box ceased to function and that busy junction also became 'semaphore free'.

The third and final scheme, costed at £45 million, required the construction of a signalling centre at Three Bridges, controlling 280 track miles and making 33 boxes redundant. The first contract was awarded to Westinghouse in 1980 and, when completed some seven years later, the Three Bridges 'empire' extended from Norbury and Anerley, where it linked up with the other two schemes, southwards to Horsham and Brighton. Also included were the Oxted line and the branches to Caterham and Tattenham Corner. The Caterham branch succumbed to colour-lights in March 1981 and Tattenham Corner's 'massive' 'A' box of 1925 closed in September 1983. (Its predecessor, incredibly, had 205 levers - a reminder of the facilities needed to handle the intensive traffic on race days). The situation at West Croydon had the makings of a 'frontier dispute' between the two signalling centres, apparently settled amicably as Clapham Junction controls the platform 2 line, leaving Three Bridges responsible for the rest of the station!

Among the many signal boxes to disappear was Gloucester Road, high on an embankment - the first of the distinctive Southern Railway 1933-designed structures to be demolished. This was in conjunction with the track alterations and resignalling at the Selhurst junctions.

Following the conversion of the Coulsdon-Redhill line the last outpost of semaphore signalling was on the Oxted line, on which colour-lights were installed in readiness for electrification in 1987. A box remains at Oxted to control the junction of the East Grinstead and Uckfield branches at Hurst Green.

SERVICES

As previously mentioned, Central Division services have always made full use of the complexity of routes available, interchanging at a number of places with the neighbouring South Western and South Eastern Divisions.

In 1948 the weekday morning peak from 06.00 to 09.00 saw 88 suburban and semi-fast arrivals on the 'Central' side at London Bridge and 69 at Victoria. During the busiest period, between 08.00 and 09.00, on average trains entered London Bridge every 95 seconds and Victoria every 2 minutes. In round figures they conveyed 30,000 and 24,000 passengers to the two termini during this hour, by the services shown in the accompanying table. Additionally, at that hour, three trains from the Sutton-Wimbledon line terminated at Holborn Viaduct and one at Blackfriars.

Once the peak hours were over, local services settled down generally to a 30-minute frequency. The Tattenham Corner/Caterham trains ran to and from Charing Cross, while a shuttle service operated between Beckenham Junction and Crystal Palace. There were also a few shuttles between Oxted and East Croydon, powered by superannuated tank engines.

At the end of the 1948 summer timetable some off-peak services were improved - between London Bridge and Streatham Hill, and with through trains between Victoria and Beckenham Junction via Crystal Palace - while the Holborn Viaduct to Wallington via Wimbledon trains were extended to West Croydon. The Streatham Hill service did not prosper, however, and was withdrawn again, off peak, by 1952. Some lightly patronised late evening services disappeared in January 1951 as part of a fuel economy drive, though a few were reinstated in the spring. Another 1950s development saw platforms lengthened on the main and branch lines at Purley, and at stations southwards to Redhill to take 12-coach trains, in response to growing outer-suburban traffic. It was during that period that passenger journeys throughout the Southern Region reached an all-time high.

In 1956 Holborn Viaduct-Wimbledon-Victoria trains were rerouted to London Bridge. In that year departures in the busiest afternoon peak hour numbered 41 from London Bridge and 30 from Victoria, each inclusive of two Oxted line steam trains.

Moving into the 1960s, DEMUs began to take over services through Oxted in March 1962 and, once the transformation was complete, the running time between that station and Victoria was reduced by 9 minutes. On a number of lines there was a gradual erosion of weekend services; on the Wimbledon-West Croydon line Sunday trains ceased running in the summer of 1965, with late evening weekday trains withdrawn two years later. In the 1967 summer timetable stopping trains on Sundays between London Bridge and Brighton were diverted via Tulse Hill and Norwood Junction to compensate for reduced local services. Similarly a 'roundabout' service in and out of London Bridge was re-routed via Crystal Palace so that other trains serving that station could be withdrawn.

The Epsom Downs branch lost its Sunday trains as from 5 May 1969, and on the same date Saturday midday peak extras were withdrawn from all routes. A more or less standard frequency of three trains hourly in the peaks and two per hour at slack times and weekends was maintained on most lines throughout the 1960s. The Holborn Viaduct-Wimbledon-West Croydon service was extended thence via the main line to Victoria, with a 95-minute timing for a round trip of 31 miles with 32 stops. Surely this is a record for an inner-suburban service, rivalled only perhaps by London Underground's Central Line?

The 1970s saw further changes, taking on board the growing importance of Croydon and the steady expansion of the outer suburbs. There was more pruning of slack-hour trains, starting in 1970 when the Victoria to Coulsdon North service was cut back to East Croydon. To minimise inconvenience through trains replaced some shuttles from Purley on the Tattenham Corner branch on which Smitham station is only a few yards from Coulsdon North. October 1971 saw 31 trains 'axed', and more cuts came in 1976, partly as the result of staff shortages. Once again Beckenham Junction lost its trains to Victoria via Crystal Palace, the more direct ex-LCDR route being available for through passengers.

On the brighter side, a threat to close the Wimbledon-West Croydon line was lifted in 1974, but peak-hour services on it were reduced. At the end of the decade the extensive alterations at Victoria caused some services to be cut back to Clapham Junction; this situation continued intermittently into 1981, for which purpose the third rail was laid for a short distance along West London tracks to facilitate

---

EARLY MORNING SUBURBAN SERVICES TERMINATING AT LONDON BRIDGE AND VICTORIA, 1948

Terminating at	From	Via
London Bridge	Crystal Palace	Sydenham
	Effingham Junction	Sutton
	London Bridge	Tulse Hill/Crystal Palace
	London Bridge	Streatham/Norwood Junction
	Streatham Hill	Tulse Hill
	Sutton	West Croydon/Forest Hill
	Tattenham Corner/ Caterham	Main line (combining at Purley)
	Victoria	Streatham Hill/Tulse Hill
	Victoria	South London line
Victoria	Beckenham Junction	Crystal Palace
	Epsom	Mitcham Junction
	London Bridge	Tulse Hill/Streatham Hill
	London Bridge	South London line
	Selhurst	Main line
	West Croydon	Crystal Palace
London Bridge and Victoria	Coulsdon North	Main lines
	Epsom Downs	West Croydon
	Brighton (semi fast)	Main lines
	Horsham	Mitcham Junction
	Horsham	Three Bridges/main lines
	Oxted	Main lines

---

reversals. While this work continued Oxted line services were concentrated on London Bridge, reverting to Victoria in 1984.

From 17 May 1982 peak-hour 'circulars' from and back to London Bridge via the Norwood Junction-Selhurst spur were withdrawn. In the Summer 1984 timetable South London line services were restricted to peak hours only and remained so for the next seven years, while off-peak services on the Tattenham Corner branch once again became 'shuttles' from Purley. As a somewhat retrograde step, the well-established off-peak 'regular interval' pattern was abandoned in the Winter 1984/85 timetable, and a further 20 trains were withdrawn, prompted by diminishing receipts. (As an example 20 per cent fewer passengers were using London Bridge in 1983 as compared with 1967.) Fortunately, regular intervals were reintroduced after two years.

One 'roundabout' service that continued to be subject to change was that using the Wimbledon-Sutton line, which was successively routed between Holborn Viaduct and Victoria, from and back to London Bridge, Holborn Viaduct and London Bridge (from the summer of 1984) and, finally, Victoria and London Bridge. The last change was prompted by the advent of 'Thameslink' in 1988, which led to the subsequent closure of Holborn Viaduct. Thus the diversion of the service between East Croydon and London Bridge via Tulse Hill into Holborn Viaduct in the Summer 1988 season was short-lived. Another innovation came when through trains between Tattenham Corner and Charing Cross were re-routed into Victoria.

After a 'Gala Weekend' on 26/27 September 1987, electric traction replaced diesel on the East Grinstead line through Oxted on 5 October. Trains ran at half-hourly intervals between East Grinstead and East Croydon, continuing alternately to London Bridge and Victoria. On the diesel-worked Uckfield branch peak-hour trains ran through to and from both London termini, with hourly connections at Oxted for the rest of the day. Subsequently off-peak East Grinstead services were concentrated on Victoria with a 36-minute journey time between Oxted and London - 6 minutes less than with diesel traction.

Thameslink trains commenced operating between the Midland and Central Divisions on 16 May 1988. Those for Brighton main line destinations use the Blackfriars-Metropolitan Junction spur, running non-stop between London Bridge and East Croydon, save for a few at peak times routed via Tulse Hill and Selhurst. Other Thameslink trains calling at Tulse Hill are those on the 'roundabout' route via Sutton and Wimbledon. From May 1990 a weekdays service was introduced of 14 trains from Luton to Guildford plus five to Sutton with a corresponding number northbound, but this has subsequently been replaced by a half-hourly service between Luton and West Croydon. Precisely 2 hours were allowed between Luton and Guildford (58½ miles) with 26 stops.

By the close of the Network SouthEast era there was a marked reduction in peak-time suburban services as compared with early BR years, partially offset by more semi-fasts including the Thameslinks. The 1993/94 timetable listed 19 arrivals at Victoria and 23 at London Bridge between 08.00 and 09.00, including two and four respectively from the Oxted line.

Although journey times have fluctuated, partly due to variations in routes and intermediate stops, there has been little change in the average speeds of suburban trains, the majority falling within the limits of 22-26 mph; in some cases the 1990s timings are even marginally slower than those of 1948. There has, however, been some improvement as regards outer-suburban services where modern traction can show its paces. The Oxted line has already been mentioned in this respect, while, as another example, semi-fasts from Redhill reach Victoria in 9 minutes less than in BR's first year.

TRACTION AND TRAINS

In spite of the steady influx of Bulleid 4SUBs in the early BR years, joined by 4EPBs from 1951, the pre-war units of Southern Railway design continued to play their part on the Central Section well through the 1950s. Indeed, some of the three-car sets of converted LB&SCR vehicles were strengthened by an additional trailer of the same parentage. (The knowledgeable could identify ex-'Brighton' stock by the long vertical grab-rails.)

The older units were displaced from the Caterham and Tattenham Corner services by 1945-built '4101' Class 4SUBs in March 1949, but elsewhere they clung on tenaciously - for instance, when some Brighton semi-fasts were routed via Crystal Palace in the late 1960s they were still worked by '4LAVs of 1931-32 construction. They also appeared on Coulsdon North services at that time.

Two other lines on which older stock lingered were the South London loop and Wimbledon-West Croydon, worked by the two-car sets designated 2SL and 2WIM, both displaying headcode '2' and dating from 1929. The side-gangway vehicles enabled tickets to be issued en route, but their 9 ft 6 in width restricted their spheres of operation to the lines for which

Two generations of two-car units meet at Mitcham Junction in about 1955, on Wimbledon-West Croydon line services. On the right 2NOL No 1837, a 1934 design converted from LSWR steam stock, is eastbound, and 2EPB No 5777 is westbound for Wimbledon. *Lens of Sutton*

they were designed, save for access to Selhurst depot via Streatham. Their replacements from September 1954 were the new 2EPBs, though both 2NOL and 2HAL outer suburban units were noted in the ensuing years. The 2NOLs also showed up on other lines including the Epsom Downs branch, until their expiry in 1959.

During the 1960s and 1970s the lion's share of duties was in the hands of 4SUBs, and EPBs in four- and two-car versions; a 4EPB disgraced itself in March 1974 by running unmanned from Caterham for 9 miles to Norwood Junction, where it was diverted into the yard! Some variety was provided by former South Tyneside Eastleigh-built 2EPBs, which came south in January 1963, while at the end of that decade outer-suburban 2HAPs - a 1957 design - were at work on several local services; they continued to be so employed into the 1980s. The all-2nd Class conversions designated 2SAP (Class 418) were seen on

the South London line in 1969, and the two branches from Purley were also stamping-grounds for two-car units. For many years the 2EPBs performed, either as shuttles from Purley, or in combination with 4EPBs on the run to London.

Although the experimental 4PEP unit No 4001 ventured on to the Central Section on training runs in July 1972, the first sliding-door stock in regular service were Class 455s, from early 1985. By this time the 4SUBs had been withdrawn (as from September 1983), but the EPBs were not to be easily ousted, particularly as 51 of sub-class 415/4, refurbished from 1979-86, were at Selhurst depot in the late 1980s. The extent of EPB activity on the Division can be gauged by Selhurst's allocation in March 1986, which still embraced 446 vehicles in two- or four-car formations. The last official run by a 4EPB was on 14 May 1993, though a few two-car units remained in reserve.

Next on the scene, as the result of the opening of the north-south line through St Pauls and Blackfriars, were the dual-voltage Thameslink Class 319 units, all 81 being allocated to Selhurst. Those not required for the through runs to and from the Midland Division do valuable work on internal Central Division rosters, their high speed being an asset on the longer journeys. At the other end of the scale, they did a short tour of duty on the South London line.

The latest - and last - EMU class to make its debut on the Division is Class 456, all 24 being employed not only on the services traditionally worked by two-car units, but also on general duties, solo or paired with Class 455s. Thus, inclusive of Thameslinks,

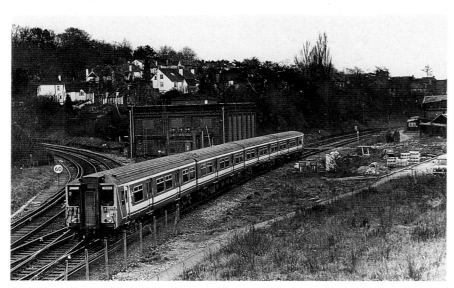

Above left A Class 455/8 unit forming a Tattenham Junction to Victoria service crosses the junction with the Caterham branch at Purley on 25 January 1989. A sub-station is in the angle of the junction and the old SECR steam shed, still intact, can just be seen on the far right. *F. Hornby*

Left A pair of Class 423 4VEPs arrive at Oxted from East Grinstead on 27 September 1987 during the inaugural weekend of the Oxted line electrification. All stations were newly painted and 'en fete' - some of them, including Oxted, rebuilt - marking the end of a quarter-century of diesel traction. *F. Hornby*

the suburban EMU strength at the close of our period in early 1994 consisted of 142 units of Classes 319, 455 and 456, plus a handful of superannuated 2EPBs. In addition, the Oxted line services, together with main-line semi-fasts, involved Classes 423 (4VEP) and 421 (4CIG), nominally allocated to Brighton but stabled at Stewarts Lane or Streatham Hill.

It would be space-consuming to catalogue in detail the wide variety of steam classes that saw service on the Oxted line until ousted by diesel traction. Suffice to say that it ranged from small tank engines at one end of the scale to Bulleid 'Pacifics' at the other, the 'West Countries' being regular performers on the heavily loaded 17.10 from Victoria, calling only at East Croydon north of Oxted. In the early BR years the trains that started or terminated at East Croydon were the preserve of various classes including 'M7' or 'H' 0-4-4Ts, and 'E4X' or 'E5' 0-6-2Ts (even a veteran 'D1' 0-4-2T in June 1948). Another class of small tanks that occasionally worked through in and out of Victoria was the Ivatt-designed Class '2' 2-6-2T. At one time or another, once the ex-LB&SCR 'I3' 4-4-2Ts and 'J' 4-6-2Ts based at Tunbridge Wells West had made their way to the scrapyards, various types of 4-4-0, Classes 'Q' and 'Q1' 0-6-0s and most Maunsell 2-6-0 Classes were recorded at one time or another. A degree of standardisation resulted from an influx of 2-6-4Ts of LMS and BR designs, but other classes obstinately continued to appear, up to BR '4' 4-6-0s.

Dieselisation brought a mixture of diesel-electric units to the line;

in 1962 Eastleigh turned out 19 three-car '3D' Class 207s specifically for this purpose, reinforcing the 1957-built '3H' Class 205s. Occasionally, around 1980, '3R' units (dubbed 'Tadpoles' as the vehicle at one end was thinner than that at the other) strayed on to the Oxted line from their normal Reading-Redhill haunts.

The first diesel locomotive seen on the line was the 'one-off' No 10800, on trial in the early 1950s, but years later the much superior Class '33' Bo-Bo diesel-electrics were regular performers, either with hauled stock or with a 'push-pull' combination of ex-SUB and BIL vehicles. The last loco-hauled trains ran on 8 May 1986, at which time Tunbridge Wells West ceased to be a stabling point, and the DEMUs were transferred to New Cross. Although the East Grinstead line was converted to electric traction, the Uckfield branch has remained loyal to diesel units, with through workings to and from London at peak hours.

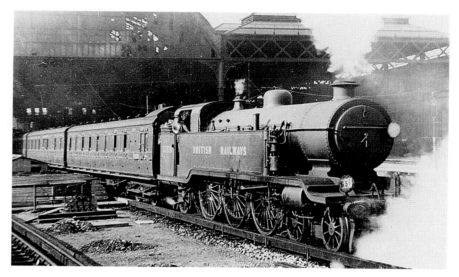

Above right A vintage scene at London Bridge on 30 September 1948 with ex-LB&SCR 'J1' 4-6-2T No 32326 heading an ex-SECR 'birdcage set' on an Oxted line semi-fast. No 32326 was built at Brighton in 1912 and named *Bessborough.* Unlike its sister engine No 32325, it was equipped with Walschaert's valve gear, and notched up nearly a million miles before withdrawal in June 1951. *B. W. Brooksbank*

Right On 25 February 1967 DEMU No 1317 of Class '3D' (later reclassified 207) pauses at Clapham Junction's down main line platform while forming the rear portion of an Oxted line train. The diesel units did yeoman service between the phasing out of steam around 1960 and electrification 27 years later. *F. Hornby*

12

SOUTHERN REGION
SOUTH WESTERN DIVISION

We conclude our clockwise tour of London's suburban railways with a close look at the South Western Division lines, which, following the example traditionally set by the timetables, are divided into two sections covering, respectively, the main line and branches and the Windsor lines.

They share a common terminus at Waterloo, with the two groups of suburban platforms on opposite sides of the station, separated by those for long-distance traffic. Their tracks keep company as far as Clapham Junction and, further out, the two sections meet at Teddington, Weybridge and Ash Vale, facilitating through services. (Another link is by the loop from Point Pleasant Junction to Wimbledon, no longer used save for empty stock movements, and shared from East Putney with District Line trains.)

Few would quarrel with the contention that the areas encompassed by these routes are among the most attractive around the Capital, enjoying as they do a profusion of parks, golf courses, race courses, stately homes and even Royal residences. Even close to Waterloo there are glimpses of the palaces of Westminster and Lambeth! Seen from the train windows, the high-rise flats of Battersea give way in turn to late-Victorian terraced houses, between-the-wars 'semis' in the suburbs, and elegant homes in the 'Stockbroker Belt'. As a glance at the map shows, the River Thames is ever prominent, and the London & South Western Railway was, from its earliest years, keenly aware of the potential of the flourishing towns along its banks.

First to open was the London & Southampton's main line from the old Nine Elms terminus out to Woking in May 1838, followed by Clapham Junction to Richmond in July 1846. The Nine Elms terminus was abandoned for passenger traffic in July 1848 in favour of a new one at Waterloo, which was destined to be enlarged piecemeal over many years. Hampton Court, Epsom, Windsor and the Hounslow loop had been added to the railway map by 1850, and Reading was reached by a westward extension from Staines - sharing SER tracks from Wokingham - in July 1856. Kingston, hitherto neglected, saw its first trains by the

indirect route via Twickenham in July 1863, with completion of the loop to New Malden six years later. In the meanwhile, doubtless with local rejoicing, the Shepperton branch opened in November 1864. (The junction south of Strawberry Hill became a triangle with the addition of a spur from the Teddington direction, first regularly used in 1901.)

One can visualise the trains of those early days, with a rake of four-wheelers behind a red-painted Beattie well tank, gradually giving way to the more powerful creations of Adams and Drummond. By then the LSWR had seen its territory invaded by the District Railway, first at Richmond in 1877, then at Wimbledon in 1889, and in due course at Hounslow in 1905. Meanwhile the railway monopoly was rudely broken by the coming of the London United Tramways around the turn of the century, prompting the LSWR to follow the LB&SCR's example by turning to electrification. The first route chosen was that from Waterloo to Wimbledon via East Putney in 1915, soon followed by others on both the main and Windsor lines, in spite of problems caused by the First World War.

After the Grouping the SR continued the process during the 1920s - to Guildford via Cobham, Raynes Park to Dorking North, and Leatherhead to Effingham Junction in 1925 - with an increase in traffic that, in a few cases, was tenfold! The remaining outer suburban routes were dealt with in the 1930s, taking the third rail to Windsor and Reading, to Alton and Aldershot, and from Virginia Water to Weybridge. Most ambitious yet was the electrification of the Portsmouth main line, passing beyond our boundaries at Guildford, while a brand new branch was opened from Motspur Park to Chessington South in 1939.

Thus, after nationalisation, the electrical engineers could turn their attention elsewhere, returning to the South Western Section for the major extension from Brookwood to Bournemouth, far beyond the suburban area, which dealt the death knell to Southern Region steam traction in 1967.

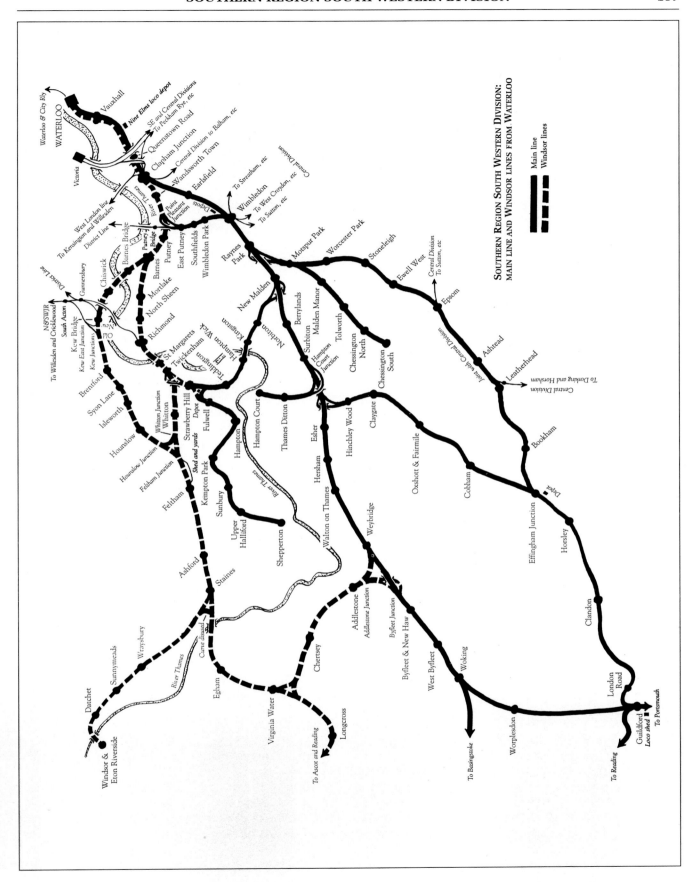

SOUTHERN REGION SOUTH WESTERN DIVISION: MAIN LINE AND WINDSOR LINES FROM WATERLOO

Main line
Windsor lines

MAIN LINE FROM WATERLOO AND BRANCHES

WATERLOO-GUILDFORD VIA WOKING
RAYNES PARK-DORKING VIA EPSOM AND LEATHERHEAD
LEATHERHEAD-EFFINGHAM JUNCTION
MOTSPUR PARK-CHESSINGTON SOUTH
NEW MALDEN-SHEPPERTON VIA KINGSTON
HAMPTON COURT JUNCTION-HAMPTON COURT
HAMPTON COURT JUNCTION-GUILDFORD VIA EFFINGHAM JUNCTION

ROUTES AND INFRASTRUCTURE

Waterloo ranks high in the London terminus league table, first in size and second only to Liverpool Street in the number of passengers using it daily. When the new station arose Phoenix-like from the rubble of the old, the first platforms to be completed were three 'islands' on the south side, averaging 700 feet long, with faces Nos 1-6 for suburban trains serving the main line and branches. Their functions remain unchanged today, over 80 years later, with Nos 1-4 reserved exclusively for the inner suburbans. Stairs from the platforms descend to a subway leading to the Bakerloo and Northern Line tubes and to the Waterloo & City Railway. Uniquely, from 1934 a small news cinema occupied a site close to platform 1, but was closed some time after a raised structure for train crew accommodation was erected across the platform barriers in 1967.

Just outside the station a small group of sidings is provided for off-duty EMUs, near the location of the long-defunct Necropolis station from which, years ago, funeral trains ran to Brookwood Cemetery. Once clear of the platforms the up and down local lines are paired as far out as the flyover, built in 1936, on the London side of Wimbledon. This rearranges the four running lines as shown in the diagram, with the local lines on either side of the fast roads.

The Waterloo & City line stock is notoriously camera-shy and appears above ground only on rare excursions to Eastleigh Works for overhaul. As an exception, new Class 487 motor-coach No 57 shows itself at Waterloo on 'Network Day', 1 October 1988. *F. Hornby*

Until the flyover was built, the local lines had flanked the fast tracks all the way to Waterloo, where conflicting movements were unavoidable. In addition, westwards from Wimbledon the present arrangement renders redundant the centre platforms at New Malden and at some stations beyond Surbiton.

Vauxhall, the first station out of Waterloo, is elevated on brick arches, with platforms for all eight main and Windsor lines. A subway, in which there is a refreshment room, connects them with the Victoria Line underground station. At Clapham Junction, 4 miles out, the main and Windsor lines veer away from

SOUTH WESTERN DIVISION 'MAIN LINE' SUBURBAN ROUTES FROM WATERLOO AND BRANCHES

Miles	Name	Opened	Closed	Notes
From Waterloo: main line via Woking				
	Waterloo	7/1848		
	Waterloo-Bank tube	8/1898		'Waterloo & City Railway'
1¼	Vauxhall	7/1848		
4	Clapham Junction	3/1863		
5½	Earlsfield	4/1884		'for Summerstown' to 1902
	Wimbledon Railway Staff Halt	1956		
7¼	Wimbledon	5/1838		
8¾	Raynes Park	10/1871		Burrowing junction opened 3/1884
9¾	New Malden	5/1838		'Malden for Coombe' to 1955; 'New' from 9/1957
11	Berrylands	10/1933		
12	Surbiton	5/1838		Originally 'Kingston'
14½	Esher	5/1838		Originally 'Ditton Marsh' then 'for Sandown Park'
16	Hersham	9/1936		
17	Walton-on-Thames	5/1838		
19	Weybridge	5/1838		
20½	Byfleet & New Haw	1927		'West Weybridge' to 6/1961
21¾	West Byfleet	1887		'Byfleet' to 6/1950
24½	Woking	5/1838		Rebuilt 1937/38
26¾	Worplesdon	5/1845		
30¼	Guildford	5/1845		
From Waterloo via Epsom				
8¾	Raynes Park			
9¾	Motspur Park	7/1925		
10¾	Worcester Park	4/1859		'Old Malden' to 2/1862; rebuilt 1937
12	Stoneleigh	7/1932		
13	Ewell West	4/1859		'Ewell' to 7/1923
14¼	Epsom	4/1859	LSWR/LB&SCR joint	New station opened 3/1929
16¼	Ashtead	8/1859	LSWR/LB&SCR joint	
18	Leatherhead	2/1859	LSWR/LB&SCR joint	New station from 1867; ex-LSWR station closed 7/1927
20½	Bookham	2/1885		
	To Effingham Junction			
'New Line' via Effingham Junction				
14	Hinchley Wood	10/1930		
15¼	Claygate	2/1885		
17	Oxshot	2/1885		Formerly '& Fairmile'
19	Cobham & Stoke D'Abernon	2/1885		Formerly 'Cobham'
21¼	Effingham Junction	2/1885		
22¼	Horsley	2/1885		
25½	Clandon	2/1885		
28¾	London Road	2/1885		
	To Guildford			
Chessington South branch				
9¾	Motspur Park			
11	Malden Manor	5/1938		
12	Tolworth	5/1938		
13¼	Chessington North	5/1939		
14	Chessington South	5/1939		
To Strawberry Hill and Shepperton branch				
9¾	New Malden			
11¼	Norbiton	1/1869		
12	Kingston	7/1863		Resited 1869; rebuild 1934-5
12½	Hampton Wick	7/1863		
13¾	Teddington	7/1863		
14¾	Fulwell	11/1864		
16½	Hampton	11/1864		
18¼	Kempton Park	7/1878		Race days only
18¾	Sunbury	11/1864		
19¼	Upper Halliford	5/1944		Originally 'Halt'
20¼	Shepperton	11/1864		
Hampton Court branch				
14	Thames Ditton	11/1851		
15	Hampton Court	2/1849		

each other, with carriage sheds and sidings fanning out between them. A start was made at laying third rails along the sidings in 1967 and numerous units

stable here. On the main line side there are five platform faces, including a sharply curved one for an up loop line, used by some semi-fast trains.

Beyond Clapham Junction the line emerges from a cutting, and is thereafter on embankments, with some intervals, for much of the way to Woking. There are no gradients of any consequence before Byfleet, 20 miles out, where a long gradual climb commences.

There is a large EMU depot between Earlsfield and Wimbledon in two distinct parts. An extension - Wimbledon East - was completed in 1974 on land previously occupied by Durnsford Road power station, which had generated current for the railway from 1916 until closure in May 1958. The two carriage sheds and numerous sidings are home to over 160 units and now rejoice in the name of 'Wimbledon Traincare Depot', with a creche for children among its amenities! Close by is the tiny Railway Staff Halt, opened alongside the up fast line in 1956 and not, of course, shown in the public timetable.

Top left Vauxhall, looking towards Waterloo on 12 August 1957, with pre-war 4SUB unit No 4316 outward-bound. This was one of 26 three-car sets built in 1925 for the Western Section, then numbered 1285-1310, which were renumbered when an extra trailer was added in 1945. *N. L. Browne*

Middle left Durnsford Road power station, near Wimbledon, was built to supply power for the LSWR electrification in 1915, and demolished in 1965 to make way for extensions to the carriage sheds. Just visible at the top of the ramp is the tiny Bo-Bo electric locomotive No 74s which was stationed there to shunt coal wagons. Earlsfield station is in the far distance on the right. *F. Hornby*

Left The South Western Division can boast the biggest and smallest stations south of the Thames, in Waterloo and Wimbledon depot's 'Railway Staff Halt', seen here on 6 October 1974. It is alongside the up main and was originally served by overnight and early morning trains. In the rear are 4EPB units resting between duties. *F. Hornby*

Wimbledon station opened with the main line in 1838, taking its present form in 1929, with rebuilding to make good war damage in 1956 and further 'facelifting' in 1992/3. There are 10 platform faces including four terminal bays for District Line trains from Earls Court. Two island platforms serve the four South Western Division through lines, with a third for Central Division trains on the lines from Streatham, West Croydon and Sutton. A recent widening of the road bridge at the western end gives an almost tunnel-like impression!

Following the quadrupling of the main line to Woking the LSWR had the forethought eventually to lay out flying or burrowing junctions for the several branches, thus avoiding conflict with the ever-busier fast lines. The first one we encounter is at Raynes Park, where a 'dive-under' was constructed for the up line from Epsom in 1884; the station has staggered platforms with the outer faces for the branch and the inner faces for the up and down local lines.

The first station on the Epsom line, Motspur Park consists of a 520-foot island platform constructed at the time of electrification in 1925; here the Chessington branch diverges. The Epsom line continues more or less due south through three stations, with a gradual climb from Worcester Park, before joining the route from Sutton. Stoneleigh was built as recently as 1932, to the same design as Motspur Park; Worcester Park and Ewell stations opened with the line in 1859, though the former was rebuilt in 1937 when local housing development was in full swing.

Above right Raynes Park has staggered platforms linked by a footbridge. This view from the up platform on 7 August 1992 shows the down line for Chessington South and Epsom curving away to the left. There are Waterloo-bound stopping trains at both the up local and up branch platforms. *F. Hornby*

Right Chessington South station, at the end of the branch from Motspur Park, had been down-graded to one platform some time before this scene was recorded on 23 September 1983. The branch formed the final piece of the South Western suburban network when opened throughout in 1939. Class 415 4EPB No 5105 is trailing a train ready to leave for Waterloo. *F. Hornby*

Mention was made in the previous chapter of the continuation from Epsom along the ex-LB&SCR/LSWR joint line to Leatherhead and thence on former LB&SCR metals to Dorking. Leatherhead station is of LB&SCR origin, at the convergence of the 4¼-mile line to Effingham Junction dating from 1885. There is still a good deal of open countryside hereabouts, protected by 'Green Belt' restrictions.

When the Chessington South branch was opened only months before the Second World War it was intended to extend it across country to join the Dorking line near Leatherhead. The extension was abandoned although some earthworks were prepared, and the line terminated in a goods yard just 33 chains beyond Chessington South. Close by is the zoo (now a 'World of Adventures') providing a source of extra revenue with, in steam days, occasional excursions hauled by 'foreign' locomotives. The line is mostly on

embankments, crossing seven overbridges and a viaduct over a river. The station buildings were futuristic for their time, with fluorescent lighting and curved concrete roofing free of columns; only one of the two platforms remains at the terminus. Coal depots at Chessington South and Tolworth generated freight traffic worked by motive power ranging from 'Q1' 0-6-0s to Bulleid 'Pacifics', and in more recent times Class 37 diesel-electrics on workings from Didcot.

Returning to the main line, New Malden is the next junction, for the loop line through Kingston used by the 'roundabout' trains, and for the Shepperton branch; this time it is the down line to the loop that does the burrowing. Norbiton, the first station on the branch, retains its LSWR building, but Kingston was rebuilt in the 1930s in the prevailing 'Southern' concrete style, with two through platforms and a west-facing bay. The Thames is then crossed on a four-arched bridge before the line swings north towards its junction with the Windsor line at Twickenham.

En route the Shepperton line diverges by means of a triangle junction between Teddington and Strawberry Hill. The car sheds in this triangle were adapted from the steam depot, which closed when Feltham shed opened in 1921. New units coming into service are frequently received by Strawberry Hill depot and tested along the Shepperton branch. The 6½-mile branch follows a sinuous course that brings it quite close to the Thames from Hampton onwards. One of the six stations, Upper Halliford, was opened in 1944 as a 'halt', while another, Kempton Park, is used for race meetings only and in consequence is semi-derelict. Shepperton station, at the end of the line, has, like Chessington South, been reduced to one platform.

Westwards from New Malden the main line runs straight and virtually level through Berrylands with its 'CLASP' buildings, and Surbiton, opened as 'Kingston' in 1838. It was rebuilt in the late 1930s with two 800-foot island platforms. The two remaining suburban branches, north to Hampton Court and south to Guildford, leave the main line 1½ miles beyond the station by flying and burrowing junctions respectively, constructed during the First World War.

The Hampton Court branch is the older and shorter, dating from 1849 and just 1½ miles long; the attractive little intermediate station at Thames Ditton opened two years later. The terminus, close to the palace and the river, once had four platform roads, together with goods sidings and an engine shed.

Above left Shepperton terminus, like Chessington South, has been reduced to one platform, which, on 6 April 1979, was occupied by 4SUB No 4631 at the end of its 21-mile journey from Waterloo via Kingston. *F. Hornby*

Left Although photographed as recently as 30 October 1992, Thames Ditton retains much of its 'wayside station' charm. Class 455 EMU No 5861 is moving away from the down platform en route to Hampton Court. *F. Hornby*

The 'New Line' from Hampton Court Junction to Guildford serves a succession of pleasant communities in outer suburbia, some still almost rural. Most of the station buildings date from the opening of the line in 1885, one of which is Claygate, seen here on 25 August 1993. The Class 455 units monopolise the half-hourly service to and from Waterloo. *F. Hornby*

Just one island platform remains, so the 'rationalisation' may be regretted when an intensive service is run for the annual Flower Festival!

The other branch, the 'New Line' to Guildford, completed in 1885, forms a diversionary route for Portsmouth trains when the main line via Woking is blocked, but in the normal way sees nothing more exciting than the regular-interval stopping service, the longest run on which inner-suburban stock has been consistently used. Hinchley Wood, the first station, is of 1930 construction with its platforms in the angle where the up and down lines from Hampton Court Junction converge. Effingham Junction, 7 miles further on, has been modernised, but the seven-road car shed there was closed in recent years. The other five stations are of uniform LSWR 1880s design, all but one serving small communities in still quite rural surroundings. The fifth and last, London Road, is in the outskirts of Guildford, and the line then curves through 180 degrees before entering the main station, where the 'New Line' trains terminate at a bay platform.

Retracing our steps to Hampton Court Junction, the four-track main line runs south-westwards for 9 miles to Woking, with long straight stretches passed for 100 mph running on the fast tracks. Between the line and the River Thames to the north there are reservoirs, until the two come closer together at Weybridge; thereafter the Basingstoke Canal keeps company with the railway to Woking. Other landmarks are Sandown Park race course, on the south side at Esher, then the remains of Brooklands motor racing track and the former airfield near Weybridge. Two of the six stations between Surbiton and Woking (Esher and Walton) still have platforms for the fast lines; the former also had platforms for race specials at the west end until 1965. Weybridge has a bay platform for the connecting line to Virginia Water, which diverges by means of a triangle junction at the country end, while West Byfleet has an island platform serving the down local and fast lines. The architectural styles vary; Esher's original 1838 building survived until 1967 and has been replaced by a 'prefab', while the booking office at Weybridge had to be replaced after a disastrous fire in January 1987.

The combined population of these communities is some 60,000, to which Woking and district adds another 85,000, having virtually doubled in post-war years. The station there was rebuilt for the Portsmouth electrification of 1938, with four 820-foot through platforms and three bays, of which only the one at the western end remains. A 'rail-air' bus link operates between the station and Heathrow airport.

The route to Portsmouth via Guildford branches away from the Bournemouth and Exeter main line half a mile west of Woking, turning south through Worplesdon and meeting the 'New Line' at the approach to Guildford station. The latter was extensively rebuilt (and much improved) in 1988-90 as befits a junction where lines converge from London, Portsmouth, Reading and Redhill, used by some 13,000 passengers daily. There are berthing sidings for EMUs on the up side, but the site of the old locomotive roundhouse is now occupied by a multi-storey car park.

There is little to choose between the two routes from London in distance - 30½ miles via Woking and 30 miles via Cobham - nor in the journey time by stopping trains, though of course the Portsmouth expresses give a much faster service.

SIGNALLING

The first appearance of a colour-light at Waterloo was in 1920 when a trial was made with an American three-position signal. At that time the enormous array of semaphores on a huge gantry was being systematically reduced, and track-circuits were being installed on the running lines. However, it was not until 1936 that any further progress was made, when a new box was opened with 309 miniature levers in three frames, one of which controlled the four suburban platforms. Colour-lights with three aspects were installed out to Loco Junction and four aspects thence to Hampton Court Junction, with route-indicating 'feathers' where needed. Otherwise pre-war advances were limited to the Woking-Guildford section, converted in 1937.

After nationalisation, schemes for the Central and South Eastern Sections took precedence and little more was done save that the Guildford area was updated in the mid-1960s. A new box at Guildford with a route-setting panel replaced 12 existing boxes, and colour-lights were installed thence to Ash and Effingham Junction, some of which were of two-aspect only. In 1970 Surbiton panel box replaced 11 manual boxes, controlling four- and three-aspect signals to West Byfleet and Oxshott, to Hampton Court and between Weybridge and Chertsey. The Chessington South branch was converted in January 1972, followed by the Kingston loop and Shepperton branch in October 1974; these latter were controlled from a new box at Feltham on the Windsor lines. The year 1978 saw AWS (Automatic Warning System) installed from Raynes Park to Epsom and Chessington South, and on the 'New Line' to Guildford.

In June 1986 a fire in Clapham Junction 'A' box, spanning the tracks at the London end of the station, caused great disruption in its aftermath, both to main and Windsor line traffic. In the event its days were numbered, as the 'Waterloo Area Resignalling Programme', started in 1990, led to its abolition in May along with others in the vicinity. Its duties were transferred to a new centre at Wimbledon, opened the previous month, which, by August, had absorbed the functions of boxes at Raynes Park, Motspur Park, Epsom and Leatherhead. Wimbledon's 1930s-style 'A' box remained in use to control the line from East Putney until 1991, and to New Malden until October 1992. Waterloo box was demolished in 1990, after regulating traffic in and out of the terminus for 54 years!

By the end of our period, in the spring of 1994, modernisation was complete. Level crossings were remotely controlled and monitored by closed-circuit TV, and semaphore signalling had been abolished in the suburban area along with the majority of the distinctive LSWR-style boxes.

SERVICES

All suburban services in and out of Waterloo on the main line side share the same pair of tracks as far as Raynes Park, so even in off-peak periods the head-ways on this section are quite close; the 1993/94 timetable listed 14 'Standard Class only' trains hourly in each direction.

In 1948 there was less consistency, some services fluctuating between two and three per hour off-peak, with those to Guildford via Cobham using the fast tracks out to Surbiton. In that year, exclusive of the Windsor line, there were 290 weekday '3rd Class only' arrivals converging on Waterloo from as far afield as Horsham (35½ miles). The greatest number - 61 - was on the 'roundabout' service via Kingston, while at the other extreme there were solitary arrivals from Chertsey and Earlsfield.

Other services, from the Basingstoke, Alton and Portsmouth lines, conveying 1st and 3rd Class passengers, using the fast tracks and calling at outer-suburban stations, accounted for a further 54 weekday arrivals. In the busiest hour (08.00-09.00) 23 stopping and seven semi-fast trains entered Waterloo from 17 points of origin. The residents of Surbiton in particular, thanks to its strategic location at the junction of three routes, had the benefit of no fewer than 140 weekday trains to town, in a journey time as short as 16 minutes by the 'non-stops'.

In addition to the foregoing, nine up trains from a variety of starting places terminated at Wimbledon in the evening, before retiring to the nearby car sheds.

In January 1951 cuts to save energy were put in force, mainly affecting evening services, with Shepperton trains operating to and from Kingston only. This particular ploy would be adopted on future occasions, although in that instance the cuts were of short duration. Indeed, it reappeared in the summer timetables from 1954-58 when paths on the local lines had to be found on Saturdays for additional Portsmouth semi-fast trains. More changes affecting the Shepperton branch were made in 1958 when Sunday trains via Richmond were withdrawn in favour of two per hour via Kingston.

Other off-peak and Sunday services were pruned in September 1958, this time to meet the cost of a staff pay increase. The next two years saw further reductions in weekend services, in response to the spread of the five-day week and, on Sundays, to the growth in private motoring. It was, however, refreshing to note that on Whit Monday 1958 trains ran at 5-minute intervals on the Hampton Court branch, before and after a race meeting at Hurst Park! Also worthy of mention in that year's timetable was a steam-hauled 03.53 arrival at Waterloo from the Bournemouth line for passengers and mails, which took 59 minutes for the 24½ miles from Woking, with four stops! (There were of course other steam-hauled Basingstoke semi-fasts, calling at Surbiton and making appreciably faster runs.)

In this view of Dorking station in March 1975 4SUB units in 'Rail Blue' livery monopolise the scene. The line continues southwards to the Sussex Coast via Horsham, but Dorking is the outer limit for suburban services. The station was opened by the LB&SCR in 1867, but has now been rebuilt in the 'modern idiom'. *F. Hornby*

The remaining Saturday peak-hour trains were withdrawn in 1963, and at the same time all weekday slack-hour services were standardised at half-hourly, involving some curtailment to those on the Epsom line. The cumulative effect of the alterations over the years resulted in a reduction of weekday suburban arrivals at Waterloo to 264. The effect was most marked on Saturdays, which in 1948 differed little from weekdays whereas by 1966 the tally was down to 204 - a 30 per cent reduction.

The Bournemouth line electrification in 1967 saw the closure of Nine Elms shed and the end of all steam-hauled trains, with a drastic revision of the whole timetable and a temporary decline in reliability until 'the bugs had been ironed out'. The end-product mirrored the changes taking place all round the Capital, with a steady exodus of population from the inner to the outer suburbs. The Leatherhead and Dorking service was a beneficiary, with ten trains in each evening peak hour, terminating at five different places and including, for a time, two per hour non-stop to Epsom.

The saga continued thereafter much as before, the 1970s being beset by strikes, unofficial stoppages and staff shortages. From October 1976 Sunday schedules were revised, with the reappearance of our old friend the 'Shepperton shuttle' and with hourly intervals on all other lines. The following year the Chessington South Sunday service was enhanced by hourly trains to and from Wimbledon, which were extended through to Waterloo in 1978. In that year also an hourly service was introduced between Waterloo and Dorking, utilising main-line stock and making only four stops, in compensation for a reduction in the frequency from Victoria via Sutton.

The May 1984 timetable introduced another Sunday variation, when 'New Line' trains operated as far as Effingham Junction only, connecting there with a Waterloo-Guildford service via Epsom and Leatherhead. This, presumably, met with some criticism as the through trains via Cobham were reinstated in due course.

Staff shortages posed an ongoing problem, leading to the temporary withdrawal of 43 daily trains in 1990 and stimulating the more widespread use of 'OPO' (one person operation) as soon as equipment could be installed at the stations.

WATERLOO 'MAIN LINE' SUBURBAN JOURNEY TIMES AND AVERAGE SPEEDS, 1948 AND 1993/94

From Waterloo to:	Distance (miles)	Stops	1948 Time (mins)	Average (mph)	Stops	1993/94 Time (mins)	Average (mph)
Epsom	14.5	5	28	31.1	8	30	29.0
Hampton Court	15.0	9	33	27.3	9	31	29.0
Shepperton	21.0	14	49	25.7	14	45	28.0
Woking (non-stop)	24.5	-	29	50.4	-	23	63.9
Guildford (via 'New Line')	30.0	10	53	34.0	11	54	33.3
Guildford (via main line)	30.5	9	54	33.8	11	56	32.7
Guildford (non-stop)	30.5	-	39	46.9	-	29	63.1

The Southern Region, as such, was replaced by three divisions within Network SouthEast as from 29 April 1991, and in the South West Division summer timetable the Dorking service from Waterloo was once again revised, with weekend trains terminating at Epsom, some for one per hour to Effingham Junction. There were improvements on the Kingston loop, where the off-peak frequency was doubled to four trains per hour, thanks to a grant from Kingston council. The next winter, however, saw cuts on Sundays back to one train hourly on the Hampton Court and Chessington South branches.

It comes as no great surprise to find that by 1993/94 the balance between 'all Standard Class' inner-suburban and '1st & Standard Class' outer-suburban services had shifted, with the weekday arrivals at Waterloo via the slow line further reduced to 229, although the Saturday figure was little changed from 1966. On the up fast line 64 trains called at Surbiton on every day of the week, many of them being booked also to stop at Clapham Junction.

There has been little change in journey times or average speeds over the years, save for a significant improvement as regards fast trains between Waterloo, Woking and Guildford. Doubtless thanks to the absence of conflicting junctions and to a main line that, beyond Clapham Junction, is generally straight and level, the average speeds compare favourably with those of the other two 'Southern' Divisions.

TRACTION AND TRAINS

Your author well remembers, as a small boy in Southern Railway days, travelling down the line from his local station at Earlsfield in three-coach units of LSWR origin, while eagerly looking out for glimpses of 'Lord Nelsons' or 'King Arthurs' racing past on the parallel tracks.

This pleasurable experience could still be enjoyed in early BR years, although most units were soon strengthened with an additional trailer and the older stock gradually gave way to Bulleid's flat-fronted 4SUBs (and the trains racing past might well be hauled by a 'Merchant Navy'!). However, the old and new units co-existed happily throughout the 1950s, and one must assume that overcrowding in the rush hours was marginally less chronic than on the South Eastern Section, as no move was made to lengthen trains to increase capacity. If a 1949 roster for a pair of 4SUBs was typical it was hardly intensive - consisting of one round trip to Guildford via Cobham in the morning and a 'roundabout' jaunt via Kingston in the evening.

The demise of pre-war stock was hastened by the advent of the 4EPB units, but their two-car counterparts were initially somewhat restricted in their use, being prohibited from working along the Guildford 'New Line'. Doubtless for this reason their numbers were also limited. No such inhibitions applied to the 4EPBs, which by 1963 had a virtual monopoly on this route, although a variety of units appeared occasionally when Portsmouth trains were diverted from the main line. In the early 1970s the older 4SUBs took over for a while and the 4EPBs were rostered to Hampton Court and Kingston 'roundabout' services. Shortly afterwards, in October 1973, 'New Line' commuters found their trains had been upgraded to 4VEPs with 1st Class accommodation.

The experimental 'High Density' 4PEP units went into service on the Hampton Court and Shepperton branches in the summer of 1973, and by the following year Wimbledon depot was host to a greater diversity of traction probably than ever before or since, comprising 4SUB, 4EPB, 2EPB, 2SAP, 2HAP, 4VEP, 4PEP and 2PEP units. With so much variety available it is remarkable that, in the winter timetable of 1977, a morning train from Chertsey to Waterloo via Weybridge consisted of eight Mk I coaches powered by a Class 73 electro-diesel or a Class 33/1 diesel-electric locomotive. In August of the same year, when part of the Shepperton branch was flooded, a Class 73 with a '4TC'

On 3 August 1974 Class 415/1 4EPB unit No 5111 in 'Rail Blue' livery pauses at platform 10 at Clapham Junction on a Hampton Court to Waterloo service. Clapham Junction's platforms are rarely free of trains for more than a few minutes save in the small hours. *F. Hornby*

Right The spotless interior of Wimbledon East depot is seen during an 'open day' on 5 May 1991. According to the stock-books unit No 4201 was the only 2HAP in sub-class 414/2, but the subtle difference from the rest of the class was not stated. All were built at Eastleigh for outer-suburban work in 1957. *F. Hornby*

Below right The two units visible in this view at Waterloo span 30 years of development - a 1950s 4SUB on the left and a new Class 508 on the right. The thousands of commuters who swarm on and off the trains at Waterloo are conspicuous by their absence in this Saturday afternoon view of suburban platforms 1 and 2 in August 1980. *F. Hornby*

push-pull set kept the service going, shuttling to and from Kingston.

By this time local freight traffic had ceased in the suburban area, the 'Clean Air Act' having put paid to most of the coal yards, save on the Chessington branch, where the depot opened in 1963 was still in use.

In early 1980 the first of the Class 508 four-car units entered service, and by the end of April all 43 were at work on the Western Division, extending their activities to Dorking in May 1982. As has already been chronicled, however, after a five-year stint they went north to the Liverpool area where they are still gainfully employed, having left behind one trailer coach per unit for further use.

The next - and so far the last - development was the introduction of Class 455 in 1982, taking up their duties the following year. By then the 4SUBs had departed from the scene, followed in 1985 by the elimination of the 2EPBs from regular activities. (This was less than popular when a four-car 455 was substituted for what had previously been a six-car EPB formation!) The ubiquitous 455s had also, from May 1984, replaced the Class 423 4VEPs on the Guildford run, depriving the locals of their 1st Class luxury once more. They also operate the main-line service to Guildford, calling at all stations from Surbiton, which was once the preserve of two-car

units. No fewer than 103 were allocated to Wimbledon East in 1986, plus 25 surviving 2HAPs near the end of their active existence - weekday services call for 91 Class 455s, allowing a rather small margin for repairs and maintenance. Both routes to Guildford were passed for 'one person operation' in June 1990.

Having seen off the EPB stock in both variations, all inner-suburban routes from Waterloo have now been monopolised by the 455s for some years. Since the only penetration of 'Thameslink' units into the SW Division territory was, for a short time, to Guildford via Sutton, and since the 'Networkers' have as yet appeared only on trials, they may well maintain their monopoly for some time to come.

WINDSOR LINES

Waterloo-Reading via Richmond and Ascot
Point Pleasant Junction-Wimbledon via East Putney
Hounslow loop (Barnes-Feltham and Whitton via Hounslow)
Twickenham-Teddington (for New Malden)
Staines-Windsor & Eton Riverside
Virginia Water-Weybridge and Byfleet
Ascot-Ash Vale (for Aldershot and Guildford)

ROUTES AND INFRASTRUCTURE

When the rebuilding of Waterloo was completed in 1922, one section of the older station survived, dating from 1884 and comprising the Windsor line platforms Nos 16-21; separated from the rest of the station by an office block, it remained undisturbed for the next 70 years. With all services electrically operated since 1938, the only steam intrusion in BR years came from an occasional parcels train.

The construction of the new International Terminal in the early 1990s caused a major upheaval with the loss of the old Windsor line platforms and a rearrangement of the running lines out to Queenstown Road. After reconstruction four platforms, Nos 16-19, became available, together with the use of No 15 when required. Track realignment has been necessary to make way for the massive flyover between Vauxhall and Queenstown Road, transferring the international tracks across to the South Eastern Division.

The station at Queenstown Road serves the Windsor lines only, with an island platform for the slow roads and a disused up platform, hemmed in at either end by viaducts carrying the Central Division main line from Victoria and the South London lines across the South Western tracks. The station exterior has been renovated, drawing attention to its LSWR origin.

Approaching Clapham Junction a triangle junction gives access to the West London line, the chord facing towards Waterloo having been relaid recently for use by 'Eurostar' trains between the terminus and their depot at North Pole Junction. The other chord is now used by the Clapham Junction-Willesden service as well as by freights and occasional 'specials'.

At Clapham Junction two island platforms, with faces Nos 3 and 4 for up and 5 and 6 for down trains, are dedicated to the Windsor line services and are separated from the other SW Division platforms by the carriage yard.

A flyover from Point Pleasant Junction, between Wandsworth Town and Putney, carried the up spur from East Putney until it was taken out of use in recent years, when the down spur was made reversible. The first LSWR electric service began operation over this loop line in October 1915 between Waterloo and Wimbledon and survived until 1941. The loop passes through the nearest tunnel to Waterloo, between East Putney and Southfields, and is still useful for empty stock movements and diver-

There are contrasts in roofing styles and in motive power in this scene at Waterloo in September 1956. 2 NOL unit No 1854 (vintage 1934) has arrived from Windsor in the old part of the terminus while an 'M7' 0-4-4T built in 1900 heads empty stock in the main station. *A. J. Pike*

Not 'Three Bridges' but a view from Putney looking towards Wandsworth Town on 3 May 1991! The nearest bridge carries the District Line, the second a road and the third the disused up line from East Putney to Point Pleasant Junction. The train is a Class 455 incorporating a trailer carriage from a 508. *F. Hornby*

sions. On summer Saturdays in the 1950s several trains were routed this way to ease congestion on the main line, as were some South Coast excursions in 1969, which picked up passengers at the intermediate stations. The latter, although under BR control, are normally served only by District Line trains and, in keeping with LT practice, the fourth rail is in place along this stretch.

On the main route the four-track section ends at Barnes, 7 miles out, where the Hounslow loop diverges from the direct line via Richmond. The station was designed by Sir William Tite for the LSWR in the 'Tudor' style with tall and ornate chimney pots. Beyond the junction a road crosses both routes on the level, to the frustration of motorists! A sharp curve, long since removed, once linked the two lines.

The first station on the Hounslow loop is Barnes Bridge, immediately beyond which the Thames is crossed by a three-span bowstring girder bridge. Kew Bridge, two stations further on, is between two junctions of a triangle leading to a 'freight only' line that connects at South Acton with the North London line from Richmond. This connection was used for a few months in 1854 by three trains each way daily between Fenchurch Street and Windsor, proving that there is nothing new in the 'CrossRail' concept! More recently it was traversed by summer weekend holiday trains between the Midlands and South Coast, using the curve between Kew East and New Kew junctions.

Until the general closure of freight yards there was a busy one near Brentford station, which attracted a variety of steam locomotives to the loop line. Another triangle junction, between Whitton and Feltham, reunites the Hounslow loop with the direct line, Hounslow station being about a mile from the apex. The loop is 7¼ miles in length, with seven intermediate stations, the newest of which is Syon Lane, opened in 1931.

Westwards from Barnes the direct line serves first Mortlake, then North Sheen and Richmond, where the busy 1930s-style station has terminal bays for the North London and District Line trains. The Thames is crossed beyond the station by a bridge, renewed in

Two Windsor line stations with contrasting architectural styles. The entrance to Wandsworth Road has been smartened up during the 1980s with a simple design using modern materials. Brentford, on the Hounslow loop, still presents a solid 'no nonsense' appearance, much as it was in LSWR times. *F. Hornby*

1906-08, with five wrought iron arches on stone piers. St Margarets and Twickenham follow, with three tracks between them; at the latter a new station was opened in 1954, to the east of the old one, with three through platforms and two bays for extra traffic occa-

South Western Division suburban 'Windsor lines' from Waterloo

Miles	Name	Opened	Closed	Notes
From Waterloo to Reading				
	Waterloo	7/1848		
1¼	Vauxhall	7/1848		
2¾	Queenstown Road	11/1877		'Queens Road' to 5/1980
4	Clapham Junction	3/1863		
4¾	Wandsworth Town	7/1846		
5¾	East Putney	6/1889		Service by District Line trains
6½	Southfields	6/1889		Service by District Line trains
7½	Wimbledon Park	6/1889		Service by District Line trains
8½	Wimbledon			Service by District Line trains
6	Putney	7/1846		
7	Barnes	7/1846		
8¼	Mortlake	7/1846		'for East Sheen' in 1948
9	North Sheen	1930		
9¾	Richmond	7/1846		Rebuilt 1936-37
10¾	St Margarets	10/1876		
11½	Twickenham	8/1849		Rebuilding completed 1954
12¼	Strawberry Hill	1874		
	(To Shepperton and Kingston)			
12½	Whitton	1930		
14¾	Feltham	1848		
17½	Ashford (Middx)	1848		
19	Staines	12/1849		'Central' until 4/1966
21	Egham	1856		
23¼	Virginia Water	10/1866		
25¼	Longcross	1942		Opened 1940 for Army only
27	Sunningdale	1856		
29	Ascot	6/1856		
29¼	Ascot West	1922	1965	Race course station
31¼	Martins Heron	1988		
32¼	Bracknell	1856		New station 5/1976
36¾	Wokingham	1849		
38¾	Winnersh	1910		Originally 'Sindlesham & Hurst Halt'; 'Halt' from 1930
39½	Winnersh Triangle	5/1986		
40½	Earley	1863		
43½	Reading	1855	1965	Date of closure of SR station; thereafter incorporated with WR station

sioned by Rugby matches at the nearby stadium - one of these is now derelict.

The Kingston loop diverges southwards by a flyover junction some quarter of a mile further on, followed by the triangle junction with the Hounslow loop previously mentioned. West of the triangle is the site on the down side once occupied by the hump marshalling yards and sheds at Feltham, home for over 70 locomotives including the four massive 'G16' 4-8-0Ts. The steam shed closed in July 1967, and the depot succumbed in August 1970, drastically reducing freight traffic in an area where, in the 1950s, there were 30 freights arriving and departing daily.

Staines (pop 52,000), 19 miles from Waterloo, has a straightforward two-platform station, named Staines Central until April 1966, with berthing sidings for EMUs. It is the junction for the Windsor branch, which runs arrow-straight in a north-westerly direction for 5 miles before describing a semi-circle and crossing the river into Windsor & Eton Riverside. Doubtless the 'South Western' envied the near-monopoly of Royal comings and goings enjoyed by

Miles	Name	Opened	Closed	Notes
Hounslow loop				
8	Barnes Bridge	1916		
8¾	Chiswick	8/1849		'for Grove Park' in 1948
9¾	Kew Bridge	8/1849		
10¾	Brentford	8/1849		'Central' 1950-80
11¼	Syon Lane	7/1931		
12¼	Isleworth	8/1849		
13½	Hounslow	2/1850		
Windsor branch				
19	Staines			
21½	Wraysbury	1848		Resited 1861
22¾	Sunnymeads	1927		
24	Datchet	8/1848		
25¾	Windsor & Eton Riverside	12/1849		
Virginia Water to Weybridge				
	Virginia Water west curve closed 6/1966			
23¼	Virginia Water	10/1866		
25¾	Chertsey	2/1848		
27¼	Addlestone	1848		
29	Weybridge	1838		
To Guildford via Aldershot				
29	Ascot	6/1856		
32¼	Bagshot	1878		
35½	Camberley	1878		Originally '& York Town'
37¾	Frimley	1878		
41	Ash Vale	1870		Originally 'North Camp & Ash Vale'
	(To Aldershot)			

the rival Great Western, but was not to be outdone, providing a respectable three-platform terminus with all-over roof, and buildings in the Tudor style dating from 1849 including a fine Royal waiting room. Freight facilities were withdrawn in 1965; all sidings have been lifted and the station has been modernised while retaining much of its character. The branch is 6 miles long, bordered by reservoirs, with three intermediate stations at Wraysbury, Sunnymeads and Datchet. In January 1981 a spur was opened from the down line into Staines West Shell oil terminal, which had hitherto been serviced by the Western Region.

After parting company with the Windsor branch the Reading line crosses the river, passes through Egham and turns south to Virginia Water, junction for the Weybridge branch. An east-west curve connecting the two lines was taken out of use in 1966 whereafter race traffic from London to Ascot via Weybridge was perforce re-routed via Staines. The branch veers away south-eastwards to join the South Western Division main line by the triangular junction west of Weybridge station, where it has its own bay platform.

Even in these days of long-distance commuting it might be considered an extravagance to include Reading, 43½ miles from Waterloo, in a London suburban survey, though as the extremity of the 'Windsor lines' it does deserve a mention. Suffice it to say that, after bearing west from Virginia Water we reach Ascot (29 miles), the junction for Aldershot via Ash Vale, then Wokingham (36¾ miles), where the old South Eastern Railway line from Guildford is joined. Trains from both routes share tracks for the remaining 7 miles into Reading, where, since the closure of the SR terminus in 1965, an island platform has been provided, integral with the WR station.

In recent years the Wokingham and Bracknell area has become a magnet for 'high-tech' industries and two additional stations were opened in the neighbourhood in the 1980s, Martin's Heron and Winnersh Triangle. However, the separate race course station to the west of Ascot closed in 1965.

Retracing our steps to Twickenham, we follow the Kingston loop for a mile or so to Strawberry Hill, junction for the Shepperton branch on which

Left Up and down Windsor trains meet at Staines on 25 July 1978, both being Class 418 2SAPs, which at that time were prominent on the section. The 35 units of the class were converted in 1976 by down-grading the 19 1st Class seats in the Driving Trailers to 2nd Class. The inverted black triangle on No 5944 indicates that there is a baggage compartment at the rear of the driver's cab. *F. Hornby*

Middle left A Class 416 2EPB unit stands alongside a 4EPB at Windsor & Eton Riverside station on 20 July 1968. Although the original roof has been replaced, the buildings are substantially as first built in 1851. One platform was removed in 1991 to make room for a car park. *F. Hornby*

Bottom left Strawberry Hill station on the New Malden-Twickenham loop line retains its old LSWR building on the southbound side. The colour-light signal on the right with the route-indicating 'feather' protects the north curve on to the Shepperton branch. *F. Hornby*

through trains to and from Waterloo via the Windsor lines operate only at peak hours. Southwards from Strawberry Hill in the Kingston direction we trespass on to territory already covered in the previous section.

SIGNALLING

Up to the time of nationalisation semaphore signalling was still in widespread use beyond Clapham Junction, controlled from conventional signal boxes, as were the level crossing gates, found in some numbers thanks to the generally flat terrain.

By February 1959 colour-light signalling had reached Richmond, but in the mid-1970s semaphores were still in use on parts of the Kingston and Hounslow loops and in the Feltham area. Track 'rationalisation', which simplified the introduction of new systems, went ahead throughout the 1960s, particularly the removal of goods yards and sidings, resulting from the wholesale withdrawal of local freight services.

Class 405 4SUB No 4632 approaches Clapham Junction on a 'roundabout' service via Richmond and Brentford on 5 April 1978. Straddling the tracks is Clapham 'A' signal box with the skeleton remains of the wartime protective roof still in place. *F. Hornby*

The East Putney-Wimbledon line went over to colour-lights in 1971, enabling three boxes to be closed, but the biggest advance was in 1973 when resignalling in the Feltham area was put in hand, the panel box there being commissioned in May 1974. The scheme was extended in September, by which time the Hounslow loop, Windsor branch and Virginia Water to Chertsey and Sunningdale had all been converted. A further stage accomplished the removal of semaphores from the whole of the Windsor lines by the end of 1974, whereafter a few boxes remained open to operate crossing gates. Richmond box also survived, but only to control the North London and District Lines!

The boxes at the notorious Barnes crossings were closed in 1976-77, control thereafter being from Barnes by closed-circuit TV. By this time all the Windsor lines were equipped with the Automatic Warning System.

SERVICES

Inevitably there have been many changes in the service patterns over the years, but perhaps the least affected are the Kingston 'roundabouts', on which bullet-nosed three-coach electric units bearing headcode 'V' commenced running in 1916. By 1948 the original quarter-hourly frequency had been reduced to three per hour off-peak, with slight deviations from a strictly 20-minute interval. The journey time for the circuit was then 70 minutes for 27 miles with 21 intermediate stops. On Sundays there were two trains hourly, with 20- and 40-minute gaps.

On the Shepperton branch, at the time of nationalisation the all-day service via Kingston was supplemented by additional trains via Richmond - three each way at peak times on Mondays to Saturdays and hourly on Sundays. The weekday trains have survived to the present time, but those on Saturdays and Sundays were withdrawn in the late 1950s.

Services on the Hounslow loop have been subject to alterations from time to time. In 1948 the long-standing tradition going back to LSWR years was still followed, with trains running round the loop and back to Waterloo every 30 minutes in each direction. Their headcodes were $\bar{O}$ for those routed outwards via Richmond, with a plain O for those outwards via Brentford; the 27½-mile round trip occupied 70-72 minutes with 22 stops, coincidentally similar to the performance of the Kingston roundabouts. Weekday peak-hour variations via the loop included two trains from Waterloo to Weybridge and Windsor, non-stop to Hounslow in only 18 minutes, with corresponding up services.

The normal service between Waterloo and Windsor in 1948 was via Richmond, perpetuating the half-hourly frequency established with electrification in July 1930. The journey time was 48 minutes for 25¾ miles - some early morning trains made additional stops and took longer. A Weybridge portion was detached at Staines, reaching its destination in 54 minutes from Waterloo (as compared with a 30-minute journey via Surbiton).

Reading saw its first public 'Southern Electric' service on New Year's Day 1939 when trains comprised of 2BIL units commenced working to and from Waterloo every 20 minutes at peak times and every half-hour off-peak and on Sundays. A rear portion for Guildford via Aldershot was conveyed as far as Ascot, giving this line a vastly improved service, while the 75-minute running time to Reading was 15 minutes less than with steam traction. In 1948 these criteria still applied, with 26 minutes allowed for the start-to-stop run between Waterloo and Staines. Nearly five million passengers were carried annually - a figure that had multiplied almost threefold in a decade.

By 1957 the Kingston 'roundabouts' were restored to four trains per hour on weekdays, alternately missing Queen's Road Battersea (later renamed Queenstown Road) and completing the circuit in 65 minutes. An interesting variation had appeared in the previous year's summer timetable when a morning train was routed out via Kingston and back via the East Putney line!

The late 1950s were marked by reductions in Saturday peak and weekday off-peak frequencies; the enhanced 'roundabout' service was one of those affected as some trains were diagrammed to operate between Waterloo and Kingston only, via Richmond. Similarly, in the 1958/59 winter timetable, Sunday trains that had hitherto made an hourly circuit round the Hounslow loop and Whitton curve were terminated and reversed at Twickenham.

During 1966 the Windsor/Weybridge service was reduced in the evenings to one train per hour with - as an omen for the future - conductor-guards issuing tickets for unmanned stations on the Windsor branch. Further cuts were prompted by the 1972 miners' strike and, for a time, the Virginia Water-Weybridge line was served by a shuttle to and from Staines. In the same year extra stops were inserted into the Reading service, at Richmond and Feltham, with bus connections at the latter for Heathrow (transferred to Staines in 1982).

Outer suburban services were recast in the 1975 summer timetable, with the innovation of separate through trains to Guildford via Ascot at 06 and 24 minutes past each hour from Waterloo, semi-fast to Staines. Reading departures were at 36 and 54, and once again a shuttle service operated between Staines and Weybridge, connecting with the 24 and 54 minutes departures from Waterloo. Although with minor adjustments this pattern was adhered to well into the 1980s, the branch from Virginia Water received more than its fair share of attention later in the decade.

In May 1986 alternate trains from Staines along this line were diverted to Woking via the Byfleet curve, leaving Weybridge with only one train hourly. The following year the half-hourly Waterloo-Twickenham via Hounslow trains were diverted to run alternately to Woking and Weybridge in place of the shuttles from Staines. In due course the Woking train was extended to Guildford, giving Class 455 units an end-to-end run of 40 miles, taking almost 90 minutes. It was, of course, not advertised as such due to the much more direct route via Surbiton, and operated only for a limited period in the early 1990s.

In the summer of 1992 the other Guildford service via Ascot ceased to run, in favour of connections at Ascot with the Reading trains. By this time we find the Windsor trains calling at principal stations between Waterloo and Richmond including Vauxhall, resulting in a journey time 6 minutes longer than in 1948, while Weybridge once again has a half-hourly

Above left A Class 455 EMU rumbles across Barnes Bridge on a fine spring morning in May 1993, overlooking the jetty for the local River Police. The original three-span bridge of 1849 was replaced in 1894 and carries a public footpath as well as the double-track Hounslow loop. *F. Hornby*

Left Richmond station offers interchange between the Windsor line through tracks on the left and terminal platforms for North London and District Line trains. In this view on 8 October 1986 a 455 unit departs for Waterloo while a former Southern Region 2EPB forms a North London service on the right. *F. Hornby*

through service from Waterloo (hourly at weekends). The Kingston 'roundabouts' are back down to half-hourly off-peak in each direction with a typical journey time of 67 minutes.

Changes in working hours over the years are reflected by the pattern of Windsor line arrivals at Waterloo during the morning peak period from 0700-0900 as follows:

	Weekdays	Saturdays
Summer 1948	31	31
Summer 1993	22	16

In conclusion it is worth mentioning that on the various occasions when services in and out of Waterloo have been interrupted - whether by engineering work or by mishaps of one kind or another - a measure frequently employed has been for Windsor line trains to start and terminate at Clapham Junction.

TRACTION AND TRAINS

From 1948 to date all regular services have been operated by EMUs, only those on the Reading and Guildford via Aldershot lines requiring 1st Class accommodation. On the Kingston and Hounslow 'roundabouts' pre-war 3SUBs were still in use, but when the platforms at Kew Bridge and Syon Lane were lengthened in 1948 it was possible to strengthen all units with an additional trailer coach. The Bulleid 4SUBs introduced from 1946 onwards gave long and reliable service, even making a 'comeback' on the Windsor branch in 1983 in an emergency!

When the four- and two-car EPB stock came into service, the latter made their debut on the two loop lines in November 1954, accelerating the withdrawal of the pre-war units. Some trains were made up to six cars comprising a 4EPB and 2EPB, but the 16.46 Hounslow loop train from Waterloo won top marks for unorthodoxy when recorded consisting of a 4SUB, 2NOL and a 2BIL!

Regular passengers on the Windsor and Weybridge services, accustomed to the 1934-built 2NOL units Nos 1851-90, had little time to familiarise themselves with the 4SUBs, which replaced them in December 1956, as they in turn yielded to EPB stock in May 1957. A batch of 2EPBs, Nos 5651-84, built in 1958 with all-saloon seating, were similarly employed from November 1959, and were joined a few years later by the 5781-95 series, which had come south from Tyneside. Yet another two-car variant appeared in 1974 in the shape of the 2nd Class only 2SAPs, which were a familiar sight on the Windsor lines after their conversion from 2HAPs.

In 1972 one of the experimental 'High Density' 4PEP units made trial runs for platform clearances on the Hounslow loop, providing useful experience for the development of the Class 508s. The first of these was delivered from BREL York to Strawberry Hill for trials in August 1979, and when more arrived they were put to work on Kingston 'roundabouts', but they were in fact 'out of gauge' for the Hounslow loop! They left the Southern Region in 1984, leaving the field clear for their successors of Class 455, which had arrived from 1982 onwards. They currently monopolise the Kingston 'roundabout', Hounslow, Windsor and Weybridge duties as well as being widely used elsewhere.

The Reading line, involving a longer run and requiring 'main-line' stock, and the Guildford via Aldershot service were worked by 2BIL side-corridor units of 1936 design until they were withdrawn in 1970-71. Thereafter the Reading line became the preserve of the popular 4CORs built for the Portsmouth electrification in 1937-8 and widely known as the 'Nelsons'. However, their stay was of short duration as the 4CIGs (Class 421) took over in 1972 and remain on this and the Guildford via Aldershot service 23 years later.

Although having no separate allocation, Strawberry Hill depot plays an important role in stabling and servicing Windsor line units, and since 1974 new stock has been commissioned here.

These notes briefly record the changes in the routine scene, which is of course enlivened from time to time by locomotive-hauled trains, both passenger and freight. The latter can still be seen, albeit in reduced numbers, particularly between the Kew and Ludgate junctions.

'Specials' over the years have ranged from Sir Winston Churchill's funeral train in 1965 (hauled by the locomotive bearing his name) to the occasional appearance of the diesel-hauled 'VSOE' Pullmans. Another famous 'Pacific', *Flying Scotsman*, was on display at Twickenham in October 1969 prior to departure for the USA, and Stanier Class '5' No 44932 was the star exhibit at a gala day at Windsor in December 1989.

Daily travellers expecting their usual 4EPB were sometimes treated to superior accommodation, as in October 1968 when a 'COR-BUF-COR' rake turned up on a 'roundabout' service, and in June 1974 when 4VEPs appeared on the Hounslow loop. The pièce de résistance was reserved for a few Sundays in February 1977, when a Class 74 electro-diesel took a turn round the Kingston loop with main-line stock and buffet car, as a means of turning the train round for its return working to Exeter.

13

CAPITAL CONNECTIONS

The primary purpose of this book has been to chronicle the changing scene on BR's London suburban network between 1948 and 1994, which we conclude with a look at the West London line, on which a modest commuter service operates along with inter-regional passenger and freight trains. However, the story would be incomplete without due recognition of the close liaison between BR and the London Transport rail system, with the two sharing stations and trackage at numerous locations.

It was, for example, impossible to do justice to the Euston-Watford DC lines without considering the Bakerloo Line service northward from Queens Park. Mention has also been made, in the appropriate places, of how District Line trains reach Richmond and Wimbledon over BR tracks, and of the Central Line's post-war extensions into former LNER and GWR territory. Other lines that qualify for examination in this final chapter are the Metropolitan, the Hammersmith & City, the District Line to Upminster, the East London line and that comparative newcomer, the Docklands Light Railway.

WEST LONDON LINE

The 6¼-mile line between Clapham Junction and Willesden forms a vital link between the railways south and north of the Thames, still heavily used by inter-regional freight traffic. The line was opened in two stages, commencing with the West London Railway from Willesden to Kensington in May 1844, with a connection on to the GWR near Wormwood Scrubs. The West London Extension was completed in 1863 with three spurs at the southern end, giving access to the LSWR and LB&SCR sides at Clapham Junction, and to the LCDR at Longhedge Junction.

During mid-Victorian years there was a heavy flow of cross-London local trains to such an extent that in the 1870s some 200 were calling daily at Kensington (Addison Road). However, this traffic gradually fell away, ceasing completely when the other four intermediate stations closed during the 1940 Blitz. The Clapham Junction-Kensington service, which had first run in 1863, was reinstated in 1946, though unadvertised in the public timetables, and in the following two decades the line was also heavily used, particularly at summer weekends, by through trains between the South Coast, Midlands and North. By 1969 the shuttle service consisted of no more than two trains each way, northbound in the mornings, south-

This scene at Kensington Olympia in September 1953 is historic in so far as the parcels sidings beyond the platform have been removed, while the District Line train from Earls Court is comprised of vintage stock dating from 1911, with hand-operated doors. *A. J. Pike*

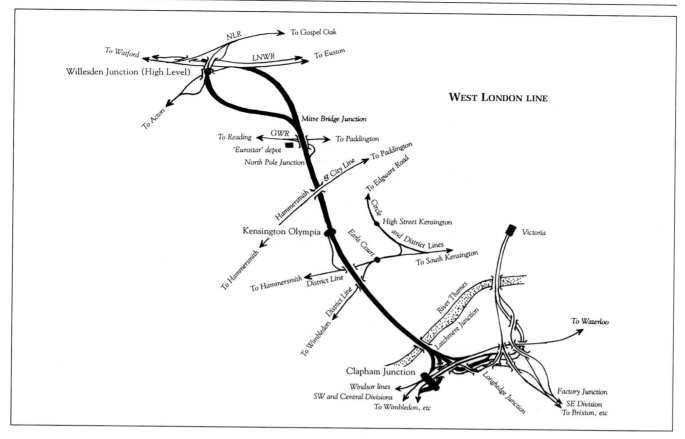

bound in the evenings and midday on Saturdays, mainly for the benefit of Post Office workers at Kensington. Eight minutes were allowed for the 3-mile journey.

Originally trains ran to and from both sides of Clapham Junction station, and the stock was stabled in Falcon Road sidings, on the 'Brighton' side of the lines, when not in use. In recent years platform 2, on one side of an island platform next to the Windsor lines, has been exclusively used - the track on the outer side of the platform has been lifted. Some freight trains still make use of the 'dive-under' on to the Central Division, as do the two through trains between Brighton, Manchester and Glasgow. Through freights to and from the SE Division use the Latchmere Junction-Longhedge Junction connection. Just after the end of the period covered by this survey - in May 1994 - a half-hourly weekdays-only service was introduced between Clapham Junction and Willesden High Level.

Between Clapham Junction and Kensington (renamed Olympia in 1946), the Thames is crossed at Chelsea, the line across the bridge having been singled for a while in recent years. After passing the London Underground depot at Lillie Bridge, Olympia is reached, now consisting only of two through platforms, plus a terminal bay for District Line trains from High Street Kensington via Earls Court. Other bay

platforms at both ends, together with a motor-rail depot that opened in May 1966, have been removed. The line came under London Midland Region jurisdiction in February 1970, but evidence of the former joint ownership persisted, and it was some years before the GWR lower quadrant signals were replaced by upper quadrants. Prior to 1958, when Olympia Middle box closed, there had been three controlling the station precincts, and the unmistakeably LNWR box at the south end outlasted the 1980s, as have the semaphore signals. However, in March 1983 colour-lights and track circuiting were installed between Clapham Junction and Olympia. The line is now controlled as far north as Mitre Bridge Junction from the Clapham Junction signalling centre, with Willesden box responsible for the remainder.

The connection on to the Western Region main line at North Pole Junction ceased to be available for normal traffic after the construction there of the depot for 'Eurostar' trains. These run empty to and from Waterloo via the West London line, making use of the restored connection from Latchmere Junction towards Queenstown Road. Freight or inter-regional passenger trains needing access to the Western Region now have to proceed via Willesden and Acton Wells Junctions.

To facilitate passage of the 'Eurostars' the third rail

On a Saturday midday in September 1958 Ivatt Class '2' 2-6-2T No 41298 of Battersea shed approaches Clapham Junction on the Central Section side with a train from Kensington Olympia. The first two vehicles are articulated saloons originally employed on the Sheppey Light Railway. *N. L. Browne*

was laid between Clapham and Longhedge Junctions and the new depot via North Pole Junction, and was energised from 8 March 1993.

Steam traction for the Clapham Junction-Olympia shuttle service was provided for some years by Stewarts Lane shed, with 'H' 0-4-4Ts commonly used until replaced by Ivatt Class '2' 2-6-2Ts. In April 1959 Nine Elms took over for a short time, rostering 'M7' 0-4-4Ts, but the duty reverted to Stewarts Lane and the Ivatts, the usual load being five or six carriages. In 1963 Classes 'U' and 'N' 2-6-0s were occasionally noted, running tender-first in one direction, but in later days BR Standard tanks were employed, the last steam working being by 2-6-2T No 82019 on 7 July 1967.

After the demise of steam traction a Class 33 Bo-Bo diesel was rostered with a six-coach corridor set, but the diesel era saw many permutations, with the coaches replaced by a more suitable 'push-pull' set,

while the '33' gave way on occasions to a Class '09' 0-6-0 diesel limited to 27.5 mph (no great disadvantage!). From October 1982 a Class 119 DMU from Old Oak depot was diagrammed, but locomotive-hauled trains still appeared, powered either by Class 33s or by Class 73/1 electro-diesels. The service was stepped up to six trains each way daily, advertised by posters at Clapham Junction from 1982, and Class 205 diesel-electric units replaced the Western Region's diesel-mechanicals.

Until 1940 the LMS had operated a Willesden Junction-Earls Court service via Olympia with electric units, and 53 years later, with the switching on of the current in 1993, the 'Kenny Belle' enjoyed a brief spell of electric traction at the other end of the line, a Class 455 EMU doing the honours from 26 July. Ironically the introduction of the through service the following year meant a reversion to diesel-mechanical units as the spur from North Pole Junction up into Willesden High Level station does not have the benefit of the third rail.

To bring the story up to date, the present service consists of 26 trips daily in each direction, with a running time of 22 minutes.

METROPOLITAN RAILWAY

For a map of the route see page 12.

The Metropolitan Railway had its origins in a 3¾-mile line between Farringdon Street in the City and Bishops Road, Paddington, opened in January 1863. Years later, with aspirations to become a 'main-line' company, it reached out into Buckinghamshire, to Chesham in 1889 and Aylesbury in 1892. Its outer limit was Verney Junction on the Bletchley-Oxford line, but passenger services to this outpost ceased in 1936.

It was over Metropolitan metals, southwards from Quainton Road, that the Great Central Railway came

to town in 1899, sharing the double track for 42 miles until quadrupling took place out to Harrow-on-the-Hill, and eventually to Watford South Junction in 1959-62. The Baker Street-Harrow section was electrified in 1905 and extended to Rickmansworth, together with a new branch to Watford, in 1925. Traffic into 'Metroland' grew, and there was even a daily Pullman service until the outbreak of war in September 1939. Steam traction was employed north of Rickmansworth; the 'Met' steam locomotives were taken over by the LNER in 1937, but were displaced from passenger duties during the war. After nationalisation BR steam locomotives were employed until the

METROPOLITAN RAILWAY

Name	Opened	Closed	Notes
Aldgate	11/1876		
Liverpool Street*	11/1876		
Moorgate*	12/1865		'Moorgate Street' to 10/1924
King's Cross/St Pancras*	1/1863		
Baker Street**	4/1863		
Finchley Road**	1879		
Wembley Park	1894		
Preston Road	1908		
Northwick Park	1923		Originally '& Kenton'
Harrow-on-the Hill*	8/1880		
North Harrow	3/1915		
Pinner	5/1885		
Northwood Hills	11/1933		
Northwood	1887		
Moor Park	5/1910		Originally 'Sandy Lodge', then 'Moor Park & Sandy Lodge'
Rickmansworth*	9/1887		
Chorley Wood*	1889		
Chalfont & Latimer*	1889		'Chalfont Road' to 11/1915
Amersham	9/1892		
To Aylesbury	9/1892		
Watford branch (Moor Park/Rickmansworth)			
Croxley	1/1925		
Watford	1/1925		
Chesham branch (Chalfont & Latimer)			
Chesham	7/1889		

* Interchange with BR station
** Metropolitan stations between Baker Street and Finchley Road closed 1939/40

third and fourth rails were extended to Amersham and Chesham in September 1961. Thereafter the stations beyond Amersham have been served exclusively by BR trains in and out of Marylebone.

A visit to Chesham in December 1950 produced an ex-GCR 'N5' 0-6-2T, which gave a lively run on the branch, with 'L1' 2-6-4Ts working between Aylesbury and Rickmansworth, where they handed over to Metropolitan electric locomotives. On another visit in 1956 a 'C14' 4-4-2T worked the branch train, which still consisted of three Metropolitan ex-electric coaches; Fairburn 2-6-4Ts were responsible for the main-line trains north of Rickmansworth. By then the electric locomotives sported their original names and crimson liveries. By the late 1950s Ivatt Class '2' 2-6-2Ts had taken over on the Chesham branch and one of these, No 41284, was in charge of the last steam train on 11 September 1960.

Baker Street Metropolitan station, overshadowed by the impressive bulk of Chiltern Court, took its present form in 1912, with the four-track through station just below the surface and the platforms for Hammersmith & City and Circle Line trains at a slightly lower level. Beneath these are the Bakerloo and Jubilee Line 'tubes'.

The Metropolitan and Jubilee Lines emerge into the open at Finchley Road where there is cross-platform interchange, and the two keep company to Wembley Park, where the Jubilee diverges to Stanmore. Since the quadrupling, interchange between Metropolitan and BR services has been restricted to Harrow-on-the-Hill, Rickmansworth and the stations thence to Amersham.

One can only presume that there are fewer vandals to the square mile in 'Metroland' than in many other areas, as the stations (if not the trains) are graffiti-free and well maintained - many even with accessible toilets! Watford and Croxley, dating from 1925, are

Left Were it not for the London Transport 'bullseye' on the left, this scene at Chesham could be mistaken for a country branch line far from the capital. Ex-GCR Class 'C14' 4-4-2T is in charge of the Chesham-Chalfont shuttle on 29 September 1956. *F. Hornby*

Middle left A southbound Metropolitan train formed of two 'A60' units hurries through Neasden on 26 January 1985. The Jubilee Line tracks are in the foreground, and just north of the station are the extensive car sheds and sidings where much of the 'Met' fleet is stabled and serviced. *F. Hornby*

Bottom left Croxley is the only intermediate station on the Metropolitan line's Watford branch, with a stylish brick building on the overbridge dating from 1925. A down train of 'A60' stock is seen there on 1 July 1989, on which day the branch was also host to a WR 0-6-0PT and 'Met' electric loco *Sarah Siddons* on specials. *F. Hornby*

excellent examples of the architecture of that period.

Twenty 1,200 hp Bo-Bo electric locomotives were built in 1904/06 and extensively rebuilt in 1922/23 by Metropolitan-Vickers. From 1925 they spent most of their working lives on passenger trains between Baker Street or the City and Rickmansworth, with one daily through working each way on the Watford branch. For a brief period around 1960 they also worked through trains to and from Chesham, but the majority were withdrawn in 1962. One survivor, No 12 *Sarah Siddons*, makes frequent appearances on special trains and has been seen as far afield as the South Coast!

In 1948 the off-peak service between Baker Street and Aylesbury consisted of two trains hourly at irregular intervals, the standard journey time for the 38 miles being 87 minutes with nine stops; 4 minutes were allowed for the changeover between electric and steam traction at Rickmansworth. At peak times the trains ran through to and from Liverpool Street, adding about 13 minutes to the end-to-end time.

Right Metropolitan Bo-Bo electric locomotive No 3 *Sir Ralph Verney* is seen at
Baker Street on 4 June 1961 ready to
take an Aylesbury train as far as
Rickmansworth. There were 20 of these
fine machines, rebuilt into the form as
shown in 1922/23 and restored to their
pre-war maroon livery during the 1950s.
F. Hornby

Middle right Before the 1959-61 widening Moor Park station boasted two platforms with rather primitive shelters. On
27 October 1956 a train of 1927-built
'T' stock calls there en route from
Watford to Aldgate. These rather elegant
teak-coloured units were retired from
service in October 1962. *F. Hornby*

Bottom right Wembley Park is one of
those latter-day London Transport stations apparently designed solely with a
T-square! On 13 December 1987 the
footbridge frames a train of Metropolitan
'A60' stock en route from Watford to
Baker Street. *F. Hornby*

The Watford services were operated by 'T' stock multiple units
introduced in 1927, in six-coach
formations enhanced to eight
coaches at busy times. The motor-
coaches were powered by four 275
hp motors producing a maximum
speed of 60 mph (5 mph less than
the locomotives). The off-peak
service consisted of four trains per
hour between Watford and Baker
Street, allowed 41 minutes with 11
stops. At peak times they ran
through to and from Aldgate.

The major works of 1959-61,
extending electrification to
Amersham and Chesham, heralded the withdrawal of the 'T' stock
and the appearance of 62 new
four-car units of 'A60' stock in silver-grey livery. Since 1981 all
trains save for the Chesham shuttle service has consisted of two
such units.

From the introduction of a completely new timetable on 18 June
1962 the off-peak service has consisted of half-hourly trains between
Aldgate and Amersham, and quarter-hourly between Baker Street
and Watford - extended to
Aldgate, as before, at peak times.

The Amersham trains are allowed 43 minutes beyond Baker Street with six stops - 13 minutes less than in 1948 - but the Watford service is only marginally faster.

Additionally to these routes, the Harrow-Uxbridge branch, electrified in 1905, had trains every 15 minutes off-peak in 1948 with a 40-minute schedule (reduced by 2 minutes in the 1990s). Between Ruislip and Ickenham on this branch, a spur gives access to the Central Line depot at West Ruislip, alongside the BR High Wycombe line. The final section from Rayners Lane to Uxbridge is shared with Piccadilly Line trains at peak hours.

The track widening northwards from Harrow-on-the-Hill involved considerable infrastructure changes, with platforms lengthened at several stations and extensive rebuilding at Northwood, Moor Park and Amersham. Many bridges were reconstructed and the signalling system was improved, including provision of a new box at Amersham. The local lines are controlled by two-aspect colour-light signals and the fast lines by three-aspects, as is also the double track section beyond Rickmansworth.

In conclusion it is of interest to note that the Metropolitan Line beyond Northwood was subject to a swingeing fare increase of 40 per cent in July 1977 when local County Council grants were not forthcoming. As examples of the effects of inflation at that period, this was followed, throughout the LT system, by rises of 10 per cent in June 1978, 8 per cent in June 1979, 12-13 per cent in September and another 19 per cent in March 1980!

HAMMERSMITH & CITY LINE

The Hammersmith & City Line is relevant to our story largely by virtue of cross-platform interchange with BR at Paddington, at Barking at peak hours, and via a long footbridge at Westbourne Park until the BR station closed in 1992.

A mixed-gauge line opened from Westbourne Park to Hammersmith in 1864 with an eastward extension to link up with the Metropolitan Railway in 1871. (The 'dive-under' beneath the main line west of Royal Oak followed seven years later.) There were spurs on to the LSWR Richmond-Addison Road line until 1914 and from Latimer Road on to the West London line until 1940.

From 1867 the Hammersmith & City was jointly owned by the Great Western and Metropolitan railways and these two companies provided the stock for electrification in 1906. Although later considered as part of the Metropolitan system and worked by London Transport from 1933, the 'Hammersmith & City' title was revived 30 years later.

At Paddington suburban station the H&C trains use platforms 15 and 16, continuing through Royal Oak, less than half a mile away, before descending diagonally beneath the BR lines to reappear at Westbourne Park. There are six intermediate stations in the 3½ miles between Paddington and

HAMMERSMITH & CITY LINE

Name	Opened	Closed	Notes
Aldgate			Line electrified 1906
Paddington*	11/1871		
Royal Oak	11/1871		
Westbourne Park*	11/1871		Old station 1/1866-10/1871
Ladbroke Grove	6/1864		'Notting Hill' to 1880; 'Notting Hill & Ladbroke Grove' to 6/1919
Latimer Road	12/1868		
White City	1/1908	10/1959	'Wood Lane' to 11/1947
Shepherds Bush	1/1914		Old station 6/1864-3/1984
Goldhawk Road	1/1914		
Hammersmith	1/1868		Old station 6/1864-1/1868

* Interchange with BR station

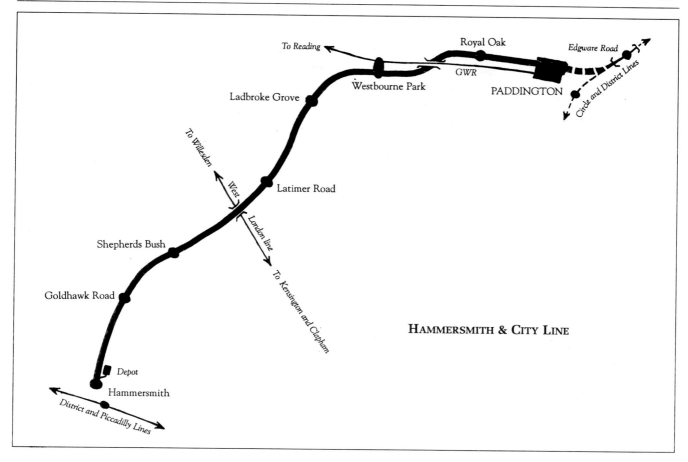

To Reading

Royal Oak

Edgware Road

Westbourne Park

GWR

PADDINGTON

Circle and District Lines

Ladbroke Grove

To Willesden

West

Latimer Road

London line

To Kensington and Clapham

Shepherds Bush

Goldhawk Road

HAMMERSMITH & CITY LINE

Depot

Hammersmith

District and Piccadilly Lines

Hammersmith, much of which is on viaducts. The car sheds are at Hammersmith, close to the three-track terminus. An item of interest, situated at Ladbroke Grove, was London Transport's last full-size lever frame, taken out of use in March 1983.

Eastwards from Paddington the line is in tunnel, sharing Circle Line tracks from Edgware Road to Liverpool Street. Off-peak services terminate at Whitechapel, continuing eastwards over the District Line to Barking in the rush hours.

Traffic has been worked successively by pre-war 'Metadyne' stock comprising two three-car units ('Metadyne' was the name of the control equipment fitted), then by 'C69' stock in three two-car formations, and from December 1977 by the new 'C77' stock. These latter,

with four sets of double-doors on each side of the coaches to expedite loading and unloading, have a reduced seating capacity compared with their predecessors. A colourful livery has been adopted, with red doors and cab fronts, and a blue band along the lower edge of the silver-grey sides. From October 1984 'one person operation' has been in use, preceding its adoption on the District and Circle Lines.

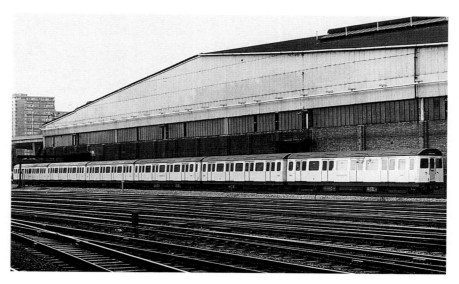

A Hammersmith & City Line train of Metropolitan 'C69' stock makes its way from Paddington to Park Royal on 6 May 1975 with the massive bulk of Paddington Goods Station as a backdrop. *F. Hornby*

DISTRICT LINE

The District Line has the distinction that it shares stations with BR at all four of its extremities, three of which are reached over tracks owned by BR or its predecessors.

At Ealing Broadway District and Central Line trains

terminate at bay platforms adjacent to those of the main-line station although there is no physical connection. Access to both Wimbledon and Richmond was originally by courtesy of the LSWR, the former from Putney Bridge and the latter from Ravenscourt Park, shared with North London line trains from Gunnersbury. Again, at both termini the District Line trains occupy bay platforms alongside the main-line stations.

At the opposite end of the system District Line activities were extended eastwards in stages, initially over joint DR/LT&SR trackage between Whitechapel

Ealing Broadway, one of the District Line's western outposts, is seen on 29 April 1967 with a train of silver-painted 'R' stock ready for the long run to Upminster. On the left are the Central Line platforms, and in the background the footbridge leading to the Western Region main-line station. *F. Hornby*

DISTRICT LINE

Name	Opened	Closed	Notes
From:			
Ealing Broadway*	7/1879		
Richmond*	6/1877		
Wimbledon*	6/1889		
To:			
Bow Road	1902		
Bromley-by-Bow	1902		
West Ham	1902		Originally LT&SR, opened 1858;
Plaistow	1902		electrified to East Ham 8/1905, to
Upton Park	1902		Barking 4/1908
East Ham	1902		
Barking*	1902		
Upney	9/1932		
Becontree	9/1932		
Dagenham Heathway	9/1932		'Heathway' to 5/1949
Dagenham East	9/1932		'Dagenham' to 5/1949
Elm Park	5/1935		
Hornchurch	9/1932		
Upminster Bridge	12/1934		
Upminster*	9/1932		Opened by LT&SR 5/1885

* Interchange with BR station

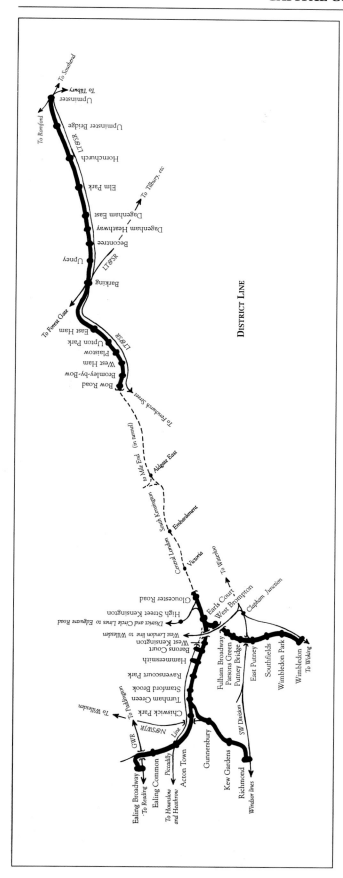

DISTRICT LINE

and Bow in June 1902, and on to Barking over a double line provided by the LT&SR in 1908. Electrification reached that point two years later, but well into BR days these tracks were sometimes used by freight trains and even, on occasions, by steam-hauled passenger trains. However, all connections with the parallel LT&SR lines have since been severed. Upminster was reached in 1932 over separate tracks made available by the LMS. Five entirely new stations were opened in the following three years, with much revenue attributable to the vast new Becontree Estate built by the LCC over ten years from 1925.

London Transport became responsible for the line's power supply from July 1955, and the stations were transferred from Eastern Region to LT control in 1970, with the exception of Barking and Upminster. At the former, extensive track layout alterations, completed in 1962, afford cross-platform interchange with the LT&S line trains. There is a bay platform for trains terminating there, and nine stabling sidings east of the station. A large new depot - replacing one at East Ham - opened at Upminster in 1959, accommodating 34 eight-car trains.

Through services operate between the western and eastern extremities although some terminate at Mansion House, Tower Hill, Barking or Dagenham East. The long and busy section between South Kensington and Bow Road is nearly all below the surface and average speeds are modest - there are, for example, 40 intermediate stations in the 30 or so miles between Ealing Broadway and Upminster; the through journey time is around 85 minutes. Traffic is heavy notwithstanding the faster service at the eastern end on the parallel LT&S line.

The stations originally built by the LSWR in the west and by the LT&SR in the east still show evidence of their ancestries, but the newer ones of LMS origin between Barking and Upminster were built in a contemporary style with 'passimeter' booking offices and 700-foot platforms.

The entire length of the eastern section between Campbell Road Junction, Bow, and Upminster was resignalled in a scheme completed in 1960, with two-aspect colour-lights throughout, controlled from boxes at Barking and Upminster. At the western end the last semaphore signals on London Transport lines, between Turnham Green and Richmond, were replaced in 1980.

District Line multiple unit stock has seen many changes since 1948, when there were still several varieties, the oldest of which was of pre-1914 vintage. Generally the longer runs were entrusted to the 'M', 'N' and 'Q' 'Metadyne' stock built from 1935-39, but large numbers of new 'R' stock came into service in

Left For evidence of the origins of East Ham station, take note of the wrought-iron 'LT&SR' insignia on each of the supports. London Transport took over full control in 1970 and the train, seen there on 6 July 1993, is of District Line 'D' stock, heading for Barking. *F. Hornby*

Below left On 24 March 1956 a District Line train for Richmond awaits departure from Upminster, a journey of nearly 90 minutes' duration. The rear coaches are clerestoried Birmingham-built 1927 'K' stock, with two leading vehicles of the more modern 'R' stock. *F. Hornby*

1949-50, supplemented ten years later by a batch in unpainted aluminium. They gave sterling service until March 1983, running at first in eight-car formation, reduced to seven cars from October 1971. A single experimental car in unpainted aluminium had first appeared in 1952, joined by others painted silver in 1956, but it was not until 1968 that the traditional red livery was finally eliminated.

The 'R' stock was replaced by six-car trains of 60-foot 'D79' stock from June 1979, roughly equalling in length the older seven-car formations. By 1983 a fleet of 75 trains was in service, each with 272 seats - or room for well over 500 with 'standees'.

EAST LONDON LINE

The East London line has its origins in a double-track railway between Wapping and New Cross Gate, opened in December 1869 and using a tunnel beneath the Thames originally opened for pedestrians in 1843. In 1880 connections were made at the south end with the SER at New Cross. In April of that year the northern end was extended to link with the GER just outside Liverpool Street, and at one time there were even through trains between that terminus and Brighton. Another spur, the St Mary's curve, affords a connection with the Metropolitan & District Line near Whitechapel; it was used by through trains until 1941 and for empty stock movements thereafter. BR trains to or from Liverpool Street continued to use the line occasionally until 1966, including football or enthusiasts' specials - your author first covered the line in September 1952 in corridor stock hauled by an ex-GER 0-6-0T! However, the connections with BR have since been removed.

The East London line took its (comparatively) modern form when electrified in 1913 and the service now consists of three trains hourly to and from each of the New Cross termini, where there are bays alongside the South Eastern and South Central Division platforms. Off-peak trains terminate at Whitechapel at the northern end, beneath and at right-angles to

EAST LONDON LINE

Name	Opened	Closed	Notes
Shoreditch	4/1876		
Whitechapel	4/1876		'Mile End' 1884-1901
Shadwell	4/1876		'St Georges East' to 1918
Wapping	12/1869		Originally 'Wapping & Shadwell'
Rotherhithe	12/1869		
Surrey Quays	12/1869		'Deptford Road' to 6/1911;
			'Surrey Docks' to 2/1989
New Cross*	4/1880		
New Cross Gate*	12/1869		

* Interchange with BR station

the Metropolitan & District station. At peak times they continue to the now single-platform station at Shoreditch, tucked away in a side turning. From the platform the trackbed can be seen climbing up to the one-time junction with the Great Eastern outside Liverpool Street.

With the closure of the docks that were close to the line on either side of the river, some of the line's raison d'être has disappeared - note that 'Surrey Docks' became 'Surrey Quays' in 1989. This station has been smartened up, thanks to the construction of an adjacent shopping complex, but the other intermediate stations, partially roofed over in deep brick-lined canyons, retain some of the gloomy atmosphere of steam days.

From 1882 the 4-mile line was controlled by a joint committee of no fewer than six companies, ultimately passing to the LPTB in 1933.

For many years services were worked by superannuated stock, with units of classes 'C' and 'D' of 1910-14 still in use around 1950. They were replaced by the all-steel type 'F' of 1920 of more modern appearance, which in turn were superseded in 1963 by 'Q' stock, the District Line being responsible for providing trains at that time. Their successors were 'C69' stock,

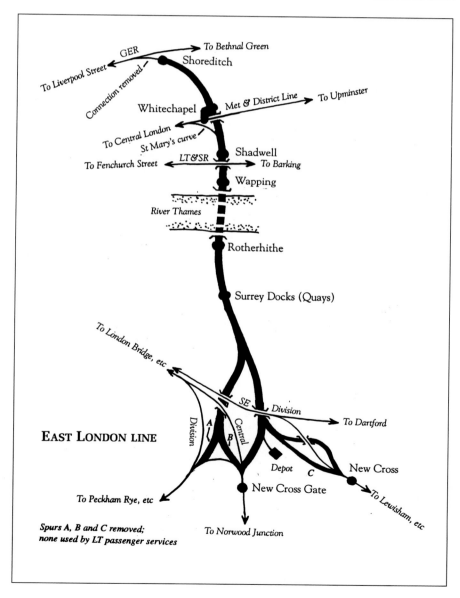

EAST LONDON LINE

Spurs A, B and C removed; none used by LT passenger services

Left Sunlight and shadows on the East London line at Shadwell on 22 May 1991 with a Whitechapel to New Cross Gate train emerging from the gloom. The mirror on the left indicates that 'one person operation' is in force. *F. Hornby*

Below left A 35-year-old train of London Transport 'F' stock approaches New Cross on the East London line in April 1955. The Southern Region's Eastern Section main line is in the foreground. *A. J. Pike*

followed for a spell in the 1970s by smaller 'tube' trains. New Cross depot received an allocation of Metropolitan 'A' stock four-car units in June 1977, but their tour of duty was interrupted in December 1982 for 2½ years while almost new 'D79' stock did the honours. The 'regulars' must have thought this too good to last when the 'A' trains returned, but several of these were refurbished around 1989-90 and repainted in blue and white with red ends, adding a welcome splash of colour. Five trains are based at New Cross, where the car sheds are at a lower level than the station.

Not surprisingly there are gradients as steep as 1 in 40 as the railway descends beneath the river; the running time between Shoreditch and both southern termini is 14 minutes with five intermediate stops.

DOCKLANDS LIGHT RAILWAY

Perhaps it is fitting that the last line to receive attention in this London suburban survey should also be the latest addition to the network, introducing a new conception of rail transport to Britain, halfway between the old street tramway and the conventional heavy-duty railway.

Designed to provide the redeveloped docklands with an effective but comparatively inexpensive 'people-mover', a measure of its success is that the original installations soon proved inadequate, so that already stations have had to be adapted to accommodate longer trains.

The contract was awarded to GEC and John Mowlem to build 7½ miles of line - all double-track save for a short section near Stratford - with 16 stations, a depot, signalling and control installations and 11 twin-articulated trains. Completion date was set for July 1987, but in the event public services commenced the following month. Current at 750V DC is collected from an outside third rail, using bottom-contact, and the driverless trains are controlled by computer from a centre at Poplar. A 'train captain' checks tickets and can, in emergencies, drive the train manually, though still subject to automatic signalling. From the front seats, once one has overcome any slight misgivings about the 'look - no hands' situ-

DOCKLANDS LIGHT RAILWAY

Name	Opened	Closed	Notes
Stratford* and Tower Gateway			
to Island Gardens	8/1987		
Bank	11/1991		
Poplar to Beckton	3/1994		

* Interchange with BR station; interchange also at Limehouse and Custom House

ation, an excellent view can be enjoyed! The units are rated at 400 hp with a maximum speed of 50 mph (37½ mph on the Bank branch), and with average speeds of 17½-20 mph. Not surprisingly (as anyone who has been involved with new computer systems would have expected), operations were far from trouble-free in the earlier days, but nevertheless the clean and colourful units and frequent service have attracted ever-increasing patronage.

The first route to be opened was from Island Gardens, on the north bank of the Thames opposite to Greenwich, through the area of the docklands redevelopment, dividing at West India Quay with one line continuing northwards to Stratford and another turning westwards to Tower Gateway. At the former

the line terminates in a bay platform at the joint BR and Central Line station, while at the latter Tower Hill (District and Circle Lines) is nearby.

At Island Gardens the station is raised some 20 feet above street level, with a glass cupola containing a staircase and lift between the two platforms. Much of the line to Poplar is elevated, using an old North Greenwich branch viaduct for part of the way, and crossing three docks between South Quay and Poplar. For over four years the trains stopped solemnly at the then non-existent station at Canary Wharf (fortunately without the doors opening!), but this is now the site of an impressive covered station with three tracks and four platforms, which opened in August 1991. There is a short four-track section thence through West India

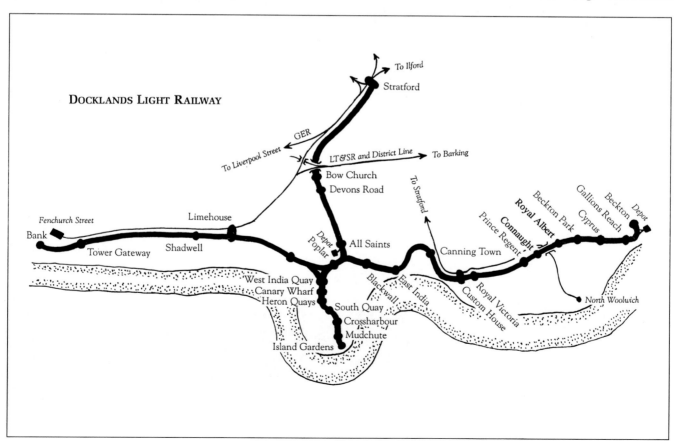

DOCKLANDS LIGHT RAILWAY

Left The outside third rail with current collected from the underside, and the concrete trackbase, can clearly be seen in this view at Heron's Quay station on 2 October 1990. Unit 07 of the original batch is 28 metres long and weighs 39 tonnes. It has since been sold to the Essen tramway in Germany. *F. Hornby*

Below left End of the line on the newest extension of the DLR is at Beckton where, fittingly, unit No 64 is of the latest Belgian-built 'B90' stock with communicating end-doors. *F. Hornby*

The Bank extension, opened in November 1991, is approximately two-thirds of a mile long. It diverges just short of Tower Gateway and descends at 1 in 16⅔ to pass below Tower Hill. At Bank station there is interchange between the DLR, the Northern and Central Lines, the Waterloo & City and - via a long pedestrian subway - with the Circle and District Lines at Monument.

Trains on both the Bank and Tower Gateway branches run at 10-minute intervals and terminate at Cross Harbour, connecting with the Stratford-Island Gardens service.

The most recent addition to the system, opened in March 1994, is the Poplar to Beckton branch, on which a self-contained shuttle service operates; it is 4½ miles in length with nine intermediate stations. As yet this line is less heavily trafficked as for part of the way it skirts the disused Royal Docks, with a good view across them to the London City Airport.

Quay to the triangle junction where the Stratford and City routes part company. The depot is at Poplar close to the station, which has two island platforms serving four tracks, and a walkway to West India Quay. The remainder of the route to Stratford is less spectacular, with the line singling after curving sharply alongside the BR tracks at Bow Junction.

The approaches to the triangle from both Stratford and the City are notable for sharp curves and steep gradients - more akin to a 'theme park' roller-coaster than to a main-line railway - and the City line descends to Limehouse on the same course as an old London & Blackwall Railway viaduct of 1840. For the rest of the way to Tower Gateway the line is alongside the LT&S tracks into Fenchurch Street. The two-platform terminus is considerably higher than street level, to which it is linked by escalators provided by a German firm once well-known as builders of steam locomotives (Orenstein & Koppel)!

The first 11 twin articulated cars - the 'P86' stock - have been sold back to Germany from whence they came. Services are now worked by ten York-built 'P89s' and by 70 'B90s' built in Belgium, with end-communicating doors, sliding passenger doors attached outside the vehicles and various minor modifications. The intention is to dispose of the 'P89s', leaving one uniform design operating all services.

By the end of 1989 there were already 30,000 daily passengers, as against just 22,000 forecast for 1991, hence the imperative need to increase capacity. Most stations can now accommodate trains of two units, save for Island Gardens where the original design prevented lengthening of the platforms.

INDEX

General

Automatic Train Control (ATC) 107
Automatic Warning System (AWS) 173
Electrification
fourth rail 38-39, 169
from Broad Street 74, 78, 80
Charing Cross/Cannon Street 118
Euston (DC Lines) 32; (main lines) 44
Fenchurch Street 106-7, 110
King's Cross 69, 72
Liverpool Street 84, 90, 91, 95, 100
London Bridge/Victoria (C) 111, 140
St Pancras 53
Victoria (E)/Holborn Viaduct/Blackfriars 133
Waterloo 111
'Eurostar' trains 168, 177
Fare increases 9, 32
'Gatwick Express' 140, 145
'Jazz' service 7, 84
'Kenny Belle' 178
Network SouthEast 9, 101
'Stansted Express' 85
Thameslink 9, 48, 50, 52, 60, 79, 123, 147

Locomotive classes
Diesel
Co-Co Nos 10000/10001 45, 83; 1-Co-Co-1 Nos 10201-03 45, 83; Bo-Bo No 10800 110, 155; DP2, *Lion* and *Deltic* 71
TOPS Class 09 178; 15 72; 20/21/23 71, 110; 24/26 45, 58, 71; 31 71, 110; 33 155, 166, 178; 35 'Hymek' 21; 37 162; 45/47 58, 71
Electric
TOPS Class 73/74 166, 175, 178; 86/3 46; Met Rly Bo-Bo 180
Steam
BR Standard: 2-6-0 30, 71, 97; 2-6-2T 47, 178; 2-6-4T 10, 30, 45, 47, 55, 108, 155; 2-10-0 83; 4-6-0 45, 55, 58, 138, 155
Ex-GWR: '14XX' 0-4-2T 10; '54XX'/'57XX'/'94XX' 0-6-0T 10, 19, 20, 30; '45XX'/'61XX' 2-6-2T 10, 19, 20, 30; 'Hall' 4-6-0 19, 20
Ex-LMS: 0-4-4T 46; ex-MR 0-4-4T 50, 109; 0-6-0 55, 58, 109; 0-6-0T 97, 109; ex-LNWR 2-4-2T 32, 46, 47; 2-6-0 45, 109; 2-6-2T 10, 45, 46, 47, 55, 57, 178;

2-6-4T 10, 30, 45, 55, 58, 70, 108, 155, 179; 4-4-0 45, 55, 57; ex-LT&SR 4-4-2T 10, 97, 108, 109; 4-6-0 45, 109
Ex-LNER: ex-NER 0-4-4T 97; 0-6-0 30, 97; ex-GER 0-6-0T 97, 186; ex-GNR and GCR 0-6-2T 10, 30, 69, 70, 84, 96, 97, 99, 179; ex-GER 'Decapod' 0-10-0T 7; ex-GCR and GER 2-4-2T 10, 70, 84, 96, 97; 'V2' 2-6-2 30, 70; 'L1' 2-6-4T 10, 30, 69, 83, 96, 97, 108, 179; ex-GNR and GCR 4-4-2T 10, 30, 70, 109; 'B1' 4-6-0 30, 70, 71, 83; 4-6-2 70, 71, 'A5' 4-6-2T 10, 23, 30
Ex-SR: 0-4-4T 130, 155, 178; 0-6-0 and 2-6-0 155, 178; Bulleid 'MN'/'WC' 4-6-2 155; ex-LB&SCR classes 155

Multiple unit classes
Diesel
BR ACV 4-wheel 30, 47; DEMU 3D/3H/3R 155; Derby Lightweight 47; ex-GWR AEC 19, 20; Wickham 99
TOPS Class 101 21, 58, 72; 104 21, 47, 58; 105 47, 58, 71, 82, 83, 110; 108 47, 72, 110; 115 30, 58; 116 100; 117 21; 119 178; 121 21, 58; 122 21, 40; 123 18; 127 58, 72, 99; 165/166 'Turbo' 22, 31; 210 22
Electric
Ex-LMS 38, 82; ex-LNWR 38, 83
Class AM2 (302) 98, 110; AM4 (304) 46, 98; AM5 (305) 98, 110; AM6/7 (306/7) 97; AM8 (308) 98, 99, 110; AM10 (310) 45, 46, 110; 312 46, 73, 98, 110; 313 39, 40, 47, 58, 72, 83; 315 98, 110; 317 46, 58, 72, 98; 'Thameslink' 319 58, 115, 139, 153; 321 44, 46, 47, 99; 501 38, 39, 82
Southern Region: ex-LSWR 3SUB 111, 113, 130, 166, 175
Ex-SR 3SUB 130; 4SUB 153; 41XX 4SUB 112, 153; 2BIL 111, 115; 2HAL 111, 115, 130, 139, 153; 2NOL 111, 115, 130, 175; 2SL/2WIM 111, 153; 4LAV 153; 4COR 175
BR 4DD 113, 130; Class 405 4SUB 113, 116, 130, 139, 166, 175; 413 4CAP 115, 130; 414 2HAP 114, 115, 130, 139, 153, 167; 415 4EPB 114, 116, 130, 139, 153, 166, 175; 416 2EPB 40, 82, 114, 116, 153, 167, 175; 418 2SAP 115, 153, 175; 421 4CIG 154, 175; 423 4VEP 115, 154, 166; 4PEP/2PEP 115, 153, 166, 175; 455 115, 153, 167, 175, 178; 456 116, 153; 'Networker' 465/466 116, 130, 139, 153; Waterloo & City 482/487 117; 508 117, 167, 175
London Transport: C, D and F stock 185, 187; M, N, Q and R stock 185, 187; T stock 181; 1938 stock 40; 1959 stock 40; A60 stock 181, 188; C69 stock 183, 187; 1972 stock 183; D79 stock 185, 188
Headcodes 117; liveries 8, 38, 40, 117